Cara Reed and Michael Reed
Enough of Experts

De Gruyter Contemporary Social Sciences

—

Volume 17

Cara Reed and Michael Reed

Enough of Experts

Expert Authority in Crisis

DE GRUYTER

ISBN 978-3-11-162075-6
e-ISBN (PDF) 978-3-11-073491-1
e-ISBN (EPUB) 978-3-11-073497-3
ISSN 2747-5689
e-ISSN 2747-5697

Library of Congress Control Number: 2022951985

Bibliographic information published by the Deutsche Nationalbibliothek
The Deutsche Nationalbibliothek lists this publication in the Deutsche Nationalbibliografie;
detailed bibliographic data are available on the internet at http://dnb.dnb.de.

www.degruyter.com

Contents

Introduction —— 1

Chapter 1: Theorizing Expert Authority —— 5
1   Introduction —— **5**
2   The Ideal Type of Expert Authority —— **6**
3   Analytically Structured Narratives: Conceptual Building Blocks —— **13**
3.1   Changes —— **14**
3.2   Mechanisms —— **15**
3.3   Outcomes —— **17**
4   Conclusion —— **18**

Chapter 2: Delegitimation —— 21
1   Introduction —— **21**
2   Structural Changes —— **22**
2.1   Economic/Technological Changes —— **24**
2.2   Political/Socio-Cultural Changes —— **33**
3   Mediating Mechanisms —— **46**
4   Substantive Outcomes —— **50**
5   Conclusion —— **51**

Chapter 3: Demystification —— 54
1   Introduction —— **54**
2   Local Subjugation and the Knowledge Apparatus —— **58**
3   Political Rationalities and Technologies under Neoliberal
         Governmentality —— **61**
4   Expert Authority and Neoliberal Governmentality —— **64**
5   Structural and Cultural Changes —— **69**
6   Mediating Mechanisms —— **71**
7   Substantive Outcomes —— **74**
8   Conclusion —— **75**

Chapter 4: Decomposition —— 76
1   Introduction —— **76**
2   Structural and Cultural Changes —— **80**
2.1   Institutional and Technical Changes —— **81**
2.2   Proliferation of New Managerial, Technical and Scientific
         Occupations —— **85**

2.3   Increasingly Fragmented and Fractured Expert Division of Labour —— **90**
2.4   Intensified Ontological Insecurity —— **91**
3   Mediating Mechanisms —— **94**
3.1   Opportunistic Strategies —— **94**
3.2   Organizational Focus —— **99**
3.3   Boundary Management —— **100**
4   Substantive Outcomes —— **102**
5   Conclusion —— **104**

Chapter 5: Covid-19 – A Case Study on Expert Authority —— 106
1   Introduction —— **106**
2   The Three Narratives on Expert Authority 'in Action' during the Pandemic —— **107**
2.1   De-legitimation and Covid-19 —— **107**
2.2   Demystification and Covid-19 —— **111**
2.3   Decomposition and Covid-19 —— **115**
3   Covid-19: The Return of the Expert? —— **119**
3.1   Re-legitimation —— **120**
3.2   Politicisation —— **121**
4   A More 'Public' Expert —— **126**
5   Conclusion —— **127**

Chapter 6: Reflexive Expert Authority and Governance —— 130
1   Introduction —— **130**
2   Democratic Theory and Reflexive Expert Authority —— **131**
3   Science and Scientific Rationality —— **134**
4   Expert Experience and Civic Epistemology —— **136**
5   Reflexivity and Risk —— **139**
6   Trust/Control Dynamics —— **143**
7   Reflexive Expert Authority and Governance —— **149**
8   Conclusion —— **157**

Chapter 7: Expert Futures —— 159
1   Introduction —— **159**
2   Meritocracy Recrudescent —— **160**
3   Technopopulism —— **166**
4   Civic/Connective Professionalism —— **171**
5   Critical Elitism —— **179**
6   Conclusion —— **183**

Chapter 8: Towards a News Social Contract ── 186
1   Introduction ── **186**
2   Non-Contractual Foundations of Contract ── **189**
3   Social Contract Theory ── **191**
4   Political Sociology of Expertise ── **199**
5   Conclusion ── **205**

References ── 208

Index ── 227

Introduction

Experts are at the heart of any fact-cultivating enterprise. ... Today, though, something has shifted: the once-stable framework of facts and reliable knowledge that has supported our liberal democracies is showing signs of fracture (Daniels 2021: 137–140).

Because the experts fill a genuine need for order in the chaotic whirl of high-tech, high-speed living, some of us remain stunningly blind to their pervasive, invasive, encroachment on the prerogatives of our private lives, as well as to the possibility that something besides pure benevolence motivates their actions (Chafetz 1995: xiv).

In this book we tell the story of the decay of institutionalized trust as the lodestone of expert authority. We also highlight the legitimacy struggles engaged in by various expert groups to revivify the latter through strategies which do not follow the orthodox 'professionalization playbook' in which a combination of formal credentialism and jurisdictional regulation are the dominant elements.

Instead of striving to restore the orthodox or received 'rational/deferential' model of expert authority, we focus on the emergence of a 'reflexive/deliberative' model which is much more open, inclusive and collaborative than the former. However, we do not underestimate how difficult it will be to make the 'reflexive/deliberative' model a reality in a socio-historical context where economic dislocation, ideological polarization and political fragmentation have cumulatively challenged and threatened expert authority in manifold ways. Insofar as contestation lies at the organizational core of the 'reflexive/deliberative' model, then so will its inherent instability, fragility and complexity. Nevertheless, we suggest that a much more open, dynamic and flexible model of expert authority and governance is required if the latter is to retain the 'adaptable resilience' needed in a world of high risks, high stakes decision-making where established conventions and predictions are scarce.

Although they are separated by more than two and a half decades, the quotes from Daniels (2021) and Chafetz (1995) which head-up this introductory chapter illustrate how far we have travelled, ideologically, politically and culturally from the 'high water mark' of established expert authority and all its core presumptions in favour of the latter as an institutional articulation of disinterested objectivity in liberal democracies. Chafetz's polemic against expert authority and its curtailment of individual liberty and weakening of collective resolve was published 26 years before Daniels' encomium for higher education as the primary institutional home of the objective expert knowledge fundamental to liberal democracy. However, he anticipates much of the excoriating critique of 'experts' which is to follow in the succeeding decades. Indeed, the very fact that Daniels feels the need to restate the case for universities as the cultivators and curators of the objective expert

https://doi.org/10.1515/9783110734911-001

knowledge required to sustain, practically and ethically, liberal democracy shows how serious the corrosive impact of more than two decades of neoliberal and populist critique has become by the third decade of the twenty-first century!

This book traces this transition from a rational/deferential conception of expert authority which rarely feels the need to justify itself – apart from the rare occasions on which it fails to live-up to its own exacting standards – to a reflexive/ deliberative model in which the demand to respond to challenges and threats to its legitimacy are ever-present. It begins by scrutinising the established model of 'professional authority' as the overarching theoretical template for understanding all forms of expertise-based legitimacy conceptually grounded in a Neo-Weberian analysis of institutionalized domination structures. This is followed by three interlinked chapters in which escalating attacks on the institutionalized trust relations which underpin the rational/deferential model are documented and evaluated within three overlapping but distinctive analytical narratives. The latter, in different ways and to different degrees, chart the fracturing of the core social, political and economic foundations on which the latter depended for its legitimacy and stability.

Chapter 5 focuses on the Covid-19 pandemic and the opportunities which it offers to expert groups to revivify their authority and status by providing the highly specialized knowledge and technical interventions whereby the extreme risks and uncertainties presented by a global disease and its highly disruptive impact on 'normal life' can be contained and mitigated. It also highlights the 'double-edged' nature of the opportunities which the pandemic offers in the 'clear and present danger' that it entails to public trust in expert authority as experts find themselves drawn increasingly into a political decision-making process in which their independence and autonomy is compromised, if not tainted, by closer association with political power. They may have no choice but 'to sup with the devil' as they become more intimately involved in high-risk mitigation and public order management, but their need for a 'long spoon' becomes more evident as the boundaries between 'expert authority' and 'political authority' are inevitably weakened and narrowed.

In the following chapter we identify the nature and significance of the emergence of a 'reflexive mode of expert authority and governance' which departs, in several crucial respects, from the institutional logic and organizational practice on which the orthodox 'rational/deferential model' outlined in chapter two rested. We see this development, with all its complexities and uncertainties, as a cumulative collective response to the mounting failings and limitations of the established model. These have become more evident over the preceding decades-long critique of the latter's pivotal assumptions concerning the inherent stability of liberal representative democracy and the unbreachable disinterested objectivity of scientific knowledge. Both presuppositions played a key role in intellectually buttressing and practically legitimating the rational/deferential model of expert authority. However, they have become subject to an intensity and scale of critique that putatively undermines their veracity and sustainability.

Reflexive expert authority and governance is presented as a more realistic and resilient model better suited to the endemic uncertainties and instabilities of political, economic and cultural life in twenty-first century societies. Yet, we cannot deny that it is also characterized by levels of contestation and tension which make it much more tendentious and unpredictable as to its functioning and the outcomes it produces. But we also contend that it is a necessary precondition for a more responsible form of expert authority and governance to re-emerge and regain the public trust on which its continued existence and effectiveness crucially depends.

The final two chapters of this book look more towards the future as they reflect on the kind of challenges which experts are likely to encounter as the twenty-first century unfolds and the need for a 'new social contract' in which that future can be potentially secured. If, as seems very likely, experts will inhabit a twenty-first century expert ecology in which negotiated conventions, understandings and improvisations, as much, if not more, than formalized rules, regulations and accreditations lie at the core of expert practice, then their reliance on their tacit interpretive judgements – mediated through reliable and relevant accumulated knowledge within and across their specialist fields – will inevitably increase over time. Of course, emerging digital technologies and new expert systems yet to be developed will also play an increasingly important role in supporting expert decision-taking. Yet the need for interpretive judgement based on tacit knowledge and 'synthetic flexibility' across a range of specialist domains is unlikely to disappear in a world where high stakes, high risk decision contexts will proliferate. Indeed, all the evidence suggests that reflexively negotiated expert interpretations and judgements are likely to become even more critical in situations where formalized rules and regulations cannot keep pace with the complexities and uncertainties of the high stakes, high risks decision-making contexts in which increasing numbers of experts will work in mid-twenty-first century societies.

During these final two chapters we also revisit theories of 'reflexive modernization' developed by analysts such as Giddens and Beck, but in much changed socio-historical circumstances from those in which they advanced their ideas at the end of the twentieth century when underlying optimism about the long-term trajectory and impact of globalization was at its zenith. In the three decades or so which have followed this 'Whig-like optimism' about the necessarily progressive dynamic inherent in the process of globalization has been severely dented, some would say decimated, by a succession of economic, political, medical and military crises that have undermined the epistemological assumptions and structural conditions on which the former depended for its intellectual authority and governmental legitimacy. We are living through much more dangerous and uncertain times in which the combined threats of global economic recession, political polarization, military conflict, cultural fragmentation and environmental degradation seem to overwhelm whatever remaining belief we have in our individual and collective capacity to deal with them in ways that enhance the 'common good'. Under these kinds of conditions, the shift from 'passive trust' based on institutionalized authority to 'active trust' grounded in openly contested and renegotiable expert legitimacy becomes infinitely more difficult to bring off as the latter can no longer rely on the natural inertia and widespread compliance built into the former.

Nevertheless, we have drawn upon theories of 'flexible modernization' because we see them are providing crucial intellectual resources for navigating a course between the extreme pessimism of visions anticipating an 'existential collapse' in expert authority or, alternatively, the obdurate complacency of those advocating a 'business as usual' take on expert futures. For us, neither of these positions can provide an understanding of and explanation for the inherent dynamism of expert authority as it struggles to reset its legitimacy and status within a socio-historical context in which many of the material and normative props which it traditionally relied upon to support its positioning have become badly corroded and decayed.

In the final chapter of this book, we set out a broad-ranging scenario for the kind of wider intellectual and political innovations which need to occur if our model of reflexive expert authority and governance is to stand any chance of being practically realizable and sustainable. We do not offer this analysis as some sort of instruction manual or recipe book as to how reflexive expert authority and governance is to be constructed and enacted. Rather, we see it as offering a 'framework of potentialities' within which the latter might find greater traction and support in twenty-first century conditions which are sure to be as, if not more, challenging than those experts faced in the past.

Chapter 1: Theorizing Expert Authority

1 Introduction

Debates about the nature, status and significance of expert authority have been dominated by a 'received model' of how the latter emerges and becomes established as a relatively stable institutional form and sustainable organizational practice (Davies 2018; Eyal 2019; Collins et al. 2020). This received model has been constructed around key structural elements of a neo-Weberian ideal type of professional occupational association and control in which the rationalization and formalization of advanced specialized knowledge and the socio-technical practices these processes generate provide a formidable mechanism of social closure and exclusion (Abbott 1988; Macdonald 1995; Larson 2013; Burns 2019; Saks 2021). By legitimating the monopoly occupational supply of and control over scarce cognitive resources and technical skills through claims to scientific objectivity, disinterested public service and practical efficacy, professional modes of association and practice became established as the institutional exemplars of 'expert authority in action' by the twentieth century.

However, it has become increasingly difficult to maintain this established or received model of expert authority in the late twentieth and early twenty-first centuries as it has been repeatedly challenged by theoretical critiques and socio-technical changes that fundamentally question its cogency and viability. If the received model of expert authority is based on a 'crown jewels' conception of science (Collins at al. 2020) and a 'liberal public service' mode of professional association and practice (Marquand 2004; Moran 2007; Davies 2018, 2020a) which can no longer be analytically sustained in anything like their ideal typical forms, then it seems we need to rethink the way in which we theorize what continues to be such a central social and organizational phenomenon in contemporary societies.

With this need for a 'radical reappraisal' of how we theorize the established model of expert authority in mind, this chapter opens with an outline of the major conceptual components of the latter and the way they were analytically integrated within the neo-Weberian ideal type of professional occupational association and work organization. Subsequently, it moves on to consider the major 'narratives' or 'theses' which have challenged the theoretical dominance and empirical sustainability of the neo-Weberian conceptualization of expert authority – that is, the 'de-legitimation narrative', the 'demystification narrative' and the 'decomposition narrative'. The chapter concludes with an assessment of the most significant divergences between the received or orthodox model of expert authority and those emerging from these three narratives as they identify an escalating crisis in the

https://doi.org/10.1515/9783110734911-002

institutional foundations and organizational forms through which the latter has been legitimated and practiced.

2 The Ideal Type of Expert Authority

Much has been written about Weber's definition and deployment of 'ideal types' in sociological research and analysis (Albrow 1990; Ray and Reed 1994; Turner 1993; Runciman 2002; Anter 2014; Reed 2020), but Parkin (1982: 28) provides a succinct and accessible summary of the former:

> Ideal types are conceptual abstractions that we employ in trying to get to grips with the complexities of the social world. Weber rightly points out that we cannot grasp social phenomena in their totality. Patterns of behaviour and institutional forms like capitalism, or Protestantism, or bureaucracy are each composed of many interconnected elements, both normative and structural. In order to comprehend any such institution or social formation it is necessary to reduce it to its core components. We do this by singling out and accentuating the central or basic features of the institution in question and suppressing or downgrading those features that could be considered marginal to it.

As Parkin goes on to point out, Weber was well-aware that there will be a significant degree of arbitrariness about which 'core elements' are selected and accentuated and those that are marginalized or even ignored. But this process of, often extreme, conceptual selection and abstraction is driven by the research questions which are being asked and the wider theoretical frameworks and philosophical traditions in which they are embedded. Thus, ideal types are seen to function as a form of 'analytical benchmark or yardstick' against which empirical cases can be compared and evaluated. The divergences, rather than similarities, between the ideal type and the empirical forms or patterns under investigation become the focus of analytical and explanatory attention insofar as the latter necessarily exhibit 'abnormalities' or 'discrepancies' from the former requiring further analysis.

Consequently, the neo-Weberian ideal type of expert authority has been constructed and developed as a distinctive form of 'legitimate domination'. Within the latter, the power of certain occupational associations and groups possessing advanced specialized knowledge and the complex repertoire of socio-technical skills emerging from them is authorized and sanctioned in ways that allows them to secure and retain monopoly control over the ways in which they are acquired and deployed. Of course, this 'authorizing and sanctioning' process is highly contested and contingent upon support from other key groups and institutions such as political and economic elites, state bureaucrats and the judiciary.

But the **paradigm case or exemplar of expert authority**, as a form of legitimate domination, consists of a set of positionings and claims, occupied and made by those who have successfully mounted what Larson (2013) calls 'professionalization projects' authorizing and sanctioning their power to control those segments or domains (Abbott 1988) of the labour market/working environment for expert services pertaining to their interests and the material and social rewards accruing from them. Not all expert occupational groups aspire to, or can realistically achieve, formal legitimation and recognition as 'professionals' – that is, as members of a formal association who accredit, license, educate, train and develop their practitioners with a relatively high degree of internal self-governance and management (Burns 2019; Saks 2021). It is also the case – as we show in subsequent chapters of this book – that 'existing forms of professional expertise are now in flux in ways not seen before' (Burns 2019: 287) to the extent that they have been commodified, rationalized and routinized by a conjuncture of economic, political and technological transformations whose cumulative impact fundamentally questions the foundations of the 'professional state' as it has been dissected and explained by successive generations of neo-Weberian researchers and scholars since the middle of the twentieth century. Indeed, it is as a result of this research and scholarship that we have increasingly been made aware of how complex, contested and contingent successful professionalization projects are, as well as of how much they depend on favourable exogenous political, economic and social conditions beyond the endogenous intra-organizational dynamics of the 'system of professions' itself (Abbott 1988; Macdonald 1995; Leicht 2016).

Yet, it is vital to remember – as Weber himself clearly recognized – that this neo-Weberian ideal typical conceptualization of 'expert authority as legitimate domination' in the labour market for professionalized expert services and the wider expert division of labour which it generates and reproduces crucially depends on the active and positive commitment of those requiring such services who are usually, but not always, in a subordinate or supplicant position to experts. The client or customer for expert services must retain a sufficient degree of trust in and commitment to the authority of those experts providing them if the latter are to remain in a position where they can confidentially expect the former to accept their commands and instructions. If this subordinate/client commitment and acceptance becomes increasingly more contested and contingent, then the danger is that expert authority begins to see its claims to legitimacy weakened and the aura masking its operation demystified and critiqued.

As neo-Weberian researchers and scholars (Parkin 1979; Freidson 1986, 1994; Krause 1996; Larson 2013; Johnson 2016; Gorman and Vallas 2020; Saks 2021) have repeatedly highlighted, successful 'professionalization projects' – as evidenced by elite professions such as medicine and law – depend on complex combinations of structural and processual factors emerging within particular socio-historical contexts supportive of the developmental trajectories they generate. Insofar as these mobility projects consist of two, closely linked, control strategies relating to monopoly control over specialized knowledge and skill within the labour market for expert services and organizational control over work domains within the workplace, then they must simultaneously engage in activities aimed at securing 'epistemic exclusion' and 'jurisdictional closure' (Larson 2013; Abbott 1988; Freidson 1994; Reed 1996, 2018). While the former relates to the capacity of an occupational group to develop and protect an exclusive cognitive/knowledge base combining high levels of theoretical abstraction and technical indeterminacy, the latter relates to its ability to translate this monopoly epistemological control into domains of specialized work activity which can be closed-off from other groups. This combination of exclusion and closure, if effectively constructed and sustained, provides a powerful structural mechanism through which occupational groups can establish and legitimate their claims to expert authority and the material and symbolic advantages which it conveys. It can also ensure that their work activity retains a relatively high degree of 'in-determination' in that it remains largely beyond the monitoring and control of externally imposed rules in ways facilitating uncertainty, even secrecy and mystery, over how it is to be performed and evaluated (Larson 2013: 41–42). Indeed, the shifting balance between 'in-determination' and 'codification' entailed within an ongoing 'dialectic of control' (Giddens 1994) between autonomous self-management and external regulation constitutes, Larson argues, the fulcrum around which legitimation struggles between expert groups claiming recognition as a 'profession' are fought out.

Epistemic monopoly crucially depends on the collective capacity of an aspiring profession and those professionals who are recognized, and recognize themselves, as its members and practitioners to claim the 'authority of science' in endorsing the standing and status of their 'expertise'. Their authority derives from the fact that their expertise rests upon an objective, universal and esoteric knowledge base from which specialized interventions directed at the disinterested identification and treatment of complex human and technical problems can be effectively undertaken. Their expertise is legitimated, at least in part, through their appropriation of scientific rationality in ways which demonstrate that the advanced, specialized knowledge which only they control, codify and co-ordinate is derived from universal principles and rigorous practices accumulated through disciplined abstraction, experimentation, testing and confirmation undertaken by scientists stretching over centuries. Larson (2013: 180–181) summaries the key features of 'epistemic exclusion' as entailing 'the capacity to claim esoteric and identifiable skills – that is, to create and control a cognitive and technical base'. By constructing and controlling a scientific knowledge base from which cognitive exclusiveness can be asserted and from which specialized technical skills can be monopolized and marketized, certain occupational groups can begin to mount 'professionalization projects' giving them the potential capacity to legitimate their domination of the working environments in which they operate.

But this 'epistemic exclusion', on its own, is not enough to realize a successful professionalizing project leading to a form of legitimate domination supportive of professional status; it must be combined with 'jurisdictional closure' through an organizational strategy bringing areas of work-related activity within which such specialized knowledge and techniques are applied under exclusive professional control. The effective implementation of the latter entails the translation of abstract theoretical knowledge and learned technique into sets of working routines or 'methodological templates' (Brown 2019) around which practical boundaries can be constructed and policed by certain occupational groups against actual or potential incursion by competitor groups. These templates of operational practices and routines provide the power base from which defined areas of work activity are relational and discursively 'closed off' to competitor groups within a complex ecology of interdependent occupational groups routinely engaged in strategies and tactics directed to the carving-out and protection of 'their' jurisdictional domain. To engage in a successful professionalization project requires the effective linking of 'epistemic exclusion' to 'jurisdictional closure' by means of operational methodologies or templates translating abstract cognitive power and control into practical workplace domains and spaces in which self-regulation over and management of 'work performances' can be routinely secured.

This combination of 'epistemic exclusion' and 'jurisdictional closure' is further strengthened through the – always contestable and contested – construction of a configuration of integrative mechanisms driving towards formal institutionalization and hierarchical organization. Thus, legally-supported accreditation and licensing, standardized career training and development provided by universities and colleges, forms of internal and external occupational regulation combining meritocracy and collegiality, as well as the extensive paraphernalia of implicit 'understandings' associated with admittance to and progression within 'the profession' bolster the drive towards institutionalizing the processes through which expert market power is transformed into professional authority. Once exclusion and closure have been effectively combined and stabilized in ways that have secured a sufficient degree of monopoly control within the marketplace and workplace, then a professionalizing project has the potential to be successfully pursued. They are the epistemological and organizational building blocks on which professionalizing projects legitimating the dominant labour market positioning and workplace control of certain occupational groups claiming expert authority are founded. When they are effectively combined, 'exclusion' and 'closure' generate the third precondition for the realization of a successful professionalization project in which expert authority is stabilized and reproduced – that is, the generation and maintenance of relatively high levels of uncertainty, secrecy and mystery in the performance and assessment of the expert group's core work activities such that they remain inherently resistant to rationalization and codification.

However, this potential is only likely to be fulfilled if two further contextual conditions are established; first, active and sustained support from political and administrative elites occupying key positions within the state apparatus and, second, the institutionalization of an ethic of 'liberal public service' in which expert occupational groups take on the public persona of trusted public servants deploying their expertise on behalf of the 'general good' or 'society-at-large' rather than their own vested interests or those of some other group.

Previous discussion has suggested that at the analytical core of the neo-Weberian ideal type of expert authority lies the idea that certain occupational groups with the capacity to access, develop and apply scientific knowledge within the marketplace and the workplace are able to 'extend their powers of self-evaluation and self-control [so]that they become almost immune to external regulation' (Larson 2013: xii). But this focus on the *internal mechanisms* through which special occupations translate expert power and control into 'legitimate domination' has been complemented by an exploration of the *external mechanisms* by means of which expert groups strengthen their market and organizational authority – that is, by gaining support from state elites and from the general public through the promulgation of an ethic of 'liberal public service'.

In the case of elite professions – in fields such as medicine, law, science, and architecture – Larson (2013: xii) insists that the sustained support of political, economic and social elites occupying or with access to powerful positions with the state's administrative apparatus was, and remains, critical to them mounting successful professionalization projects:

> Professions ultimately depend on the power of the state, and they originally emerge by the grace of powerful protectors. The privileged position of a profession is thus secured by the political and economic influence of the elite which sponsors it ... an account of the process by which professions emerge illuminates the fact that professions gain autonomy; in this protected position, they can develop with increasing independence from the ideology of the dominant social elites. The fact remains, however, that their privileges can always be lost.

This remains as true today as it has since the emergence of 'expertise' as a key source of occupational power and organizational control from the late seventeenth century (Johnson 1994; Krause 1996; Davies 2018). The translation of the latter into 'legitimate domination' still crucially depends on the capacity of proto-typical expert groups claiming special privileges within labour markets and work organizations being able to secure state support for cognitive, normative and organizational strategies directed at enhanced autonomy and self-management within the jurisdictional domains or fields in which they operate. So, as Larson (2013: 3) notes, 'knowledge of Latin distinguished the "learned" professions from the craft guilds that developed in the towns between the eleventh and thirteenth century [because it] increased the aura of mystery surrounding the professions' esoteric knowledge, while Latin clearly associated them with the world of the elites.' In a similar fashion, contemporary expert groups require state support for formal accreditation and licensing, regulation of their relationships with clientele, and self-management of their conduct and performance in ways that distinguishes them, indeed sets them apart, from actual or competitor groups. In the twenty-first century, expert groups need the state to support – legally, administratively and ideologically – their claims to 'special status and esoteric knowledge' and the privileges which flows from them in much the same way as medieval priests, scribes and schoolmen appropriated linguistic access to and control over religious, bureaucratic and educational resources vital to the work of the fields in which they operated.

In addition to state support, the neo-Weberian ideal typical model of expert authority also identifies the securing of 'institutionalized' or 'passive' trust (Giddens 1994) within the wider community as a precondition for reproducing and stabilizing expert power and control. Traditionally, this has been achieved through the development and communication of a generic conception of 'liberal public service' in which experts play the vital role of accruing, codifying and ministering the esoteric knowledge and practical technologies through which social order and the general wellbeing of the people – particularly in the face of crisis conditions – can be maintained (Davies 2018, 2020a; Marquand 2004; Moran 2007; Collins et al. 2020). By demonstrating how dependent 'we' are on the knowledge, skills and technologies that experts can deploy to sustain our 'normal, everyday lives', particularly when they are threatened by events radically undermining and destabilizing the, usually unnoticed, foundations on which the later routinely relies, 'we' can see how much we need them to prevent, or at least contain, the Hobbesian 'war of all against all' that lies just beneath the surface of our routine existence. By trusting experts to use the best of their cognitive, technical and organizational capacities to maintain and protect the social communities and institutions in which they are embedded – what Larson (2013: chapter 5) conceptualizes as their service or 'civilizing function' as opposed to their power or 'market-closure function' – 'we' give them the authority to deploy their knowledge and skills in whatever way they think appropriate to secure and sustain order and discipline.

As we shall document in succeeding chapters of this book, 'institutionalized trust' in expert power and control has become increasingly difficult – some would say impossible (see chapter 2) – to sustain in a context where, say, dominant political discourses and movements have fundamentally undermined the credibility of 'experts' to speak and act on behalf of 'the people' or the competition from other expert groups has become so intense that trust can only be 'actively and continuously' achieved in limited temporal phases and social situations (Giddens 1994; Beck 1999; Eyal 2019). Nevertheless, attaining and retaining 'institutionalized trust' remains a key strategic objective for any group claiming expert authority within contemporary political economies and societies insofar as it establishes a relatively secure and resilient form of legitimation that is portable and transferable across temporal and spatial boundaries. If an expert group has secured a position of 'institutionalized trust' within the societies and communities within which it operates, then it is much better placed to realize and maintain the substantial political, economic and social influence which it conveys. Any power struggles emerging over 'epistemological exclusion' and 'organizational closure' – with actual or potential competitor experts or with clients and customers increasingly aware of their capacity to go to the latter for whatever services they need – are likely to be much more containable, if not winnable, if they are in a position to support claims to generalized high trust relations with those communities and groups that they serve as they have become socially and ethically embedded over many generations.

The five key structural features of the neo-Weberian ideal type of expert authority are listed in figure 1 below. They summarize the theoretical benchmark against which the emergence, development and impact of challenges and threats to this established model of expert authority are reviewed and evaluated in subsequent chapters of this book in relation to three analytically structured narratives of 'de-legitimation', 'demystification' and 'decomposition' which are outlined in the next section of this chapter.

Figure 1: The Neo-Weberian Ideal Type of Expert Authority

---

(1) Monopoly control over markets for expert services through 'epistemic exclusion'
(2) Organizational control over expert work domains through 'jurisdictional closure'
(3) Autonomous self-management and regulation of core work practices by combining (1) and (2) in ways that preserve 'in-determination' in performance and evaluation
(4) State support from political, economic and social elites located within or access to the administrative apparatus through which 'legal rational' legitimation of cognitive, technical and organizational strategies of control can be secured
(5) Institutionalized trust in the power and control legally and administratively delegated to expert groups through generalized acceptance of the conception of 'liberal public service' geared to the protection of social order and the preservation of general wellbeing of the population at large.

---

3 Analytically Structured Narratives: Conceptual Building Blocks

The preceding section of this chapter has specified the key analytical components of the Neo-Weberian ideal type of expert authority. This conceptual abstraction treats the latter as a form of legitimate domination based, primarily, on marketplace and workplace control over the provision of advanced specialist cognitive and technical services buttressed by a range of secondary trust-building mechanisms ensuring a substantial degree of moral commitment from those dependent on such services. In this way, the Neo-Weberian ideal type of expert authority is based on a logic which analytically abstracts and combines cognitive, technical and organizational elements in order to generate a model that integrates the endogenous/internal and exogenous/external aspects of such a form of legitimate domination.

In this section we focus on the overarching analytical architecture of the three narratives that have been developed over the last two decades or so insofar as they seriously call into question the theoretical viability and empirical sustainability of the Neo-Weberian model of expert authority – that is, the 'de-legitimation narrative', the 'demystification narrative' and the 'decomposition narrative'. Each of these narratives is discussed and evaluated in more detail and depth in the following three chapters, but, in this section, we focus on their conceptual framing and rationale insofar as they reveal an underlying configuration of analytical components which they share and around which their 'storylines' are collectively constructed. While the former diverge in several fundamental respects, they also share overlapping concerns and components as they strive to develop cogent understandings and coherent explanations as to 'how' and 'why' the received or orthodox model of 'expert authority' is no longer tenable in a socio-historical context where the 'conditions of possibility' sustaining the latter have been eviscerated.

Each of the narratives unpacked in the next three chapters are constructed around three conceptual components: first, a shared focus on a critical conjuncture of structural **changes** which have, collectively, transformed the economic, political and social conditions under which expert authority can be institutionalized; second, a concern with the underlying **mechanisms** through which the longer-term impacts of these changes have been mediated and interpreted; finally, an attempt to identify the substantive **outcomes** which the complex interplay between structural change and mediating mechanisms has generated. Each narrative theorizes these three key elements of 'changes', 'mechanisms' and 'outcomes' in very different ways and accounts for the interplay between them by reference to contrasting explanatory logics. Yet, they also reveal a collective sensibility to a transformative 'paradigm shift' in the material, ideological and political 'rules of engagement' through which expert power and control is rewarded, legitimated and organized. While they vary considerably in their judgements and estimations of the scale of the challenge and threats which the established form of expert authority faces, they agree that 'business as usual' is no longer a viable option for the latter in a world where its social and cultural foundations have been profoundly de-stabilised, and its structural integrity substantially eroded.

3.1 Changes

If expert authority is a form of legitimate domination based on effective market-place and workplace control over the possession and provision of expert services, justified in terms of their technical efficacy and moral trustworthiness, then all three narratives agree that it is in serious trouble today and for the foreseeable future. Collectively, the latter begin their analyses of 'why' and 'how' expert authority has been weakened and diminished by focussing on the deep-seated structural transformations generating instability within the wider socio-historical context in which it is embedded. These changes – such as neoliberal austerity, authoritarian populism, state-driven deregulation, elite fragmentation and invasive technologies of surveillance and control – are regarded as entailing systemic, long-term de-stabilizing changes to the ideological consensus and political settlement that under-pinned the rise of the post-Second World War social democratic/welfare state and the key role which experts, technocrats and professionals were given in building and legitimating its institutional foundations and infrastructure (Blyth 2013; Raco 2013; Swarts 2013; Wilks 2013; Crouch 2016; Hurt and Lipschutz 2016; Davies 2018, 2020a). In particular, the 'hollowing out of the state' and the changing balance between 'public' and 'private' power – such that the latter effectively entails the privatization and marketization of public power in ways which radically weakens the authority and influence of scientific experts and elite professionals in government policy making circles – are seen to generate a much more 'hostile environment' within which a 'shadow elite' of policy brokers and fixers emerge in ways that side-line and marginalize mainstream expert authority (Wedel 2011, 2014; Davies 2017; Navidi 2017; Davis 2018; Geoghegan 2020; Callison and Manfredi 2020).

Overall, underlying structural transformations in the political economy of expert authority that have been developing since the early 1980s – but which have been intensified and reinforced during the decade or so following the financial crisis of 2008 and the global, neoliberal-driven 'austerity' policy regime that emerged in response to the latter – are seen to generate an ideological and political context in which 'abstract expert systems' (Giddens 1994; Beck, Giddens and Lash 1994;

Koppl 2018; Eyal 2019) are subjected to much higher levels of public criticism and distrust.

Under the 'bureau-professional' governing regimes (Clarke and Newman 1997; Newman and Clarke 2009; Noordegraaf and Steijin 2013; Pollitt and Bouckaert 2011) which came to dominate post-1945 social democratic welfare states in Europe and North America (Whitley 2000; Mizruchi 2013; Streeck 2016) until the early 1980s, a hybrid structure of legitimate domination was established in which economic, political and administrative elites effectively shared power with technocratic, professional and managerial elites. They governed within an overarching ideological and policy framework in which a wide range of stakeholder interests were balanced off against each other in order to ensure that the gap between 'winners' and 'losers' never became so great as to undermine public faith and confidence in the capacity of the system to deliver outcomes which kept everybody reasonably happy. Experts played a critical role in providing the objective knowledge and specialist techniques through which this delicate balancing act could be sustained over the long term in ways that minimally guaranteed every stakeholder's vested interest in keeping the system going by refusing to engage in forms of collective action that potentially threatened its institutional foundations.

In the next three chapters of this book, we review the various structural changes documented by each of our respective narratives as they identify the triggers that transformed the wider socio-historical context in which expert authority operated in ways that radically undermined the 'bureau-professional' governing regime on which the social democratic welfare state had depended for its ideological legitimacy and political sustainability. Taken together, they highlight a 'stealth revolution' (Brown 2015) whereby 'bureau-professionalism' is eaten-away from the inside as a result of exogenous changes in its wider political economy which invalidated the 'producer-dominated cartels' that it legitimated in favour of 'consumer-driven markets' in which private corporate power becomes the only acceptable conduit for individual consumer choice.

3.2 Mechanisms

The second conceptual building block – on which our three analytical narratives describing and explaining the 'crisis in expert authority' depends – relates to the mechanisms by which the key structural changes referred to in previous discussion are shaped and directed in ways that contribute to the emergence of major threats to the latter's sustainability as a system of legitimate domination. These mechanisms mediate and interpret the impact of structural change by providing the relational forms and discursive modes through which the demands and messages contained within the latter are organized and carried. In this respect, the 'imperatives' contained within structural change don't operate according to some deterministic logic that imposes itself on actors in a mechanistic fashion. They are always and everywhere shaped and reshaped by the relational networks in which actors are embedded and through the discursive narratives which give them meaning and value. Nevertheless, the mechanisms through which societies and organizations mediate and interpret social change are often, if not usually, difficult to identify and analyse because they do not present themselves in any obvious and simple way. Indeed, they are usually extremely difficult to discern and 'unpack' since they are inherently complex in their internal makeup and their external impact is subject to a wide range of contextual variation and diversity.

As previously indicated, these mediating mechanisms are best conceptualized as socio-material hybrids which provide the discursive frameworks through which major structural transformations are narrated and the interlinked disciplinary regimes through which the latter are translated into organizational realities. In many ways they play a 'simplifying' role to the extent that they filter out competing discursive and organizational translations in ways which justify and operationalize dominant interpretations of what structural change entails and means for those social actors who must grapple with its impact and implications. However, they simultaneously 'complexify' the socio-historical contexts within which structural change is necessarily embedded by opening-up a range of alternative analytical optics through which the latter might be refracted and viewed. Mediating mechanisms attempt to limit the analytical and organizational options through which structural change might be interpreted and implemented but in the very act of doing so they make possible the emergence of creative and innovative alternatives that escape the embrace of temporarily dominant narratives.

Consequently, mediating mechanisms provide the dominant narrative and organizational frames through which structural changes can be captured and coordinated as necessarily following certain 'institutional logics' (Thornton, Ocasio and Lounsbury 2012) and the 'strategic action fields' within which they are operationalized and sustained (Fligstein and McAdam 2012). However, the degree of interpretive and strategic closure which mediating mechanisms achieve through formalizing and normalizing the narratives and frames they wish to project in relation to certain 'institutional logics' or 'strategic action fields' are, at best, partial and contested. They are always open to counter interpretations and interventions that challenge and potentially over-turn the conventional orthodoxies which the latter have striven to establish and legitimate. Whatever their stabilizing potential, mediating mechanisms are inherently dynamic and flexible socio-material forms subject to competition and contestation from alternative narratives and frames telling very different stories justifying contrasting courses of social action to those project-ed by proponents of the mainstream view.

In this way, mediating mechanisms frame the socio-material context in which social actors intervene in the ebb and flow of social life in pursuit of certain out-comes favourable to their values and interests. They promote and justify certain courses of social action directed to the realization of social actors' preferences and inclinations as they emerge out of successive phases of social struggle and en-gagement aligned, however well or poorly, with their desire to bring about situa-tional outcomes in which their hopes and aspirations have some chance of being translated into social realities.

This takes us to the final conceptual component around which our three ana-lytical narratives are constructed and promoted – that is, the concept of 'out-comes', and the role it plays in shaping the latter.

3.3 Outcomes

Each of the analytical narratives discussed in the following three chapters of this book develops an account of the complex dynamics whereby key structural changes, refracted through the primary mediating mechanisms they identify, im-pact on established forms of expert authority in ways that threaten the latter's ideological legitimacy and organizational integrity. Consequently, they, individually and collectively, document substantive outcomes which change, and in some cases fundamentally transform, the 'conditions of possibility' for the emergence, stabili-zation and reproduction of expert authority in ways that radically move us away from the established Neo-Weberian model. As such, they suggest that we have in-herited a model of expert authority, largely based on our understanding of modern professions – and the core occupational and organizational mechanisms through which the latter establish and sustain 'legitimate domination' – which is no longer conceptually equipped to deal with the complexity it now confronts. Not only do they insist that the 'conditions of possibility' under which the orthodox form of professionally based expert authority was established have been transformed in ways which undermine its credibility and sustainability, but also that new forms of expert power and control have emerged which cannot be accommodated within its theoretical parameters. Indeed, they emphasize that the proliferation of groups and organizations claiming expert authority and status, as well as our continued belief in and dependence on 'expertise' – however conditional and contingent they may be in practice – have generated a much more crowded and competitive marketplace for the services they provide, so that 'trust' must be pro-actively se-cured and renewed by those claiming it. 'Taken-for-granted' assumptions about institutionalized trust in expert authority are no longer sustainable in a world in which the ideological foundations and political scaffolding on and through which the latter was sustained have become so insecure and corroded as to be 'unfit for purpose'. As we shall explore in chapter five of this book, this may even be the case in the context of a major public health crisis where our, literally 'life and death dependence' on expert knowledge, skill and technology may be pre-eminent, but the dangers which this global emergency entails for those anticipating a renewal of expert authority should not be dismissed or underestimated.

Thus, the third element of the heuristic framework through which the next three chapters of this book are organized relates to the current condition of expert authority and what this might mean for its prospects. In some cases, both the analysis and prognosis as to its present state and future possibilities are very bleak insofar as they identify a collapse in the institutionalized trust relationship between 'experts' and 'citizens' which is irreparable due to the latter's scale and significance. Other analytical narratives are somewhat less apocalyptic than this to the extent that they envisage the emergence of a more realistic public understanding and appreciation of the inherent limits of expert knowledge and the technological and practical interventions which it makes possible. Still others anticipate the evolution of a 'hybridized' form of expert authority embedded within a much more complex system of expert ecologies in which experts become much more open and sensitive to their 'necessary connectivity' to those whom they serve (Noordegraaf 2020; Reed 2020).

Yet, however much they may differ, indeed disagree, over the scale and depth of the crisis which expert authority is currently facing, they share a common appreciation of the need for a theoretical approach to our understanding of how expert power and control are legitimated under very different conditions to those in which professions became established as the primary occupational carriers and organizational expressions of institutionalized trust in modern societies. Together, they point the way to the need for the development of a theoretical approach to our understanding of expert authority that recognizes and expresses the inherent complexities and realities of its constitution and articulation in twenty-first century societies which we outline in the penultimate chapter of this book.

4 Conclusion

In this introductory chapter we have set out the key features of the Neo-Weberian ideal typical model of expert authority – as it has been developed by industrial and political sociologists and organizational theorists over half a century or more – and of the heuristic underpinnings of the three analytical narratives which have questioned the latter's continued theoretical and empirical relevance to twenty-first century forms of expert power and control.

This model of expert authority presumes a stable structural alignment between 'epistemic exclusion' and 'jurisdictional closure' which has become increasingly difficult to sustain in a socio-historical context characterized by escalating economic insecurity, social fragmentation and political polarization. The mediating mechanisms through which this alignment has been traditionally secured experience declining integrative and coordinative effectiveness as they are exposed to intensifying competitive and fragmenting pressures in both the marketplace for expertise and the workplaces within which it becomes organized. While the former becomes hyper-competitive and fractured within a deregulated socio-political context in which institutionalized trust is weakened and diluted, the latter begin to lose their capacity to organize and police conventional occupational boundaries and hierarchies as they are forced to adapt to new technologies that undermine and eradicate the divisions on which they were previously established.

As a result, the 'deus ex machina' of expert authority – that is, its capacity to maintain the 'in-determination' of its esoteric knowledge base and technical skills from public exposure by retaining its mysterious, even 'god-like' or sacred quality from all but those 'few' who are admitted into its inner sanctum through prolonged socialization and training (Grace 2014) – becomes progressively subjected to the unremitting rationalizing impulses of externally imposed market discipline, technological deskilling and remote organizational control. The 'god in the professional machine' is dragged, kicking and screaming, into the full glare of public exposure and its symbolic trappings stripped away to reveal something much closer to human beings in all their frailties and failings. But this, potentially, creates serious problems for professional authority insofar as it its claim to 'special status' over and above its claims to expert technical/functional expertise is stripped-bare of its key legitimating identifier – that is, its unique capacity to resolve the moral and ethical dilemmas which professional practice necessarily entails. If professional authority – as the paradigm case of expert authority – is reduced to its technical/functional effectiveness, then securing and retaining all forms of expert authority becomes much more problematic in an environment where a 'low trust' dynamic seems to have become the dominant social, political, and cultural reality.

Insofar as the independent, self-regulating professional occupation and the institutionalization of exclusive specialist knowledge and socio-technical practices on which its legitimacy rested has become the exemplar of expert authority, then it must be critically reviewed and re-evaluated at a time when the ideological and material pre-conditions on which it depended have been destabilized and transformed. This is not something which has happened overnight; indeed, it is more appropriately viewed as a long-term process in which several structural and discursive changes have coalesced to form a 'critical juncture' within which the cogency and viability of the established theoretical model of expert authority is increasingly open to question.

As the forthcoming chapters will demonstrate, white-collar, middle-class professionals, technocrats and managers – what Galbraith (1967) called the 'corporate technostructure' – find themselves increasingly subjected to the levels of job insecurity, ubiquitous organizational control and low-trust workplace relations once the preserve of working-class, blue-collar workers. Elite groups of experts within the established professions, central governmental regimes and global corporate technocratic networks have managed, so far, to insulate themselves from the worst excesses of the new disciplinary regimes routinely experienced by middle and lower-level personnel. However, they are also beginning to 'feel the heat' from encroaching employment market insecurity and technological/organizational rationalization in ways that eats away at the liberal public service social contract between 'them' and 'us', consequently undermining the institutionalized trust on which their authority had once been legitimated. The more they strive to insulate themselves – in both non-work and work settings (Bishop 2009) – from the rest of us, the more isolated and remote they become, reigniting and reinforcing populist critiques of socially remote and economically privileged 'elites' who no longer deserve our trust and support in exchange for the vital public services they supposedly provide. In turn, this populist critique of expert authority has gained increasing political traction as it reveals the social reality of a 'meritocratic society' in which core norms such as 'equality of opportunity' are exposed as ideological mystifications for the social reproduction of elite privilege and power (Sandel 2020; Frank 2020).

In a hyper-competitive, deregulated and low trust political economy and society, expert authority is now regularly exposed to levels of social critique and political suspicion previously unknown to those groups who claim it. They can no longer bask in the luxury of political, economic and cultural support from within governmental, corporate and media elite circles, nor in the certainty of automatic or 'passive trust' from those that continue to depend on their services but with escalating levels of distrust and dissatisfaction.

In the next three chapters of this book, we provide an exposition and evaluation of the three analytical narratives – based on the conceptual building blocks outlined in the previous section of this introductory chapter – that have challenged, to varying degrees and intensities, the theoretical and empirical sustainability of the Neo-Weberian model of expert authority as a form of legitimate domination based on a stable structural alignment between 'epistemic exclusion' and 'jurisdictional closure' as exemplified in modern professional associations and occupations.

Chapter 2: Delegitimation

1 Introduction

Of the three narratives reviewed in this book, 'de-legitimation' provides the most pessimistic, even 'existential', evaluation of the current condition of and prospects for expert authority. This is the case insofar as it signals a fundamental breakdown in the institutionalized 'trust relationship' between experts and those whom they serve, while signposting a future developmental trajectory in which attempts to repair the former are doomed to fail.

If the legitimation of expert power – and its subsequent transmutation into 'expert authority' – rests on a generalized acceptance of its pivotal contribution to the 'greater good' and public wellbeing within society, then the de-legitimation narrative insists that the structural, ideological and political preconditions necessary for this transformation to occur no longer exist. It advances a set of arguments and supporting evidence which contend that these necessary preconditions have been decimated by a 'critical conjuncture' of systemic changes fatally undermining the former's credibility and sustainability.

In short, the de-legitimation narrative supports the view that expert authority is in the throes of a 'legitimation crises' from which it is highly unlikely to recover in anything like its established form as outlined in the previous chapter. Considered in this way, the crisis in expert authority is interpreted as a key element of a wider, macro-level crisis in liberal democracy and capitalist modernity which is deracinating the economic, political and social foundations on which such a form of authority was once established and reproduced.

This narrative draws on, broadly speaking, neo-Marxist and neo-Weberian theoretical traditions in political economy and sociology to generate a substantial body of literature which, analytically and historically, locates the crisis in expert authority as an institutional expression of a deeper, systemic crisis in the overarching structures and relations through which modern capitalist accumulation and its governance are sustained (Habermas 1976, 1985; Jessop 2008, 2016; Schneider et al. 2017; Streeck 2014, 2016; Levitsky and Ziblatt 2018; Runciman 2019; Scott 2020; Vormann and Weinman 2021; Müller 2021).

Consequently, the de-legitimation narrative analytically focuses on the exogenous structural changes generating a systemic crisis in the institutional architecture and normative infrastructure through which contemporary capitalism and its supporting state regimes are legitimated and reproduced. The crisis in expert authority is interpreted as an integral feature of this wider implosion of authority structures in contemporary capitalism and liberal representative democracy gen-

https://doi.org/10.1515/9783110734911-003

erated by the extreme and unrelenting pressures imposed on them by exogenous changes in economy, polity and society. In this way, the de-legitimation narrative rejects the more optimistic and pragmatic assessments of those researchers and analysts operating within the 'decomposition' narrative (reviewed in chapter 4). They have failed to appreciate the scale and significance of the transformation that contemporary capitalism and liberal democracy are undergoing and *the existential threat it poses to established forms of expert authority.*

Following the analytical framework developed in the previous chapter, this chapter proceeds to identify the **structural changes** which are transforming contemporary capitalism and liberal democracy, followed by a discussion of the **mediating mechanisms** through which they are selected and interpreted, concluding with an evaluation of their **substantive outcomes** for established forms of expert authority.

2 Structural Changes

As previously indicated, the de-legitimation narrative offers a transformative, rather than adaptive or incremental, account of why and how expert authority is being attacked in ways that irrevocably tear-up and destroy, root-and-branch, its normative foundations and institutional integrity. It identifies a systemic breakdown of collective trust and belief in the moral foundations of the economic, political and social relations through which modern capitalism and its regulatory order are maintained such that a tsunami of epistemological and ethical 'nihilism' threatens to engulf whatever remnants of scientific rationality and procedural justice are left in a world dominated by 'might is right' (Mair 2013; Davis 2018; Applebaum 2020; Davies 2020a; Geoghegan 2020). Insofar as 'organized irresponsibility' (Beck 1999; Tooze 2021) – that is, a systemic disregard for the escalating levels of global, national and local risk and instability created by 'organized economic and political power' on the part of both public and private authorities – becomes the dominant ethos of ruling elites, then experts are relatively powerless to do anything about it. The technocratic dream of a world in which 'intractable questions of ethics [and politics] become matters of expert judgement' (Gray 2007:106) has mutated into a nihilistic nightmare in which nobody and nothing is to be trusted as a source of dependable knowledge and belief as a basis for 'going on' in ways which accommodate divergent, and often conflicting, values and interests. Instead, the Hobbesian vision of a 'war of all against all' beckons as the 'new normal' in a polity where the 'rules of the game' decay and the groups expected to uphold them retreat into their gated communities safe in their conviction that they can withstand whatever mayhem results (Bishop 2009; Müller 2021), whereas the 'left behind' are expected to fend for themselves as best they can as 'strangers in their own land' (Hochschild 2016).

Thus, the de-legitimation narrative identifies a 'critical conjuncture' between changes in several 'system-critical domains' which generates a system-wide transformation in authority structures and their strategic role in managing socio-political order. This 'critical conjuncture' is conceptualized as a 'coming together' of a configuration of economic/technological, political and socio-cultural changes which generates a chain reaction of transformative, rather than incremental, innovation in the core power structures through which societies are organized and managed. It entails a complex recombination of systemic changes creating an existential crisis in which established institutions and the overarching pattern of relations between them are subject to ever-increasing levels of instability and uncertainty that cannot be contained by the 'steering mechanisms' on which modern capitalist states have normally depended (Babones 2018; Jessop 2016; Guillén 2015; Kennedy 2016).

In relation to economic/technological changes, the de-legitimation narrative identifies four interrelated 'system-critical and system-wide developments: first, the global diffusion of neoliberal capitalism as the dominant form of economic organization; second, the 'fourth industrial revolution' entailing the exponentially developing power and influence of new technologies such as AI, big data, robotics and data harvesting and their destructive impact on the world of work; third, the rise of what some analysts have identified as 'surveillance capitalism' (Zuboff 2019) and others as the 'surveillance state' (Strittmatter 2019; Susskind 2020) in which vastly expanded powers or 'affordances' (Susskind 2020) of centralized, remote monitoring and decentralized, micro level control are made available to ruling groups within private corporations and public bureaucracies; and, finally, the intensification of 'distributional conflicts' between social actors as socio-economic inequality widens and deepens.

Moving to political/socio-cultural changes, the de-legitimation narrative focuses on five linked changes: first, declining ideological and political elite support for forms of expert power and authority which 'get in the way' of ineluctable progress towards a market society and the crucial role which a reconstructed 'neoliberal state' must play in both advancing and protecting the political process whereby universal market principles come to dominate all aspects of socio-economic life (Mirowski 2013; Davies 2014); second, the recrudescence of authoritarian populism and its rejection of pluralistic modes of interest articulation and coordination; third, recurring expert failures/scandals and their corrosive impact on public belief in and support for 'objective expertise' as a crucial and trusted source of shared knowledge and intervention; fourth, the secular decline of the public sphere/sector under neoliberal policies and programmes driven by marketization, privatization and deregulation; finally, the perceived rootlessness and remoteness of self-selected and self-reproducing professional/technocratic elites who increasingly remove themselves from the rest of society.

In the next section of this chapter, we will consider each of these changes in turn before moving on to a discussion of the mediating mechanisms through which they are brought together to form carriers of destructive and innovative institutional transformation.

2.1 Economic/Technological Changes

2.1.1 Neoliberal Capitalism

Several analysts and researchers have identified the 'disorganizing dynamic' at the core of neo-liberalization as it has uprooted the social foundations and dismantled the structural architecture through which post-1945, neo-Keynesian/neo-Corporatist managerial capitalism was constructed and sustained until the 1980s (Harvey 2005, 2011, 2015; Jessop 2008, 2016; Peck 2010, 2015; Blyth 2013; Ban 2016; Crouch 2016; Swarts 2013; Schneider et al. 2017; Streeck 2014, 2016). Streeck (2016: 14 – emphasis in original) identifies this 'disorganizing dynamic' at in the following terms:

> Contemporary capitalism, then, would appear to be a society where system integration is critically and irredeemably weakened, so that the continuation of capital accumulation – for an intermediate period of uncertain duration – becomes solely dependent on the opportunism of collectively incapacitated *individualized individuals*, as they struggle to protect themselves from looming accidents and structural pressures on their social and economic status. Under-governed and under-managed, the social world of the post-capitalist interregnum, in the wake of neoliberal capitalism having cleared away states, governments, borders, trade unions and other moderating forces, can at any time be hit by disaster.

However, he also notes that the destructive force of neoliberal capitalism – as evidenced in the systemic disintegration of the 'system stabilizers' that defined post-war, managerial capitalism and the overall system breakdown which this generated – is regarded as 'historical progress towards individual liberty and a free society' (Streeck 2016: 15) by political and economic elites occupying dominant positions within neoliberal political economies and their 'ideological cheerleaders'. In this way, the dismantling and weakening of the managerial structures and regulatory regimes through which post-War coordinated capitalism was stabilized and steered – what Jessop (1994: 13–37) summarizes as entailing the hollowing-out of the welfare state and its replacement with a neoliberal workfare state – sets in motion a process of institutional destabilization and social dislocation which threatens all those who, actually or potentially, stand in its way. The latter can be identified with a number of interrelated structural changes and strategic policy shifts directly associated with the emergence and development of neoliberal capitalism since the 1980s such as: the rapid deregulation of the financial sector and the increasing power of 'finance capital' (Cahill and Konings 2017; Lapavitsas 2013; Vogl 2017); long-term austerity-driven economic policy and programmes generating much higher levels of unemployment or 'underemployment' and socio-economic inequality (Blyth 2013); the transference of public power to large-scale private corporations and the marketization of public services which resulted (Hurt and Lipschutz 2016); the imposition of a system of 'private government' in which state and corporate power are fused into one and transferred to non-accountable domains in which public scrutiny is very difficult, if not impossible, to realize (Brown 2015; Anderson 2017); and the emasculation of public bureaucracies by undermining their statutory independence and diluting their organizational autonomy by drastically reducing the quality of their employees' employment conditions (Malin 2020; Newman and Clarke 2009).

Cumulatively, these structural changes and policy shifts fundamentally alter the balance of power between 'capital' and 'labour' in favour of the former such that neoliberal capitalism becomes, at least potentially, 'a victim of its own success'. By routing its opponents in both the economy and civil society (trade unions, local governments, social movements etc.,), neoliberal capitalism has removed, or at least drastically weakened, any effective sources of 'countervailing power' (Galbraith 1967) to its rule. Yet, its victory leads to increasing levels of economic inequality and deprivation, intensified distributional conflicts, and rising levels of socio-political dislocation and rootlessness which may be uncontainable within anything resembling 'democratic due process' and a gradual but unmistakable shift towards much more authoritarian and populist forms of governance. Indeed, the latter have the potential to slow, if not reverse, many of the structural transformations entailed in the emergence and reproduction of neoliberal capitalist political economies insofar as they reject the modernizing and globalizing thrust inherent within them in favour of a much more traditional and nationalistic outlook.

2.1.2 Fourth Industrial Revolution

Alongside the ever-accelerating process of 'creative destruction' unleashed by over four decades of neo-liberalization – driven by an ideological vision and political project determined to impose market discipline in every nook and cranny of socio-economic life – a new configuration of informational and social technologies emerged over this period which further destabilized the normative and structural architecture through which expert power and control were legitimated. Traversing a wide spectrum of innovative and exponentially advancing technologies, encompassing social media, data mining and extraction, robotics, and artificial intelligence, this 'fourth industrial revolution' seems to dovetail with neo-liberalization to constitute an existential threat to a form of expert authority based on claims to exclusive, indeterminate, objective, and specialized knowledge putatively 'beyond the reach of non-experts or machines' (Susskind and Susskind 2015; Susskind 2020, 2022; Crawford 2021; Johannessen 2020; Ford 2021). Not only this, but the combination of free market zealotry and socio-material technologies geared to 'massified individualism' and 'surveillance capitalism' pushes conventional, state-centric politics and the established professions and technocrats on which it depends for its routine administrative functioning even further on to the margins of socio-political life (Zuboff 2019; Benanav 2020). In their place, a new cadre of management consultants or 'calculative experts' emerges to take over the key strategic positions and operational roles once occupied and performed by professional administrators, scientists and technocrats who are no longer deemed to have 'history on their side' (Raco 2013; Eyal 2019; Sturdy, Wright and Wylie 2016; Sturdy and O'Mahoney 2018; Malin 2020). Indeed, the former can be seen as constituting an informal 'shadow elite' supporting their political masters occupying formal positions of authority within a streamlined neoliberal state apparatus and simultaneously winning out on the jurisdictional power struggles occurring within established administrative and professional hierarchies (Wedel 2011, 2014; Reed 2018; Heusinkveld et al. 2018). Johannessen (2020: foreword) summarizes the key 'power shift' generated by the fourth industrial revolution as entailing an economic and political polarization between an exclusive elite of 'innovation and knowledge workers' enjoying the material and social benefits once taken-for-granted by professional staff and an expanding 'precariat' of insecure, marginalized and alienated workers:

> Robots will have destroyed bureaucratic hierarchies and torn apart the middle classes. What will remain is contract workers with insecure jobs ... slightly further into the future, we can see a major transformation in professional environments. Doctors will be medical engineers; nurses will be nursing assistants accompanied by robots. Teachers will be replaced by robots and holograms ... the Fourth Industrial Revolution will decimate the middle classes.

However, there is more than a hint of technological and historical determinism in this kind of analysis, which is mirrored in the, at times almost messianic, ontological and epistemological commitments to be found at the analytical core of neoliberalism as a political ideology and project. The latter seems best articulated as a theoretical hybrid of economic determinism and social constructionism which seems incapable of recognizing the philosophical and political contradictions barely contained by its ideological patina of 'individualized individualism (Mirowski 2013; Davies 2014 Springer 2016; Streeck 2016; Cahill and Konings 2017). Nevertheless, the combination of exponentially unfolding economic, political and technological disorganization generated by successive waves of neo-liberalization and auto-mation since the 1980s is very likely to have 'fateful consequences' for institution-alized forms of expert authority exemplified by the established professions, senior civil servants, scientists and other members of the top echelons of the once dom-inant social democratic state.

As Crawford (2021: 217) reminds us, there is nothing particularly new or inno-vative about technologies such as AI and robotics. Building on Hardt and Negri's (2019) distinction between 'abstraction' and 'extraction' in neoliberal/informational capitalism – that is, between 'abstracting away the material conditions of produc-tion, while extracting more information and resources' – she proffers an analysis of AI stressing its critical role as an industry that integrates technology, capital and power in much deeper and more inscrutable ways than earlier forms of capital accumulation. By accelerating and deepening the global 'disorganizing dynamic' at the core of neoliberal capitalism, the AI industry abstracts and distances itself from the economic and political imperatives which drive it through the promulga-tion of 'discourses that support its aura of immateriality and inevitability' (Craw-ford 2021: 217). In so doing, it also obscures the underlying shift of power and au-thority away from, at least partially, accountable public officials, professions and technocrats towards private elites and corporations who engage in a form of 'hy-brid rule' as 'the state harnesses the private sector and generates a new pattern of state-capital or government-business relations that redefine our understanding of political authority and power' (Hurt and Lipschutz 2016: 3).

Crawford's identification of the indelible link between globalized neoliberal capitalism and AI is supported by Ford's (2021) analysis of robotics and its role in advancing AI as a disruptive and dislocating technology vastly expanding the surveillance capabilities of both corporations and states (Pasquale 2015). He also suggests that organizational roles requiring relatively high levels of creative, com-plex and coordinating knowledge and skills may have some degree of protection from the 'rationalizing and downsizing' impact of these new technologies. Howev-er, they are unlikely to escape unscathed. Indeed, the likelihood of these, relatively privileged and protected, knowledge/expert workers finding themselves enrolled within advanced control systems and governance regimes even more pervasive and intrusive than anything experienced under managerial capitalism is very high. In an age when 'super-intelligent machines' pose an emerging, if still some-what 'futuristic, existential threat to even the most creative and complex organiza-tional roles (Ford 2021; Susskind 2020) – particularly in a political environment where 'transparency' and 'regulation' are viewed by neoliberal political and eco-nomic elites with deep suspicion if not disdain – then the downgrading, if not elim-ination, of these roles to subordinate 'technical' and 'supervisory' functions located outside the organization's core labour market is an ever-present threat.

Beyond the workplace, other commentators (Gurri 2018; Amoore 2020; Daub 2020) highlight the complex ways in which globalized social media has undermined the authority of established expert elites in the eyes of the general public and advanced the political causes of, mostly right-wing, authoritarian populist leaders and regimes. By challenging any claims to truthfulness, rational analysis and objective knowledge – especially that claimed by institutionalized forms of expertise in government and public service more generally – and encouraging widespread disbelief in 'public authority', those organizations and groups who own and control globalized digital platforms have created a public sphere in which a 'culture of nihilism' becomes more evident. As Daub (2020) suggests, the communitarian politics initialling shaping the development of social media has been highjacked by a 'libertarian counterinsurgency' dismissive of governments and experts who do not, indeed cannot, understand the driving forces behind neoliberal capitalism and their 'entrepreneurial champions' such as Peter Thiel, Egon Musk and Richard Branson. Rather than leading to a transformation, even transcendence, of modern capitalism into something called 'hyper-capitalism', the combination of neoliberal capitalism and the 'fourth industrial revolution' have accelerated and replicated the power dynamics on which capitalist exploitation always depended. But they have done this in even more authoritarian and anti-democratic forms profoundly unwelcoming to anything and anybody representing publicly accountable 'expert authority'.

2.1.3 Surveillance Capitalism/State

As they become structurally aligned, neoliberal capitalism and the fourth industrial revolution can be seen to generate a new configuration, indeed fusion, of economic and political power in which greatly expanded surveillance technologies and their associated governance regimes gradually replace the formalized bureaucratic control systems typical of managerial capitalism.

Zuboff (2019) analyses these developments as entailing the move to a form of 'surveillance capitalism' in which the 'Big Digital 5' (Apple, Google, Amazon, Microsoft and Facebook) have created a new and unprecedented mode of accumulation and surveillance through four interrelated mechanism or processes: first, the discovery and manipulation of 'behavioural surpluses' (the traces we leave behind) into surveillance products/assets sold to advertisers; second, the translation of the latter into surveillance revenues through the construction of 'prediction factories'; third, using AI to generate even more accurate prediction products by forecasting what users will feel, think and do; and finally, the trading of these prediction products on 'behavioural futures markets' not limited to advertisers, This regime of behavioural surveillance and commodification is then imitated by many second and third tier digital corporations.

She further contends that this move to 'surveillance capitalism' has been made possible through two, interrelated, structural transformations uniquely favourable to its emergence and advancing dominance: first, the capture of the US governmental machine by neoliberal economic and political elites no longer committed to the 'checks and balances'/'countervailing power' model of governance accepted by post-1945 governing elites as they become more fragmented and factionalized (Mizruchi 2013), while moving toward a more confrontational mode of economic and political governance in which 'winner takes all' at a global and national level (Giridharadas 2018); second, the suspension of previously accepted and normalized democratic rules and constraints on government action legitimated by the 'war on terror' released by the aftermath of the 9/11 attack and the sharp tilt to exclusionary and intrusive surveillance regimes that it encouraged. Levitsky and Ziblatt (2018) proffer a wider analysis of this shift to more authoritarian modes of governance as exemplified in Trump's administration and the abdication of the Republican Party in the face of a rising tide of right-wing populism in which the unwritten rules and constraints within which liberal representative democracy normally operate are 'subverted from within' rather than by a classic coup d'état.

For Zuboff (2019: 100), the commodification of private behaviour made possible by the pivot towards surveillance capitalism under neoliberal/populist ruling elites in Anglo-Saxon political economies points towards a future in which 'market power is protected by moats of secrecy, indecipherability and expertise … In this future, we are exiles from our own behaviour, denied access to or control over knowledge derived by its dispossession by others for others'. The rise of a new 'corporate feudalism' under the twin drivers of neo-liberalization and technological rationalization which Zuboff identifies is anticipated in Wolin's (2004:588) analysis of a 'revolution from above' in which corporate elites impose a political economy in which 'the state and the corporation have become partners in the process; each has begun to mimic functions historically identified with the other'. Within this new corporate feudalism – ironically, if not tragically, driven by a political ideology and economic doctrine meant to release us from the bondage of collectivist feudalism by the creatively destructive forces of unrestrained market competition and exponential technological change – experts and their expertise become subordinated to massive concentrations of knowledge and power in which 'powerful private interests are in control of the definitive principle of social ordering in our time … it is the surveillance capitalist corporations that know … It is the competitive struggle among surveillance capitalists that decides who decides' (Zuboff 2019: 192). Experts are reduced to the level of 'mechanics' and 'fine tuners' who maintain and recalibrate the digital machinery which makes surveillance capitalism a material and operational reality, but they have little, if any, say in the strategic goals and underlying productive logic determining how the latter will be used.

Kotkin (2020) also provides an analysis of the 'coming of neo-feudalism' in the form of reconfigured concentrations of wealth, knowledge and power that are ruled by a new form of aristocracy or oligarchy which has the dominant influence over the government and culture, while closing itself off from access to all but a tiny minority through the erection of economic, educational and political barriers to entry defeating most aspirant candidates. He sees these ruling economic and technocratic elites in terms set out by Daniel Bell (1960, 1973, 1976, 1999) in his analysis of 'a new priesthood of power' emerging under the driving force of capitalist-led post-industrialization from the mid-1970s onwards and their advocacy of a new 'technocratic authoritarianism' replacing the inherent messy trade-offs of liberal democracy with a new form of unaccountable 'rule by experts' but under the tutelage of a remote plutocratic elite. Runciman (2019: 180 – 201) sees the latter potentially evolving into a 'new epistocracy' entailing not rule by mechanics and engineers but by 'the people who know best'; that is, a 'net-archy' (Thompson 2003; Savage and Williams 2008) in which networks of technical experts in a wide range of institutional domains find themselves subordinated to the hierarchical rule of a plutocratic elite who allow the formal trappings of public accountability to be maintained, while ensuring they don't get in the way of 'getting business done' in ways which reinforce plutocratic power and control (Davis 2018; Guilluy 2019).

This is also the analytical juncture at which 'surveillance capitalism' meets the 'surveillance state'; the authoritarian pragmatism characteristic of Putin's Russia (Belton 2020) or Xi's China (Strittmatter 2019; Hamilton and Ohlberg 2020) also depends upon the right combination of concentrated economic-cum-technocratic power and centralized political-cum-social control in order to ensure, as far as possible, that citizens are intensively monitored and closely watched in all aspects of their lives. Such a 'surveillance state' also facilitates an 'elite kleptocracy' in which a system of elite stealing and expropriation becomes so pervasive and dominant that 'everyone [becomes] hostage to the system' (Belton 2020: 498), from the plutocrats and oligarchs who are the powerbrokers of the overall system to the technocrats and professionals who provide the technical expertise required to keep it functioning. While the underlying institutional logics of surveillance capitalism and the surveillance state may differ considerably in relation to their 'system imperatives' – that is capital accumulation and private appropriation as opposed to political domination and social control – they both demand that expert authority is subordinated to the dictates of ruling elites who are driven by their determination to reproduce the structure of power relations through which their rule is protected and to sustain the vast economic rewards it generates for them.

2.1.4 Distributional Conflicts

Yet, neoliberal capitalism, technological rationalization and the rise of surveillance capitalism/state have not had everything their own way. Resistance, individual and collective, disorganized and organized, sporadic and sustained, has been evident throughout their evolution over the last forty years or so. But the 'creative destruction' wrought by neo-liberalization, automation and the advance of surveillance capitalism/state has been so disruptive and dislocating as to make collective, organized and sustained resistance to the imposition of neoliberal rule and governance extremely difficult to mobilize and maintain.

As Streeck (2014, 2016) has maintained, the combination of neoliberal capitalism and technological rationalization have had the cumulative effect of reducing growth rates, increasing socio-economic inequality, steepening levels of public and private indebtedness, enhanced reliance on a pumped-up money supply through continuous quantitative easing and intensified competition between states, corporations and regions have cumulatively generated more severe 'distributional conflicts' and widespread cynicism as to the capacity of governments to manage them. In place of the 'give and take' bargaining between vested interests and the 'deal making' characteristic of neo-corporatist intermediation and managerial capitalism, neoliberal capitalism entails 'substituting modern co-operative problem-solving by experts for old-fashioned class conflict' (Streeck 2016: 23). Demands for ever increasing 'labour market flexibility' and the precarious forms of employment which such policies inevitably promote leads to increasing division and conflict between and within social classes and status groups such that the mitigating and moderating influence of the 'checks and balances' enjoyed under social democratic governance and coordinated modes of capital accumulation are denuded of their restraining influence.

Expert occupational groups and organizations are very much 'part and parcel' of this intensified distributional conflict created by the destructive dynamic underlying neo-liberalization and its embrace of more openly class-based and confrontational modes of conflict resolution. In many respects, they are located at the fulcrum of the latter to the extent that they provide the expert labour required to design, operate and administer the expert systems on which neoliberal capitalism increasingly relies, while constituting a highly significant financial cost and organizational risk to its corporate owners and controllers (Raco 2013; Leicht 2016; Sturdy, Wright and Wylie 2016; Spencer, Voulgaris and MacLean 2017; Reed 2018). Organization-level research has also suggested that middle-ranking experts constituting the occupational core of the 'corporate technostructure' (Galbraith 2007) are willing to engage in forms of workplace resistance which are directed at creating and defending physical, mental and social 'spaces' in which more communal and collective modes of action can flourish – even in the face of the individualizing and fragmenting dynamic which drives neo-liberalization (Fleming and Spicer 2007; Currie et al. 2012; Newman 2013; O'Reilly and Reed 2011; Reed and Wallace 2015; Courpasson, Younes and Reed 2021). These conflicts often revolve around issues related to the standards and quality of work that expert workers wish to see protected against the worst 'deskilling' and 'de-professionalizing' impacts of economic and technological rationalization. They also relate to expert workers roles as 'knowledge brokers' and the leverage this still gives them in intra-organizational political processes focused on strategic decision-making over new markets, products, technologies and performance regimes.

Although neoliberal corporate bureaucracies have significantly reduced the autonomy and power of expert workers through economic marketization, technological rationalization and organizational surveillance, this does not mean to say that pose no risk, indeed threat, to the dominance of ruling economic and political elites. The prevailing mode of institutional and organizational governance emerging under neoliberal capitalism entails a hybridization of 'private' and 'public' power in which a novel configuration of relations and practices aimed at bringing these two orders or worlds into alignment sit rather uneasily together. Expert workers continue to play a vital role in 'making the hybrid happen' (Reed and Wallace 2015) to the extent that they are simultaneously the agents driving such a process on, but they are also expected to provide the vital co-ordinating and integrating expertise when hybridization threatens to overwhelm neoliberal corporate bureaucracies, in both the public and private sectors, with unmanageable uncertainty, complexity and chaos. Thus, the hybrid rule which becomes dominant under neo-liberalization also becomes more and more ambivalent, vague, disconcerting and disorienting for those subject to its bureaucratic complexities and uncertainties and those expected to make it work in the face of the latter. As Hibou (2016:76) concludes, neoliberal bureaucratization articulates and redefines the contradictions, tensions and conflicts which lie at the organizational core of neoliberal governance, but they do this in such a way as to impose even more pressure and stress on expert workers to make them work without the normative, regulative and political steering mechanisms on which co-ordinated/managerial capitalism could depend when 'the going gets rough'. Expert workers now occupy the organizational spaces in which the contradictory forces released by neo-liberalization collide, spaces in which they can carve-out some degree of autonomy and control, but only if they continue to provide the co-ordinating and integrating expertise through which the destruction and chaos inherent within the former can be at least mitigated and contained, if not exculpated.

2.2 Political/Socio-Cultural Changes

As previously indicated, the de-legitimation narrative identifies five key political/ socio-cultural changes which, when aligned with the economic/technological changes discussed in the previous sections of this chapter, irreparably undermine expert authority. This seen to be especially case when the 'mediating mechanisms' through which these changes have been interpreted and implemented – as reviewed in the latter sections of this chapter – are seen to be incapable of recognizing, much less 'making good', the destructive impact of neo-liberalization on the normative and structural pre-conditions on which the legitimation of expert power and control has been based under the established neo-Weberian model outlined in the previous chapter. These five key political/socio-cultural changes can be summarised as entailing 'elite withdrawal', 'authoritarian populism', 'expert failure', 'public service decline' and 'expert secession'.

2.2.1 Elite Withdrawal

Streeck (2016: 35–37) suggests, that social orders only implode when their ruling elites are no longer prepared to do the hard work necessary to sustain them. If true, then those researchers and analysts supporting the 'de-legitimation narrative' insist that this is exactly what has occurred under the governance regimes imposed by neoliberal economic, political and cultural elites who have carried neo-liberalization forward since the late 1970s/early 1980s in Anglo-American political economies (Harvey 2005; Peck 2010; Peck and Theodore 2015; Leicht 2016; Springer 2016; Davis and Williams 2017; Busch 2017; Nichols 2017; Vogl 2017; Cahill and Konings 2017). At the core of the neo-liberalization process and project lies the ideological and political imperative of reconstructing the capitalist state in ways that 'purge it' of any remaining neo-corporatist/social democratic traces or residues and remaking it in the light of an unerring commitment to the universalization of market principles that know no boundaries or limitations as to their unqualified application and guaranteed success (Davies 2014, 2018; Dardot and Laval 2013; Smets et al. 2017). Market competition and the economic discipline it imposes must become the dominant institutional logic pervading all spheres of social life. Consequently, the neoliberal state must play the central political and administrative role in ensuring that government policies and programmes become carriers of this market logic and that nothing must be allowed to compromise, much less contest, its realization right across the ever-expanding spectrum of economic, social and cultural domains in which such a state must encompass. As Gamble (2009, 2014) so brutally and eloquently expressed it, 'a free market needs a strong state' and that state must have the political will and administrative capacity required to remove any and every obstacle that stands in the way of realising the ideological nirvana of a 'market society' (Frank 2001, 2020).

No matter how compromised these hard ideological principles, and their emergent political logic may become under the grinding pressures and tensions of everyday governing in political economies subject to recurring crises and failures (Peck 2010; Davies 2014), they identify where potential opposition may located and how it is to be dealt with by those ruling elites charged with making the neoliberal state an organizational and administrative reality. Expert authority – and those groups deemed to be carriers of the legitimate powers and capacities which it gives them – are always likely to be treated with suspicion, if not contempt, by ruling neoliberal elites because they are deemed to embody an institutional logic of independent, or at least quasi-independent, 'professional' autonomy and control ideologically resonant of the social democratic/neo-corporatist state and the support it gave to their self-governance and management. This is, and will always be, a source of deep political concern for ruling neoliberal elites and their remaking of the modern capitalist state because 'professional experts', or for that matter any experts not under the effective control and direction of such a state, remain a potential and powerful source of opposition and contestation to the untrammelled imposition of market-driven policies and programmes. Whatever form 'embedded neoliberalism' takes in different countries, regions or localities at different historical periods (Swarts 2013; Cahill 2014; Peck and Theodore 2015; Ban 2016), the power, authority and status of professions and professionals are a potential source of countervailing interests and values to those prioritized by neoliberal governance regimes if they cannot be incorporated within the surveillance technologies and administrative systems on which the latter depend to secure the former's acquiescence, if not commitment.

Indeed, as several scholars have noted (Peck 2010; Mirowski 2013; Swarts 2014; Davies 2018, 2020; Reed 2018), ruling neoliberal elites have a 'schizophrenic' attitude towards the modern nation state and the experts on which it depends for its strategic steering and operational viability; on the one hand, they are extremely suspicious, almost paranoid, about the power of state-supported professionals, officials, technocrats, scientists, and mangers to frustrate and even undermine the neo-liberalization project by indirectly and subtly blocking and slowing its progress and momentum; on the other, they are acutely aware of their dependence on these strategically-located expert groups to ensure that neoliberal ideology is translated into state-backed policies and programmes which are practically sustainable and politically effective.

This simultaneous 'hate/love' relationship between ruling neoliberal elites and the public/private experts and their expertise on which they have to rely to get the neo-liberalization project moving as a deliverable set of policies and programmes means that they have implemented a series of 'state make-overs' in which the latter comes to resemble, as far as possible, the neoliberal ideal of a private business corporation in relation to its corporate culture, structure and systems. Thus, a running series of neoliberal state reforms – such as 'new public management', 'private finance initiative', 'public-private partnerships', 'internal markets', 'performance management', 'competitive outsourcing', 'continuous auditing', 'entrepreneurial leadership' and 'extra-judicial regulation' – have been undertaken over the last four decades or more across a range of Anglo-American political economies with the aim of ensuring that the administrative apparatus of the neoliberal state and the 'calculative/corporate experts' who run it remain committed to the imposition of competitive market discipline in all areas of socio-economic life (Du Gay 2005; Moran 2007; Wilks 2013; Raco 2013; Swarts 2013; Peck and Theodore 2015; Ban 2016; Eyal 2019 ; Reed 2019; Malin 2020; Plehwe, Slobodian and Misrowski 2020).

What we are seeing here is a gradual but persistent ideological and political withdrawal of neoliberal elite support for established forms of 'professional' expert authority and the occupational groups legitimating their power and control around the indispensable role they play in delivering an ideal of 'public service' which is no longer recognized or valued by the neoliberal state, While the social democratic state and its ruling elites broadly supported the growing power, authority and status of professionals, technocrats, experts and managers because of their functional indispensability, collective responsibility and technical reliability, neoliberal state elites have no qualms about placing the latter in a much more 'arm's length' relationship and subjecting them to a wide-range of intrusive and demeaning surveillance and control regimes having little or no time for 'due process' or 'professional autonomy'.

This withdrawal of neoliberal elite ideological and political support for expert authority has major implications for professionalized modes of occupational control and social closure. So, it is worth reiterating Larson's (2013: xii) argument that:

> Professions ultimately depend on the power of the state, and they originally emerge by the grace of powerful protectors. The privileged position of a profession is thus secured by the political and economic influence of the elite which sponsors it … an account of the process by which professions emerge illuminates the fact that professions gain autonomy; in this protected position, they can develop with increasing independence from the ideology of the dominant social elites … The fact remains, however, that their privileges can always be lost.

Larson may be developing her argument on the state-delegated and removable nature of professional power and authority, but this is true of 'expert authority' in general (Johnson 1994). Insofar as political, administrative, legal, and social elites acting in the name of the state remain the ultimate source of 'authorization' for those individuals and groups claiming such a status in relation to their expertise as an occupation, trade or skill, then they remain dependent on the former's continuing ideological and institutional support. Nevertheless, this sponsorship and support can always be withdrawn, particularly in a socio-historical context in which a new cadre of state elites remain profoundly suspicious of those forms of established expert authority which obstruct, dilute, or even oppose the disciplining force of unrestrained market competition. More than four decades of neo-liberalization has generated a very different economic, political and cultural environment in which multiple forms of expert authority – and especially professional authority – now find themselves exposed to state elites claiming to represent the interests of individual customers and users – or even more powerfully, 'the people' – against the self-interested interests and powers of elitist expert cartels.

Indeed, the emergence of 'mutant' strains of neoliberalism – forming hybrid ideological combinations of libertarianism, communitarianism, nationalism and technocracy – have been identified by a growing number of researchers as they plot the rise of more 'authoritarian populist' neoliberal political regimes exchanging globalism for 'autarky' and national self-reliance (Hurt and Lipschutz 2017; Callison and Manfredi 2020; Bickerton and Accetti 2021; Vormann and Weinman 2021; Reed 2022).

2.2.2 Authoritarian Populism

The recrudescence of a more 'authoritarian populist' ideological, political and economic strain of neoliberalism – as the latter 'mutates' in response to a changing global, national and regional environment in which accepted orthodoxies seem to be consistently overtaken and undermined by events (like a global financial crisis in 2008/9 and world-wide pandemic in 2020/21!) – has been tracked and traced by scholars researching 'populism' over the last decade or so (Müller 2016, 2021; Judis 2016; Mudde and Kaltwasser 2017; Fieschi 2019; Moffitt 2020). However, other researchers have argued that this 'authoritarian turn' in populist ideology and politics is by no means ineluctable and argue for a more progressive, 'centre/left' version that is supportive of more egalitarian and democratizing policies (Srnicek and Williams 2015; Mouffe 2018; Frank 2020). Either way, the recent rapprochement between neoliberalism and populism creates a potent ideological and political mix from which new and innovative governance regimes emerge that pose major challenges, not to say threats, to all forms of expert authority and those groups, organizations and movements claiming to exist and act in the name of their expertise.

Much like neoliberalism, populism is inherently distrustful and critical of those claiming authority based on their specialist expertise and its crucial role in protecting 'the public' against a wide range of threats to its wellbeing. By elevating the latter above the primacy of 'the market' or 'the people', claims to expert authority threaten the unitary ideologies on which neoliberalism and populism rest by admitting a plurality of, often contradictory and conflicting, interests and values which cannot be easily accommodated within a monotheistic view of the world in which 'money' or 'folk' constitute the one 'true god' (Frank 2001). In this respect, both neoliberalism and populism are ideologies which are anti-elitist, anti-pluralist, anti-liberal and pro-moralistic in their political ontologies in that their commitment to 'the will of the people' refuses to acknowledge the possibility, indeed probability, that their symbolic construction and interpretation of the latter will be contested by other political epistemologies (Müller 2016, 2021). As unitary social constructionists (Mirowski 2013; Müller 2021), both neoliberals and populists find it very difficult, if not impossible, to admit to the existence of political ontologies celebrating diversity, difference and debate because this fundamentally contradicts their belief that only they have direct access to 'real people' and their 'real needs'.

Thus, the emergence of a mutant form of 'populist neoliberalism' entails 'double jeopardy' for expert authority because it's much more authoritarian ideological strains and their implications pose a double-edged threat to the latter; any sources of expert authority not prepared to accept the policies and programmes of political regimes speaking in the name of 'populist neoliberalism' literally become 'the enemy' and, as such, deserving of contempt and ridicule because of their unwillingness, or inability, to see the error of their ways.

Neoliberalism is an inherently complex, dynamic and unstable political doctrine and practice whose 'ideological fault-line' lies at the point where its 'libertarian' and 'authoritarian' strains come into direct contact and struggle to establish their dominance (Hurt and Lipschutz 2016; Frank 2020; Callison and Manfredi 2020; Vormann and Weinman 2021; Reed 2022). While the libertarian strain has been dominant since the emergence of neoliberalism as a governing ideology and practice promoted and enacted by political, economic and social elites from the late 1970s/early 1980s, the authoritarian strain has become stronger over the last decade or so as national political leaders have attempted to exploit economic and political crises and the growing sense of unease, anxiety and rejection which they generate (Fieschi 2019; Moffitt 2020; Applebaum 2020; Müller 2021). This authoritarian strain combines populism and nationalism to legitimate a communitarian political ideology and a package of economic policies and programmes geared to improving the material and social conditions of 'real people' overlaid with an exclusionary and polarizing culture of identity politics in which multinationalism and multiculturalism are rejected as fatally undermining communal traditions and values.

The recent ideological and political pivot towards an 'authoritarian populist' strain of neoliberalism is extremely bad news for all forms of 'expert authority'; it polarizes 'the people' against 'the experts' by rejecting the legitimacy of the latter as entailing false claims to superior intellectual and technical capabilities at the expense of making 'ordinary people' seem incompetent and incapable of making decisions for themselves. As Frank (2020: 250–254) puts it, populist egalitarianism seeks 'to undermine [professional] elites by making ordinary people capable' and by refusing to accept the meritocratic doctrines through which expert hierarchies are legitimated and reproduced (Sandel 2020). By disempowering ordinary people by making them unable to function without their expertise, experts become an integral, if not essential, part of a 'conspiracy against the laity' undertaken by elite ruling groups to ensure that their political, economic and social dominance is secured – even in crisis situations where their authority may be directly challenged by events and circumstances beyond their control.

This anti-meritocratic 'turn' in the 'authoritarian populist' mutation of neoliberalism is often, counterintuitively, combined with a technocratic logic of contemporary democratic politics in which hybridized forms of 'techno-populism' come to dominate the latter across a wide range of historical and geographical contexts (Bickerton and Accetti 2021). By claiming to legitimate modes of political representation through appeals to both technical competence and popular mobilization, techno-populist discourses and movements/parties politicize expertise in ways which unavoidably challenge the independence and neutrality of established social democratic/corporatist state bureaucracies and professional associations. The latter cannot sustain claims to embody, directly and incontrovertibly, the 'will of the people' and/or the 'right to govern' because they are compromised, if not tainted, by their intimate links with and dependence on ruling elites who are more than happy to manipulate and betray 'the people' in furtherance of their unearned wealth and power. On the other hand, authoritarian/populist political movements and parties are more than happy to concentrate power and control around a relatively small cadre of 'experts' who are trusted to carry forward their long-term strategy and objectives because the latter are appropriately imbued with its ideological mission and governing mentality. Yet again, we see, an admittedly fragile and unstable, fusion of putatively opposed political ideologies/discourses and organizations which broaden and deepen the attack on established modes of expert authority based on claims to 'competence' and 'objectivity' accumulated through protracted education and training accredited by independent occupational bodies and state institutions.

Such an authoritarian populist challenge to the legitimacy of expert authority is likely to become even more protracted and acute in a context where repeated and escalating 'expert failure' becomes more socially visible and politically inde-fensible.

2.2.3 Expert Failure

Scepticism over the capacity of 'elitist experts' to deliver on their promises to keep us safe, secure and satisfied has widened and deepened as trust in 'expert systems' wanes as a result of recurring failures to predict, control and manage the risks and uncertainties we face as individuals and communities (Hanlon 2016; Koppl 2018; Hopkin 2020). This accusation of recurring 'expert failure' resonates with the ideo-logical and political inclinations of an increasingly populist and authoritarian strain of neoliberalism in which market fundamentalism and cultural nationalism come together to challenge the meritocratic credentialism of experts.

We seem to have come an awful long way since theorists of 'reflexive modernization' predicted a future in which expert systems come to 'de-contextual-ize' and 'dis-embed' our lives through steering mechanisms entailing 'the evacua-tion of the traditional or customary content of local contexts of action and the re-organizing social relations across broad time-space bands' (Beck, Giddens and Lash 1994: 85). While accepting that such a future would inevitably involve 'living in a world of multiple authorities' and the potential for some groups to become 'disen-chanted with all experts' (Beck, Giddens and Lash 1994: 86–87), such theorists were confident that pre-modern, traditional and communal cultures rejecting ex-perts, expertise and expert systems would be unable to resist the globalizing and 'de-traditionalizing' dynamic inherent in modernization. However, it is those very traditional and communal cultures and ideologies which seem to have come back to haunt us as we struggle to navigate our way through a succession of crises in which the reality of 'expert performance' falls far short of what experts have led us to expect.

As Beck insists (Beck 1999), living in a 'risk society' necessarily means that we become more dependent on the expert systems through which the, exponentially increasing, risks endemic to such a society are managed and mitigated in ways which we usually don't understand and indeed don't want to understand. If they work, then we are happy for them to 'go about their business' without needing or wanting to bother too much about how they work or what we do when they show increasing signs of failing to function in the usual way. Indeed, experts seem more than happy to allow us to maintain our collective state of 'blissful ig-norance' if it protects them from intrusive interference from an increasingly self-aware and critical public. However, in a situation where the effectiveness of those very expert systems through which dangers and threats, often of an existen-tial kind as in the case of a pandemic or climate collapse, seems to be rapidly waning and, even worse, they come to be viewed as 'risk enhancing' in their own right, then these escalating systemic failures add 'ideological fuel to the flames' of those who denounce expert authority as a charade masking the vested interests and prejudices of remote and uncaring ruling elites.

In this way, escalating critiques of and attacks on expert authority become enrolled in what Hopkin (2020) calls 'anti-system politics' – that is, an attack on a way of doing politics combining liberal market economies and social democratic governments in which experts adjudicate between conflicting interests and values to produce workable compromises supportive of a progressive status quo. This 'politics as usual' system, and the key role which experts play in sustaining it, is seen to have failed to protect most citizens against the economic disorder and social dislocation unleashed by over four decades of neo-liberalization because it is geared to reproducing itself rather than changing things in ways that benefit the majority.

Experts are now viewed as key operators within state systems and organizations failing to protect the general welfare of most of their citizens since they are driven by a technocratic imperative to impose 'scientific' systems of knowledge on unequal and divided societies which cannot be 'made whole' by their ministrations. They cannot but fail to deliver on the vastly inflated expectations placed upon them – and which they have also positively encouraged as part of their 'mobility strategy' – because their claimed expertise has been found seriously wanting in the face of the frighteningly complex problems and crises we now face. Indeed, they increasingly pose a threat to the survival of 'popular democracy' as they become more deeply embedded as a 'shadow elite within a deep state' that has near monopoly access to and control over expert advice which no longer addresses the everyday concerns of common people (Koppl 2018).

Thus, across a broad spectrum of biological, ecological, medical, social and cultural domains, 'politics as usual' – in which experts play the key role of 'honest brokers' bringing opposing positions into some sort of practical alignment as a basis for 'moving forward' – is no longer viable as a way of responding to 'disintegrating institutions' (nuclear families, labour markets, nation states), 'manufactured uncertainties' (pollution, poverty, over-population) and 'environmental crises' (pandemics, species extinction, recessions). Ultimately reassuring 'expert narratives' about our collective capacity to cope with the existential threats which these 'new realities' present seem increasingly unconvincing in a world where their stories are perceived as self-interested, contradictory and technocratically-driven (Beck 1997, 1999). In a world where 'hazards themselves sweep away the attempts of institutional elites and experts to control them' (Beck 1999: 150), the 'risk assessment bureaucracies' in which so many experts now seem to hide away from their failures to predict and contain the escalating threats which confront us seem riper than ever for downsizing, merging and even culling.

This is even more true at a time when 'public services' and the 'public domain' in general have been in serial decline as neoliberalism and populism cut into their ideological capital and cultural support seemingly without fear of political cost or electoral retribution.

2.2.4 Public Service Decline

As public services have been 'hollowed out' by the marketization, financialization, and outsourcing dynamic driven by several decades of neo-liberalization (Raco 2013; Wilks 2013; Bowman et al. 2014; Bowman 2015; Anderson 2017; Brown 2019), so the authority and status of the established professionals who provide those services has been in decline (Newman 2013; Reed 2019; Malin 2021; Wallace et al. 2023). Emerging cadres of 'calculative experts' or 'corporate professionals' have been incrementally positioned with key roles within marketized and outsourced public services in order to ensure that the policy priorities and programme directives of neoliberal state elites dominate organizational decision-taking (Raco 2013; Eyal 2019; Christensen 2017; Reed 2018; Sturdy, Wright, and Wylie 2016; Malin 2021).

This rising cadre of calculative/corporate experts design and manage the new organizational technologies whereby the political, financial, and performance imperatives imposed by neoliberal state elites are translated into appropriate operational targets and plans. They incrementally displace the 'old guard' of public service professionals who are no longer trusted to subordinate their expertise and skills to the requirements of a new regime in which deregulated markets becomes the ultimate arbiters of value and worth. Indeed, established public service professionals are increasingly seen as potential obstacles to, if not subversive of, this new calculative and judgemental regime insofar as they refuse to accept their subordinate position within the latter and continue to contest its allocative priorities and distributional outcomes. Malin (2021: 209) summarizes this process of devaluing, displacing and de-professionalizing public service professionals in the following terms:

> Neoliberalism, involving a remaking of the state, reconfigured to serve the demands of capital, has meant some professionals may have lost their authority because the state has lost its authority. Instead of celebrating the virtue of professional expertise, a system based on neoliberal ideas tends to view profession as a raw material within a general commodification process. … [A]cross areas of the public sector there has been a loss of autonomy in professional practice.

This general commodification of professional expertise and the dilution of expert authority and autonomy – based on liberal/social democratic state norms of 'service to the public' and their embeddedness within a wider cultural matrix of values associated with communal wellbeing through collective agency – which it necessarily entails, can be understood as part and parcel of a wider macro-economic shift towards 'rentier capitalism' in which 'rent-seeking' becomes the dominant economic driver to be facilitated and protected by the neoliberal state. Christophers (2020) analysis of 'rentier capitalism' suggests that, viewed in a wider socio-historical context, the re-emergence of this neoliberal-led form of capitalist political economy can be seen as the revitalization of an old/new 'dominant bloc' within contemporary elite power structures in which the interests of landed aristocracy/property and global financial conglomerates come together to prioritize 'profit making and capital accumulation through the holding of assets' rather than from sustained increases in productivity through technologically and organizationally enhanced human labour. In the Anglo-American economies, such as the UK, US, Canada, Australia and New Zealand, there has been a common 'revivification of finance' under neo-liberalization and a much more pronounced process of deindustrialization since the early 1980s in which 'rentierization' has been the dominant structural trend. Leading corporations have become 'rentiers' in which economic rents derived from control over exclusive assets, rather than from investing in new technologies, training, and organizations in order to achieve long-term increases in the productivity of their employees' labour, becomes the driving force for strategic decision making over the allocation of large-scale resources.

Moving to 'rentier capitalism' under neo-liberalization has entailed fateful consequences for the public sectors of the Anglo-American political economies to the extent that 'outsourcing' public services to private business corporations has emerged as one of the, if not 'the', dominant mechanism through which corporate control over exclusive assets and the long-term rents/profits to be derived from it has been realized. Christophers (2020: chapter 5) detailed analysis of 'outsourcing and contract rents' right across diverse sectors such as health, education, care, welfare, crime, construction and governing documents a process in which 'fake competition' becomes the new unstated rule and corporate providers an emerging 'shadow state' of unregulated and unaccountable rentier capitalists (White 2016). These 'impenetrable organizations' not only seal themselves off, as far as is possible, from external scrutiny and transparency, but they also subject their employees – and particularly those employees occupying expert and managerial roles generating and assessing information concerning the corporations' performance and impact – to much more extensive and intensive surveillance regimes. Professional/expert labour, like any other forms of labour under rentier corporations, is squeezed, casualized and controlled, because it, in part, is the rationale for outsourcing and because rentier institutions and organizations thrive on near monopoly power in which any relatively expensive and problematic resource, such as expert labour, must be exploited like any other exclusive asset.

Thus, the institutional logic on which neo-liberalized rentier capitalism thrives demands that expert work and the workers performing it become embedded in a matrix of power relations – which at the organizational level can be identified as 'neoliberal new public management' (NPM) (Reed 2019) – in which exclusive domination over and control of all assets by those corporate elites acting on behalf of it becomes the norm. The latter are empowered to sweat and exploit the assets which the former generate – esoteric specialized knowledge, scarce technical skills, complex managerial technologies, and informal tacit understandings – under rentier capitalism because it ensures that vast unearned rental income and profits are maximized and sustainable. As Crouch (2016: 68–69) puts it, the neoliberal form of 'new public management' (NPM) (Reed 2019) which has become dominant under rentier capitalism 'converges on an attack on the idea of public service professionalism and its associated ethic … subjecting a professional activity to market discipline means stripping away ethical inhibitions in the cause of increased profitability'. In this way, neoliberal NPM under rentier capitalism has a corrupting influence over the generation and application of professional knowledge within public services in which the distinction between, 'public value' and 'private interest' effectively collapses to legitimate corporate profitability as the only criteria for assessing the performance of public institutions and organizations.

This does not mean to say that public service professionals have simply 'rolled over' in the face of the new managerial technologies through which marketized and outsourced public services have been neo-liberalized at the level of service organization and delivery. Even under the latter, public service professionals play a critical role in 'keeping the show on the road' when the congenitally 'failing forward' dynamic that neo-liberalization consistently reproduces (Peck 2010) also generates all sorts of damaging fallout which only they can pick-up and rectify (Buchanan et al. 2007; Kirkpatrick et al. 2005; Currie and White 2012). This 'repair and recovery work' in which public service professionals are routinely engaged inevitably opens institutional niches and organizational spaces which they can, and do, exploit in the furtherance of their own values and interests which often run counter to what neoliberal NPM regimes may be striving to impose of them (Newman 2013; Reed and Wallace 2015; Reed 2018). Professional service logics and expert values/practices are not eradicated by neoliberal NPM under rentier capitalism but, to a considerable extent, they do 'go underground' and are forced to adapt to the dominant market-driven managerial logic which the latter regime legitimates and proscribes as the solution to 'bureaucratic inertia' and 'professional sclerosis' prevalent under social democratic forms of managerial/stakeholder capitalism.

Overall, the long-term decline of the concept of the 'public sector/service' as entailing a distinctive institutional logic and form in which a wide range of expert occupational groupings, encompassing professionals, scientists, administrators, and managers, work on behalf of the general wellbeing of society as a whole and the extremely diverse communities that it encompasses has meant a fundamental weakening of the legitimacy of expert authority across swathes of contemporary public life. But arguably, expert workers have made matters even worse through the 'secessionist' strategies in which they have engaged, often in response to the depredation of the public service ethos and the exalting of private interest, both within and without the contemporary workplace.

2.2.5 Expert Secession

Müller (2021: 20 – 41) deploys the concept of 'secession' to identify the process whereby the most privileged groups within contemporary Anglo-American political economies and those expert groups designing, building, and operating the physical infrastructures and technical systems sustaining them spatially insulate and socially isolate themselves from the larger societies in which they exist. Indeed, he argues there has been a 'double secession' through which elites 'are to retreat from any real dependence from the rest of society. Not everyone of them literally lives in a gated community, but the underlying trends of 'self-sorting', and homogenization in wealthy enclaves are clear enough; the well-educated and the well-off marry each other, live one another, and reproduce many of their privileges over the generations' (Müller 2021: 22 – 24). This 'first secession' becomes a 'double or invisible secession', Müller contends, when elites and their expert cadres undertake various structural and cultural strategies to exclude disadvantaged groups from effectively participating in the political decision-making processes through which key choices impacting on their lives are taken and legitimated. These strategies can include a raft of options making it much more difficult for, an already alienated and insecure body of people within the wider economy and society, to vote, to plan for their or their children's futures, or to access basic health, welfare, and educational services.

As Müller (2021) also concedes, many of those expert occupational groups located within an 'increasingly stressed middle' will find it difficult to maintain their economic security, social status, and cultural standing in the face of technological and organizational rationalization which threatens livelihoods and identities. Yet, the seemingly resilient positions occupied by an upper-middle class of professionals, managers, and technicians – who support the economic, political, and social elites who have benefited most from neo-liberalization and rentier capitalism – proffers a powerful aspirational example for those located in the middle echelons of the expert occupational hierarchy to follow and imitate. This reinforces the ideological and political power of authoritarian populist leaders and parties who wildly oscillate between condemnation of 'metropolitan elites' and support for them once they begin to follow what seem like policies and programmes grounded in nationalist autarky and monocultural exclusion.

Müller's (2021) identification of the 'double secession' in which expert elites have been routinely engaged in recent years has been supported by Bishop's (2009) analysis of the demographic restructuring through which increasingly socio-economically homogenized communities have emerged in the US over the last thirty years or so and Mandel's (2020) interpretation of the complex ways in which 'meritocratic credentialism' has come to be the 'last acceptable prejudice' surreptitiously legitimating a 'success ethic' which is self-confirmatory and justificatory for upper-middle class professionals and middle-middle class technocrats alike.

Bishop (2009) historically tracks and contemporaneously documents the economically and politically driven demographic transformation which the US has undergone during the last three decades which has drastically reduced social and cultural diversity, while emaciating political life to a Hobson's choice between two equally unacceptable ideological tribes. Building on Florida's (2003) research on the rise of the creative class in the US since the 1960s/70s, Bishop identifies the 'big sort' as a long-term demographic process through which high-wage expert workers in communications, engineering, education, and entertainment have clustered in socially homogenized demographic groups, primarily located in high tech city-regions, through migratory movements transforming the country's social landscape. This creative class of expert workers have driven the geographical and social mobility whereby communities have been 'sorted' into segregated and homogenized groups who no longer have any shared, collective sense of their identities and futures. In turn, these demographic and socio-economic transformations have generated various cultural shifts in which division and polarization, rather than unification and consensus, have come to dominate contemporary politics in which a growing 'populist backlash' against educationally and culturally derived power and status has gathered political momentum and force (Frank 2020).

Sandel (2020) focuses on the ideological and political resources which the creative class, both in the US and other capitalist political economies, have drawn-on to legitimate the economically and socially advantageous positions which they have come to occupy, and even treat as a 'natural right', under an increasingly segregating and polarizing set of socio-economic structures. As they have reshaped the demographic/urban landscape in ways that secure and protect their material and social advantages from external competition and challenge, so expert occupational groups have become increasingly dependent, ideologically and politically, on 'meritocratic credentialism' as the crucial legitimating device through which 'the professional classes have figured out how to pass their advantages on to their children, converting the meritocracy into a hereditary aristocracy' (Sandel 2020: 119–120). Once seen as a route for economic advancement and upward social mobility, credentialism becomes an exclusionary mechanism and justificatory rationale for elite professionals and middle-ranking expert groups determined to 'seal-off' their positions and privileges from 'uncontrolled accesses' from lower order groups who may attempt to usurp their power and authority.

No wonder authoritarian populist leaders and movements have found their attacks on 'cosmopolitan elites' such fertile ideological and political soil when the latter are seen to corrupt the ideal of 'meritocratic credentialism' in such a blatant and consistent manner.

3 Mediating Mechanisms

As discussed in chapter one, the configuration of structural changes reviewed in this chapter do not impose themselves on social actors in a deterministic manner. They are mediated and interpreted through a range of mechanisms which provide the relational forms and discursive modes through which the 'messages' which they contain are organized and carried. These mediating mechanisms constitute socio-material hybrids through which structural change is translated into organizational realities which need to be 'acted on' in various ways. They simplify and filter structural change in ways that prioritize and justify certain 'translations' rather than others so that they become the dominant interpretive frameworks through which individual and collective action is legitimated. Yet, their stabilizing and legitimating role is always open to counter arguments which contest the dominance of established orthodoxies to some degree or another.

Within the de-legitimation narrative, three, interrelated mediating mechanisms are identified which are seen to play a pivotal role in shaping the structural and discursive context in which the crisis in expert authority must be understood and explained. First, the rise of a **neoliberal state** which replaces the core 'steering capacities' associated with the social democratic/neo-corporatist state and its emphasis long-term economic planning and administrative co-ordination through centralized bureaucratic management. Second, the emergence of a **radical individualist** political ideology and discourse legitimating the policy regimes and programmes mobilized by a neoliberal political elite who effectively control the state structures and systems through which the latter are pursued. Third, the increasing political power and cultural influence of **hybrid or 'mutant' political discourses** recombining selected elements of radical individualization and authoritarian populism which promote 'individual resilience' and 'communal restoration' as the basis for national success and collective protection in a violent and disordered world.

As Mirowski (2013: 56, emphasis in original) reminds us, 'a primary ambition of the neoliberal project is to redefine the shape and functions of the state, *not to destroy it.* [Neoliberals] are inclined to explore new formats of techno-managerial governance that protect their ideal market from what they perceive as unwanted political interference'. These new formats of techno-managerial governance are legitimated as entailing 'shrinking the state', but the political and administrative reality is of modes of quasi-market-based regulation which are bureaucratically more complex and unwieldly than anything they have replaced.

Jessop (2008, 2016) argues that the neoliberal state and the techno-managerial modes of governance that it legitimates and authorizes involves the emergence of a 'strategic-relational approach' in which the 'Keynesian Welfare State' (KWS) gives way to a 'Schumpeterian Workfare State' (SWS) ideologically driven by the political imperative to eliminate, systematically and structurally, any alternative state capacities and modes of policy making and implementation standing in the way of neo-liberalization (Jessop 1994). In addition, the SWS relies on a complex configuration of relational power networks through which political and economic elites work to ensure, as far as they possibly can, that a neoliberal policy regime in which market liberalization and the extensive bureaucratic apparatus which it requires – now extensively outsourced to private sector corporations rather than 'insourced' by public sector agencies – remains 'on track'. These relational power networks give the semblance of decentralization and delegation, but they mask the political and administrative reality of sustained concentration of state power and control within a formally streamlined governance apparatus. Within these relational power networks, certain groups of technical and organizational experts – like management consultants and a whole army of 'corporate professionals' – may play an important role in ensuring the effective functioning of the new modes of regulation emerging under the neoliberal/SWS state. Yet, their role as 'technicians', 'fixers' and 'brokers' is subsumed within a wider governance structure in which they remain under the control and direction of the political, economic and administrative elites ensuring that neo-liberalization continues to unfold, even when, indeed particularly when, it seems to falter and fail (Peck 2010; Peck and Theodore 2015; Springer 2016).

The 'strategic-relational state' emerging under neo-liberalization is supported by a 'radical individualist' political ideology and discourse in which the collectivist forms of individualism that dominated the post 1945 social democratic welfare state are progressively denigrated and dismantled (Streeck 2016; Bevir 2016; Cooper and Szreter 2021). This ideological paradigm shift occurs through the incremental intellectual seeding and political imposition of an individualist/libertarian value system in which market-based competition between 'rational actors' driven to maximize their rewards in a Hobbesian/Darwinian 'struggle of all against all' becomes the universal analytical and ethical template against which all forms of 'governing' are to be evaluated and legitimated (Dardot and Laval 2013; Davies 2014; Brown 2015, 2019). Individuals are ideologically cut adrift from a supportive welfare state which is effectively disempowered of its critical role in protecting them when they are at their most vulnerable and exposed to the full disciplinary force of unrestrained market competition. Instead, they must learn to become resilient in the face of such challenges and threats to their livelihoods, indeed existence, by psychologically accepting and internalizing the mental strength and skills required to pursue, ruthlessly and unbendingly, their self-interests within a struggle for survival in which 'everybody is reduced to fending for themselves' (Streeck 2016: 40). But this dismantling and disempowering of 'collectivist individualism' and the socio-political institutions and governance regimes through which it was legitimated must be made to look as if it is the outcome of 'spontaneous necessity' rather than of intentionally planned and calculated political intervention on behalf of the elite economic and political interests for which it is enacted and sustained. As Cooper and Szreter (2021) suggest, the 'collectivist individualism' which underpinned the Keynesian Welfare State did not implode in on itself as a result of underlying, impersonal structural forces un-connected to all and any form of socio-political agency. Instead, it succumbed to a 'virulent' form of extreme libertarian individualism propagated by neoliberal economic, political and cultural elites – and their 'media cheerleaders' – over several decades who constituted a governing coalition or bloc determined to overturn the ideological orthodoxies underpinning the post-1945 social democratic consensus from which the 'expert classes' had benefited so much materially and socially.

However, and particularly of late, libertarian individualism has not had everything go its own way. Indeed, the more recent 'authoritarian turn' in neoliberal ideology and political discourse signals a growing unease with the single-minded pursuit of unrestrained market rationality and the re-emergence of neoliberalism's 'pathological tendencies.' Several analysts (Babones 2018; Callison and Manfredi 2020; Vormann and Weinman 2021; Bickerton and Accetti 2021; Reed 2022) have argued that the authoritarian/populist strain within neoliberal ideology has become more discursively active and politically impactful in recent years as the latter has mutated in response to worsening economic and social conditions within advanced political economies since the financial crisis of 2008/2009 and the austerity policy regimes which dominated the following decade. As this, inherently unstable and fragile, ideological hybrid of libertarianism, authoritarianism and technocracy has gathered political momentum, so its impact on the organization and functioning of the neoliberal state has intensified.

This has entailed strengthening the power of the executive arm of government at the expense of the legislative arm, as well as concentrating the capacity to direct and control policy making and implementation within a centralized administrative apparatus dominated by a 'state party' and its elite supporters within big business and other leading sectors of the economy and society (Jessop 2016: 222–237). Enhanced executive power and single party dominance is reinforced by a weakening of the authority of the judiciary and its pivotal role in upholding the rule of law as populist leaders are empowered to speak and act on behalf of 'the people's will' or 'protecting national interests'- particularly in crisis situations calling for immediate and drastic government action unencumbered by democratic probity or legal restraint.

Thus, the re-emergence of the authoritarian/populist strain within neoliberal ideology has reinforced the idea that 'technicians, experts and professionals can replace professional politicians' (Bickerton and Accetti 2021: 56). It has also, simultaneously, 'demobilized professional knowledge workers whose empowerment threatens the authority of administrators and managers' (Callison and Manfredi 2021: 18). They, in turn, are only trusted insofar as they continue to act as the technocratic conduit for populist leaders above the hubbub of party politics and the confusion it inevitably sows in a naïve and manipulable public.

Experts, like everybody else, become the subjects of an authoritarian/populist variant of neoliberalism entailing an extremely uneasy ideological partnership between an ethic of unrestrained individual freedom and remote technocratic rule, governed by a political elite who claim the right to speak and act on behalf of 'the people' irrespective of democratic norms or legal restraints. As Bickerton and Accetti (2021: 30, emphasis in original) suggest, authoritarian populism promotes 'a *politicization of expertise*, one that can be used as a legitimizing resource for the purpose of succeeding within the electoral game itself … the politicization of expertise that comes with rise of a techno-populist logic can result in a conflict with the expansion of technocratic power associated with depoliticization'. Claims or appeals to technocratic competence or expertise are always subordinated to the populist ideologies and movements in which they are embedded and from which they take their political meaning and value. Experts become the servants, rather than the masters, of the populist political leaders and movements who empower them to design the policies, programmes and technologies through which 'the people's interests' will be protected and advanced.

4 Substantive Outcomes

Refracted through the mediating mechanisms of a neoliberal state, libertarian individualism and authoritarian populism, the crisis of expert authority can be understood as the outcome of a complex interplay between structural changes and strategic agency which has irretrievably eroded the legitimacy of expert power and influence. At its intellectual core, this revolt against expertise is rooted in deep-seated controversy and uncertainty over the epistemological foundations of 'true knowledge' and a growing incapacity to distinguish between 'fact' and 'fiction' in a world in which populist iconoclasm is valued above consensus-building within expert communities and between them and the wider publics they serve (Collins et al. 2020). It's 'institutional fall out' is to be found in the breakdown of the social structures and political forms through which a diverse plurality of, often contrasting and conflicting, values and interests were previously coordinated and integrated to form a sustainable consensus over the compromises and 'trade offs' necessary to make it work. This has reinforced the trend towards more concentrated economic and political power in parallel with a fragmenting and fracturing of expert jurisdictional work domains and a secular decline in the legitimacy and efficacy of expert-based forms of governing and organizing. As the latter have become progressively colonized by political ideologies and discourses inherently suspicious of expert claims to disinterested objectivity and practical efficacy on behalf the collective interests of the communities in which they are embedded, so they have become increasingly subservient to the power and control of the political and economic elites who rule in the name of 'the market' and/or 'the people'.

Considered in this way, the de-legitimation narrative documents and interprets a long-term process of socio-historical decline in which the social contract between experts, society and the state that ideologically sustained and politically articulated the social democratic consensus of the post-1945 era has imploded under the combined pressure of structural change and social agency as it turned the latter to its advantage in order to destroy the obstacles standing in the way of its vision of a 'market society'. For those who adhere to this de-legitimation narrative, 'there is no way back' to resurrecting that social democratic consensus and the three-way stakeholder social contract it legitimated because their moral foundations and institutional infrastructure have both been eviscerated by the cumulative impact of the underlying structural movements and strategic political interventions documented in previous sections of this chapter.

5 Conclusion

In his book, *Legitimation Crisis*, first published in English in 1976 (Habermas 1976), Habermas identifies what he sees as an irreparable breakdown in the 'steering mechanisms' which had enabled post-1945 capitalist political economies to manage threats to their continued operation and reproduction. While the latter had been relatively successful in developing organizational forms and techniques which enhanced their capacity to absorb challenges and threats to their continued existence, these 'steering mechanisms' were no longer able to co-ordinate and integrate the complex economic, political, and social systems through which the accumulating problems facing them could be effectively managed and contained. As a result, the underlying legitimacy and acceptability of advanced capitalism was exponentially eroding as its capacity to respond to its citizens demands and needs – for secure employment, decent welfare and housing, educational opportunity for their children, and the protection of basic human and civil rights – was exponentially weakening under the unrelenting pressure for sustained capital accumulation and corporate profitability.

In particular, the ability of the state under 'managerial capitalism', to 'substitute government functions for market functions' (Habermas 1976: 51) in ways that mitigated the worst excesses of unregulated free market capitalism, such as mass unemployment and increasing poverty, was being questioned as the 'corporatist modes of interest intermediation' between business associations, trade union organizations, and government policy makers was coming under sustained political pressure. Even the 'state-monopolistic capitalism' which had developed in the German Democratic Republic in the post Second World War period was undergoing a deep-seated economic and political crisis as its organizational capacity to manage the systemic contradictions between 'socialized production' and 'market rationality' was being openly questioned and critiqued. This *displacement* of the fundamental structural contradictions of capitalism on to the state administrative system had worked for a while, but the latter was increasingly incapable of dealing with the contradictory 'steering imperatives' that it was required to absorb, such as the need for long-term planning and control set against the requirement for unrestrained market competition as a precondition for sustained capital accumulation. Repeated failure of the state administrative system to deal with these strategic, steering imperatives was generating an ongoing 'legitimation crisis' in which the political authority and cultural coherence of the former was dissipating as a result of its inability to produce meaningful and acceptable understandings of its 'validity claims' to act on behalf of the collective interests of the public at large.

Habermas' book, like all academic texts, was very much 'a product of its time' (Milstein 2021: 29). However, it signals a growing awareness, both within the academic/intellectual community and the wider polity and society, that the Keynesian Welfare State (KWS) 'had not eliminated capitalism's crisis tendencies; it merely *displaced* them' (Milstein 2021: 29, emphasis in original). For Habermas, both intellectuals/academics and politicians/publics had seriously over-estimated the capacity of the modern, post-war social democratic/KWS – and it's administrative/technical/expert elites – to transform corporate capitalism into a socio-economic system in which the imperative need for compromises and trade-offs between the competing demands and claims of a wide-range of stakeholder interests and values could be ideologically and institutionally embedded within its overarching administrative architecture and decision-taking processes. Indeed, what we have witnessed in the decades since Habermas' book was published is how fragile and weak that social democratic consensus has proved to be in the face of a succession of economic, political and cultural crises which have undermined its legitimacy and authority.

In this chapter, we have documented and reviewed what the unravelling of the social contract between experts, publics, and states has meant for the legitimacy and authority of expert power in a contemporary world in which 'financialized', rather than 'socialized', forms of capitalist political economy have become dominant and have reinforced underlying political and cultural tendencies treating claims to 'expertise' with increasing suspicion and contempt. In many ways, exponents of the de-legitimation narrative build on Habermas' original analysis of the inherent weaknesses of the 'validity claims' on which the legitimacy of liberal/social democratic state capitalist systems and the authority of those experts responsible for managing them have proved to be. As they have been even more fully exposed to the instabilities and dislocations generated by intensifying economic pressures and political demands unfolding since the late 1970s/early 1980s, so their capacity to deal effectively with the challenges which the latter pose has repeatedly failed to live up to expectations (Schneider, Schmidtke, Haunss and Gronau 2017).

For analysts working within this de-legitimation narrative, the long-term damage inflicted on expert authority by the complex conjunction of developments outlined in this chapter poses an existential threat which 'the experts' are repeatedly failing to meet. For them, there is no way back to the institutionalized relationship between experts, publics and states which emerged in the post-war period and came to frame the wider socio-political context in which expert power could be confidently legitimated and authorized.

In the following two chapters, we consider narratives which, while accepting some of the analysis that exponents of the de-legitimation narrative advance, are not in agreement with their highly pessimistic conclusions. For them, 'de-legitimation' is a synonym for a process whereby expert authority has been demystified in ways which have, eventually, revealed its socio-political reality, or the former has grossly exaggerated the extent to which the decomposition of the expert division of labour necessarily entails the demise of expert authority as it adapts to a new ecology of expert work.

Chapter 3: Demystification

1 Introduction

Our discussion of the de-legitimation narrative in the previous chapter identifies an irreversible long-term decline in the legitimacy of expert authority generated by a sustained erosion of the institutionalized trust on which it had depended on for its resilience in the face of escalating attacks on and threats to its probity and veracity. A wide range of structural, political and cultural changes have come together to form a complex socio-historical conjuncture in which established expert authority finds itself unable to cope with a 'perfect storm' of systemic instabilities and uncertainties eradicating the core institutional foundations on which its integrity and capability rests.

In this chapter, we review and evaluate an alternative demystification narrative which rejects the theoretical presuppositions informing the de-legitimation narrative, as well as its analytical scaffolding that frames its account of the 'the crisis in expert authority'. Rather than interpret the crisis as an outcome of an irrevocable breakdown in institutionalized trust and the draining away of the legitimacy which it once provided, this demystification narrative sets out a very different account that progressively strips away the conceptual prostheses and explanatory legerdemain on which the de-legitimation narrative trades. Instead of assuming that expert authority rests on socially given and 'naturalized' trust relations which automatically bestow legitimacy on expertise and those who claim it, the demystification narrative removes these artificial theoretical presuppositions and the explanatory sleight-of-hand which they entail. It analytically positions and historically locates the 'political rationalities and technologies' through which claims to expertise and the power which flows from them at the very centre of the discursive practices and organizational processes 'normalizing' expert power and control (Johnson 1994; Dean 1999; Burrell 2006; Miller and Rose 2008; Davies 2011).

In this way, the demystification narrative identifies a nascent structural determinism and neo-evolutionary functionalism at the theoretical core of both the de-legitimation and decomposition narratives (see the following chapter); they both presume that an underlying 'institutional logic' is at work reproducing the conditions under which expert authority is legitimated. While the de-legitimation narrative sees the strength and impact of this institutional logic as being fatally weakened by structural changes undermining its coherence and stability, it still remains blind to the 'political rationalities and technologies' that are required to deliver and sustain expert authority as a viable mode of organizational governance

https://doi.org/10.1515/9783110734911-004

due to its myopic analytical focus on 'sovereign power' as embodied in the institutional apparatus of the centralized state (Miller and Rose 2008; Jessop 2010, 2016). Thus, the analytical focus on 'governmentality' – that is, the conduct of government in all its various forms and levels from the most 'local' to 'global' and the wide range of 'political technologies' through which it is made possible (Burchell, Gordon and Miller 1991; Jessop 2010; Brown 2015) – is central to the demystification narrative as it strives to sensitize us to the innate contradictions and tensions which expert work necessarily entails.

As Davies et al. (2022) have recently noted in their book on the Covid-19 pandemic, Foucault analysed how a new political logic of 'hygiene' emerged in the eighteenth century and the 'political technologies' through which its unruly and disruptive impact was to be contained. A wide range of 'experts' also emerged over the next two centuries – in public health, housing, medicine, law, government and commerce – whose power and authority flowed from their putative capacity to design, operate, maintain and recalibrate the political technologies through which the risks and threats posed by disease, poverty, crime and recession could be propitiated and contained to maintain social order. They also note that the twenty-first century Covid-19 pandemic generated a wide range of hybrid political technologies and new forms of expertise required to develop and implement them, such as more advanced digital surveillance regimes and monitoring systems needed to 'track and trace' infectious citizens or, more mundanely but nonetheless significantly, the repurposing of hotels to form physical and spatial sites in which the latter could be contained and confined (the pandemic and the demystification narrative is discussed further in chapter 5 of this book).

In this way, the demystification narrative demands a rigorous analytical and substantive refocusing on the organizational strategies through which expert groups design and promote the various political technologies needed to contain social disorder and the material and symbolic advantages they derive from their positioning in key nodes of the relational networks of power emerging from the latter's implementation. There is no a priori presumption or analytical tilt towards the institutionalized trust relations through which expert authority is routinely legitimated and reproduced because this is conceptualized as being inherently contested, unstable and politicised by the continuous struggle for power in which its necessarily embedded. It is only by stripping away these institutional trappings and discursive ideological mystifications can we begin to understand how claims to expertise and the power which they authorize are dependent on the development of political rationalities and technologies and the forms of knowledge-based subjugation which they unavoidably entail (Foucault 2003). They are and remain socio-historical formulations and instantiations of expert power which may or may not become sufficiently normalized and stabilized to establish the preconditions under which modes of governmentality congenial to expert authority can be sustained.

Given these preliminary remarks on the conceptual and theoretical terms on which the demystification narrative trades, this chapter will proceed on a similar basis to that developed in the previous and next chapters of this book.

First, we consider the analytical refocusing on endogenous, rather than exogenous, changes which have led to the emergence of more openly contested modes of expert-led governmentality in which 'the material operations, forms of subjugation, and the connections among the uses made of local systems of subjugation on the one hand, and the apparatuses of knowledge on the other' (Foucault 2003: 34) are the central explanatory concern. This entails, we suggest, the move to a 'bottom up', rather than 'top down', logic of analysis in which attention shifts away from macro-level systemic or structural changes prioritized by the de-legitimation narrative *towards localized forms of political technology and the modes of governmentality which they make operationally possible.* 'Sovereign power' is analytically dethroned (Miller and Rose 2008) in favour of a sustained explanatory focus on the disciplinary networks which expert political technologies make possible through their capacity to, literally, 'see into our souls' and to reconstruct our subjectivities and identities as they do so. It is not forgotten, much less ignored, but it is not allowed to dominate the analytical frame to the exclusion, or at least marginalization, of much more mundane, 'material operations and local subjugations' as they simultaneously reproduce 'apparatuses of knowledge' but in ways that also stretch them far beyond their original rationales and capacities.

Second, we assess how this fundamental analytical refocusing influences the demystification narrative's understanding of 'neoliberalism' as a distinctive mode of governmentality made possible through the mobilization of various interrelated political technologies and their impact on the everyday processes and practices through which organizational discipline and population regularisation is generated (Springer 2016; Brown 2019). Rather than seeing neoliberalism as a distinctive form of political economy supported by specialized macro-level steering mechanisms emerging from the breakdown of the social democratic/neo-corporatist consensus from the 1980s onwards, the demystification narrative signals a reconceptualization of 'neo-liberalization' as a process or project driven by new micro-level political technologies as they become propagated within everyday life and come to govern the terms on which it is lived. Of particular significance in this context, are the innovative surveillance and accounting technologies whereby organizational discipline and population regularisation under neo-liberalization comes to take on a much more insidious and abstract, but nonetheless 'normal' and 'routine', character as they seemingly detach themselves from any kind of anchoring in physical realities and the direct constraints they impose on everyday existence.

Third, we concentrate on the analysis which the demystification narrative provides of the role which 'experts' play in designing and operating political technologies through which neo-liberalization can come to have a 'saturating effect' (Brown 2019) throughout contemporary societies as they become populated by 'neoliberal subjects' who have a very different relationship with the state and its associated agencies than that envisaged under social democracy (Chandler and Reid 2016). This is seen to entail 'a continual process of preventive management of society, based on the indirect shaping of the adaptive capacities and conduct of its individual members' (Chandler and Reid 2016: 81–82) so that their subjection to society's requirements, as mediated through the political technologies on which 'preventive management' relies, becomes softer, more nuanced, and less brutal than under older governmentality regimes based on bodily incarceration and physical punishment including torture and death (Garland 1990).

Here, the 'governmentality school' of research on new forms of expertise emerging under 'advanced liberal regimes' has alerted us to the significance of the role which experts in the social and human sciences play in 'democratizing' specialized knowledge and skill in contemporary organizations (Johnson 1994; Dean 1999; Burrell 2006; Miller and Rose 2008; Davies 2011). At one level, this entails an 'opening-up' to external scrutiny, particularly to the discipline imposed on expertise by new forms of state-mediated regulation in which proxies for market competition – such as competitive tendering, internal markets, service outsourcing and performance management – play an increasingly prominent role in subjecting experts to innovative modes of surveillance and control (Raco 2013; Christophers 2020). Yet, it also involves a weakening of the established formal, legal, administrative and occupational regulative architecture to which expert power and authority were previously subjected, to the extent that expert authority is marginalized by a new 'system of judgement' in which the state becomes 'a neutral enforcer of competition, without regard to the consequences' (Davies 2014: 172).

Finally, and has been the case in the preceding and succeeding chapters of this book, we will consider what the overall implications of the demystification narrative might be in relation to the **key structural and cultural changes** which it identifies, the **mediating mechanisms** through which they are articulated and experienced, and the **substantive outcomes** they produce for experts and their status as they become even more tightly integrated into neoliberal modes of governmentality.

2 Local Subjugation and the Knowledge Apparatus

Drawing extensively on Foucault and the work of the 'governmentality' school of thought in organization studies, the demystification narrative develops a very different understanding of 'neo-liberalization' to that offered by the de-legitimation or decomposition narratives. It suggests that neo-liberalization entails a transformation in both the way the conduct of governing is carried out and the emerging relationship between 'the state' and 'the subject' under neoliberal governance regimes based on this new mode of governmentality (Dardot and Laval 2013; Springer 2016; Chandler and Reid 2016; Brown 2019).

As Miller and Rose (2008) suggest, neoliberal governmentality entails the shift to a very different form of political rationality and technology to that prevailing under social democratic/neo-corporatist regimes in which a relatively loose and fissiparous configuration of state-delegated, and formally non-state agencies, become the primary organizational mechanisms for securing neoliberal rule. In turn, this entails a political strategy aimed at displacing and marginalizing the core institutional structures and organizational delivery mechanisms on which the social democratic state and neo-corporatist interest intermediation depended – such as a universal health and welfare system and its supporting progressive taxation regimes administered by an independent and autonomous civil service – so that a new overarching political rationality and governmental technology could become dominant. In Miller and Rose's terms (2008: 24–25 emphasis added):

> [Advanced liberal democracy] *seeks to de-governmentalize the state and de-statize practices of government* ... it seeks to govern, not through 'society' but through the regulated choices of individual citizens, now construed as subjects of choices and aspirations to self-actualization and self-fulfilment ... as an autonomizing and pluralizing form of rule, this form of rule is dependent upon the proliferation of little regulatory instances across a territory and their multiplication, at a molecular level, *through the interstices of our present experience.*

How does this neo-liberalizing displacement and marginalization strategy work and what are the conditions under which it proved to be so effective?

Foucault's work has highlighted a number of different varieties or 'modalities' of power (Foucault 2003: 249), which operate on different levels or scales and using different technologies (Foucault 1980). Foucault notes that in the modern era, two great technologies of power are in operation: disciplinary power and bio-power.

Biopolitics represents a distinct form of power, concerned with regulating society: '... the set of mechanisms through which the basic biological features of the human species became the object of a political strategy, of a general strategy of power' (Foucault 2007: 16). In various texts (notably, the History of Sexuality, Vol. 1 (1980) and his lectures at the Collège de France (2003, 2007, 2008)), Foucault delineates bio-power from the earlier juridical form of sovereign power. Sovereign power is the 'right to decide life and death' (Foucault 1991: 258), where power is an expression of 'deduction' (Foucault 1991: 259), i.e., a repressive power of suppression, deprivation and denial of property, services, even life. Contrasting with this, this new mode of power, bio-power, emphasises a generative or productive form of power, oriented towards organising and developing human life. Moreover, bio-power represents not only a new and distinct form of power but also a distinctive form of government, at the heart of which is concern for social regulation and individual self-governance. This new form of power does not replace sovereign power, rather it subsumes it, rendering this power – in the form of law and justice – one element of a wider set of the apparatus of bio-power (Foucault 1980), with an emphasis on establishing the norm and normalising. Bio-power represents therefore a constellation of techniques of power 'in which modern human and natural sciences and the normative concepts that emerge from them structure political action and determine its goals' (Lemke 2011: 33). At the organisational level, 'biocracy' (Fleming 2014a, 2014b) emerges where 'life itself' is a key area of exploitation in the contemporary neo-liberal organization.

Coupled with this, Foucault accounts for the emergence of 'disciplinary power and panopticon control' in which ever-expanding domains of individual and collective life are subjected to political technologies directed to the subjugation of bodies – particularly in rapidly expanding urban areas where the ever-present threat of social disorder and moral breakdown must be contained (Foucault 2003: 135–145). Gradually, from the mid-late eighteenth century onwards, the 'sovereign power' of the centralized state apparatus becomes increasingly dependent on and displaced by more adaptable, agile and accountable political technologies in prisons, schools, asylums, clinics, workhouses, factories, barracks and hospitals in which 'discipline organizes an analytical space' (Cousins and Hussain 1984: 185). Thus, the emergence and reproduction of 'disciplinary power' is made possible through a complex network of interrelated spatial, temporal, observational and normative practices whereby internalized self-surveillance and discipline are routinely secured without the extensive bureaucratic machinery on which the 'sovereign power' of the centralized state depends for its legitimacy and efficacy. As Merquior (1991: 113) puts it, 'unlike random sovereign power, which was chiefly exercised over the earth and its products, disciplinary power concentrated on human bodies and their operations. So, instead of discontinuous levies, modern man [sic] got constant surveillance'.

Analysts of neoliberal modes of governmentality build on Foucault's original account of disciplinary power and biopower and the political rationalities and technologies through which it they are made possible as *a distinctive form of statecraft by means which the everyday lives of 'neoliberal subjects' can be regulated in unobtrusive and self-empowering ways* (Davies 2011; Bell 2015). This suggests that neo-liberalization entails a 'recoding of the place of the state in the discourse of politics' (Miller and Rose 2008: 80) where the neoliberal state becomes 'a decentred state-at-a-distance' in which government policies and programmes are refocused on the 'personal life' of the individual consumer/client rather than the 'public life' of the producer/citizen. These neoliberal policies and programmes, as well as the bio-political and disciplinary technologies through which they are to be realized, 'promise to create individuals who do not need to be governed by others but will govern themselves, master themselves, care for themselves' (Miller and Rose 2008: 24 see also Foucault 2008). With it, comes the regularizing and normalising of the population (Foucault 1980, 2003, 2007) establishing characteristics and norms that can then be measured, ranked, and shaped (Lemke 2011) by 'stressing desirable outcomes' (Fleming 2022: 1991). These are also supported by disciplinary technologies to provide normative expectations of behaviour that are subject to regular monitoring and control (Hook 2007).

Under these internal transformations, the sovereign power of the social democratic state can no longer be relied upon as new political rationalities and technologies, dominated by neoliberal discourses which ideologically valorise 'power without a centre', come to displace the institutional apparatus on which the former relied for its legitimacy and relevancy. Since the 1980s, the social democratic sovereign state is transformed from a relatively well-integrated and centralized administrative mechanism into an increasingly fragmented and fractured mode of governmentality entirely dependent on new tactics, technologies and trade-offs to make and remake 'neoliberal subjects' who are practically and emotionally equipped to cope with the heightened uncertainties and insecurities which they must face in a 'market dominated society'. It becomes merely one agency, amongst many others, now relocated organizationally and discursively within a network of governmental relations and technologies, which operate without any overall directing strategic logic but are instrumental in making 'actors complicit in their own subjection to rules, norms and practices' (Davies 2011: 70).

As should be clear by now, the demystification narrative provides an analysis of expert power and status under neoliberal governmentality that foregrounds the role of endogenous change in political rationalities and technologies generating the reconfiguration of discursive and material conditions under which 'expert authority' is legitimated. The latter is progressively stripped bare of its sacred and mystical qualities and socially downgraded into a much more mundane, everyday legitimacy claim subject to the same ideological struggles as any other claim to special status and reward. By deconstructing the neo-Weberian sovereign state as a unique form of 'rulership' whereby military, political and juridical power are integrated to provide the dominant institutional mechanism through which a legitimate monopoly of the means of violence within a geographic area is secured (Jessop 2010; Anter 2014; Fligstein and McAdam 2012), governmentality theorists provide a radically different understanding of the status and role of the state under neo-liberalization by redefining it as *one agency competing with many others to claim and control certain areas of activity and resources.* Any presumption, analytical or ideological, in favour of the state as the locus classicus of a Hobbesian 'sovereign power' guaranteeing social order against incipient disorder and decay is rejected as an abstract, mythical construction unable to comprehend the intricate webs of discursive and socio-technical power defining the neoliberal world (Davies 2011; Springer 2016). Over forty years of neo-liberalization has left us with a very different form of 'disciplinary' and 'bio', rather than 'sovereign', power in which the conduct of government requires political rationalities and technologies aligned with the new realities of deregulated market competition, hollowed-out public services, private sector corporate control and government policies and programmes directed at retraining an often recalcitrant and obdurate workforce (Hurt and Lipschutz 2016; Callison and Manfredi 2020; Vormann and Weinman 2021).

Both the role and status of 'experts' under this neoliberal governmental regime also become much more contested and problematic as the 'reflected glory' which they once enjoyed as technocratic 'public servants' to a sovereign state wane quite dramatically. They are now under constant pressure 'from above' – from political, economic and administrative elites to deliver on whatever promises they are making to their populations – and 'from below' – from populaces who feel increasingly remote from and excluded by those very same public servants who are supposed to be their technocratic saviours.

However, before discussing this issue we need to attend in a little more detail to the political rationalities and technologies through which neoliberal modes of biopower, disciplinary power, and governmentality are generated and sustained.

3 Political Rationalities and Technologies under Neoliberal Governmentality

Foucault highlights the emergence of much more complex networks of specialist organizations and occupations as a precondition for neoliberal modes of governmentality in a wide array of fields such as medicine, law, science, education and administration (Clegg 1998). They are both products and carriers of a new 'political rationality' – that is, a loosely integrated set of ideas focused on the creation and management of 'obedient and/or regularised subjects/bodies' within large and diverse urban populations who must be governed through the promulgation and internalization of discursive practices conducive to self-correction and control. In this respect, 'the discourses of neoliberalism reflected a major shift in how politics could be understood or contested ... neoliberalism shrinks the understanding of human subjectivity, removing the foundational sphere of rational autonomy' (Chandler and Reid 2016: 81). Neoliberal subjects cannot be left to their own devices to develop and grow autonomously into their lives through the acquisition of better knowledge and understanding. This is because they cannot be relied upon to adapt to the continually changing demands and pressures presented to them in their everyday lives within market-dominant economies and societies in which much of the public support once provided by the state has been hollowed-out and transferred to the private sector. Instead, they must be continually subject to the 'preventative management' which neoliberal governmentality provides if they are to develop and retain the 'self-resilient adaptability' on which individual survival and advancement depends. In turn, this reduces the neoliberal subject to a socially isolated 'rational decision maker' who is driven by the imperative to maximize on the outcomes of their decisions by subjugating the latter to the dictates of a market-determined rationality dominated by the pursuit of rational self-interest (Davies 2014, 2018).

As a political rationality, neoliberalism requires a 'technology' which translates its, rather abstract and theoretical, discursive commitments into practical, on-the-ground changes whereby state power – it's capacities, responsibilities and authority – is redefined in ways consistent with the dominance of market forces and the much more self-resilient subjects they depend upon for their legitimacy and efficacy (Springer 2016). This is seen to entail a proliferation of non-state agencies which increasingly assume a wide array of functions previously located in central state bureaucracies and gradually come to replace the latter as the locus of political power and decision-making. In this way, by creating an innovative ensemble of rationalities and technologies which displace and replace the sovereign power of the central state with the disciplinary power and biopower of neoliberal governmentality, a neoliberal system of rule emerges in which 'local subjugation' and 'strategic knowledge' are recombined in ways beyond the comprehension, much less realization, of social democratic state elites.

A plethora of organizational technologies, reinventing and recombining local control and central domination in novel ways geared to reproducing 'obedient and/or regularised subjects/bodies', have been developed under neoliberal governmentality. Often, these consist of 'private/public hybrids' which retain the carapace of bureaucratic regulation and control but only insofar as it helps, rather than hinders, the enhanced disciplinary power and biopolitics of privatized modes of governance unrestrained by extra-market sources of authority and mediation (Davies 2011, 2018; Anderson 2017; Brown 2019). Rather than being imprisoned within a

Weberian 'iron cage' of bureaucratic rules and conventions, the neoliberal subject becomes self-enclosed within a 'panopticon gaze' of surveillance and control technologies prioritizing 'biopolitical life' as the strategic terrain on which a panoply of micro-level interventions is required to ensure it either conforms or regularises to neoliberal governmentality norms. In particular, the combination of disciplinary power and panopticon control provides this new regime with a matrix of semi-integrated governance systems and management mechanisms that spatially, temporally, physically and socio-psychologically contain the 'neoliberal body/subject' in ways consistent with a political rationality legitimated around asocial utility maximizing rational actors (Reed 1999).

Private corporate government, and the supporting governance systems and management mechanisms which make it possible, becomes the institutional and organizational template for neoliberal governmentality because it protects biopower and disciplinary power from any unwanted external interference making its operation more open to scrutiny and critique. Consequently:

> Government is 'bettered' by becoming less visible because it manifests itself in forms of authority less detectable than hierarchical forms of government (there is no sovereign entity that governs, only networks of 'experts') and it is more ingrained because it is in place in the very operational practices of these expert bodies, in the collection of information and data (statistics). (Sokhi-Bulley 2011: 266)

This power thrives on secrecy, opacity, complexity and confusion because they cloak it in a veneer of everyday 'naturalness' and taken-for-granted 'common sense' that make it very difficult, if not impossible, to challenge. If such challenges emerge – from the legal system or from civil society organizations and voluntary movements, for example – then these can be weakened and contained by recourse, not to the mundane nature of its functioning but, conversely, to its highly rarefied and esoteric workings only accessible and understandable to those specialists and experts well-versed in its arcane complexities and mysteries. Thus, much of the organizational innovation associated with the transition to neoliberal governmentality – 'network-based governance', 'project team working', 'hybrid domestic and office working', 'knowledge management', 'platform micro-working' and 'corporate social responsibility' – can be interpreted as masking, or what Burrell (2022) calls 'camouflaging', the underlying political reality of privatized disciplinary power and biopolitics in which resistance, individual or collective, is by no means impossible, but extremely difficult and costly to mobilize (Martí et al. 2017). Once privatized, corporate government is allied with the advanced information and surveillance technologies now routinely available to neoliberal elites in politics, business, culture and public services, then it becomes doubly difficult to take on the biopower and disciplinary power embedded in neoliberal governmentality regimes due to the considerable risks and costs that it involves for individuals and organizations alike (Reed 2019).

This also raises the question of what happens to 'expert authority' under neoliberal governmentality as experts seem to become even more central to the latter's operational legitimacy and efficacy but simultaneously more dispensable as their roles and status are exposed to incessant technological and organizational rationalization.

4 Expert Authority and Neoliberal Governmentality

Experts should do well under neoliberal governmentality as it is usually seen to enhance 'the significance of the "rule of experts" and technocratic knowledge elites' (Springer 2016: 25). As Springer goes on to suggest, this can be seen as a self-reinforcing and reproducing process in which experts come to occupy the nodal positions within globalized 'power/knowledge networks' playing a strategic role in ensuring that the primary role of the neoliberal state is 'to unleash market forces wherever possible, as well as via the locus of state authority and its increasing circumspection of political decision-making' (Springer 2016: 25). Both disciplinary power and biopower embroil experts within their technologies, often providing the knowledge base from which to discipline or regularise (Ransom 1997). Thus, neoliberal governmentality ostensibly enhances the power and authority of experts by placing technocratic knowledge elites at all levels of the governance process and ensuring that they design and operate the discursive and material technologies whereby free market ideology and policy becomes generally accepted as 'the only game in town' (Reed 2019). They also play a strategic role in providing the expertise and skills whereby the 'streamlined/strategic state' can become an organizational reality by promoting policies and programmes, such as market deregulation, service outsourcing, employment flexibility and internal competition, which shift the burden of scrutiny and accountability away from central government towards organizations and individuals who can no longer rely on the latter as the primary source of institutionalized trust and order.

Insofar as neoliberal governmentality constitutes an ensemble of political rationalities and the technologies needed 'to make them real' in a constantly moving and unstable environment in which there is a premium on adaptability and resilience in the face of failure (Mirowski 2013; Peck 2010; Peck and Theodore 2015), then we would expect it to place the production and dissemination of expert knowledge at the organizational core of its legitimation and operation. As its dependence on the latter grows, we would also expect the body of experts and expertise which it draws on for intellectual, technical and political inspiration to become more complex, inclusive and heterogeneous encompassing an ever-expanding range of officials, technocrats, advisors and professionals who often offer conflicting advice on 'what is to be done' or, even more importantly, 'what is not to be done' (Gamble 2009, 2014; Jessop 2010; Loveridge 2013; Reed 2012; Savage and Williams 2008; Wedel 2011, 2014).

However, this increasingly diverse and influential, if not powerful, configuration of overlapping, contesting and colluding expert circles – increasingly drawn from the private corporate sector and often at odds with established public service senior officials and managers – plays a critical role in sustaining neoliberal governmentality as a viable mode of governance and management in which 'the state' may become smaller but nonetheless even more 'strategic' (Jessop 2008, 2010, 2016; Morgan et al. 2015). In many ways, neoliberal governmentality comes more closely to resemble Dahl's (1971: 8) model of 'polyarchy' – that is, a political regime which has been 'substantially popularized and liberalized, which is highly inclusive and extensively open to public contestation' but ruled by competitive elite minorities who have been forced to allow a widening range of interest groups 'voice' as they contend for their electoral support. Experts play an increasingly strategic role within this neoliberal/polyarchic governmentality regime to the extent that they provide the specialist knowledge and technologies which frame and legitimate the 'offerings' that ruling minorities make to the electorate in order to sustain their power in government (Wallace et al. 2023). They blend ideology and pragmatism in discourses and technologies which are aimed at retaining political power and authority within a state apparatus which becomes increasingly fragmented and fractious but nonetheless sustainable as a mechanism reproducing elite rule. As a hybrid of oligarchic rule and pluralistic stakeholder participation, neoliberal governmentality/polyarchy provides neo-liberalization with a viable state form and strategy which can secure its longer-term survival so long as it retains its inherent flexibility and adaptability.

Experts remain central to retaining this capacity to blend ideology and policy in ways that enable that ensemble of rationalities and technologies we call 'neoliberal governmentality' to continue to do its job of reproducing the power relations and interest coalitions on which it depends for its legitimacy and authority. It has proved to be highly resilient in its capability to rationalize its mistakes and failures (Davies 2011) over a period of five decades or more by deftly combining 'hard' and 'soft' power. This is achieved through the construction and maintenance of an extensive and complex infrastructure of surveillance and control in parallel with the promulgation of 'discursive imaginaries' promoting the successes and advantages of the regime and marginalizing any negative views of its performance (Fairclough 2010).

This is where experts 'come into their own' under neoliberal governmentality in that they provide the specialist knowledge and skill through which interrelated systems of surveillance and control can be developed alongside discursive narratives promoting the inevitability and normality of policies and programmes venerating free market ideology and its inherent drive to deregulate, privatize and marketize (Bowman et al. 2014, 2015; Swarts 2013; Ban 2016). A range of empirical and investigative studies have demonstrated the crucial role that experts – lawyers, accountants, public relations and communications consultants, lobbyists, academics, statisticians, social media specialists, think tank associates and journalists – play as 'technocratic fixers' and 'political brokers' mediating between competing factions within neoliberal elite circles to ensure that neoliberal governmentality sustains its underlying ideological momentum and political drive in the policy regimes and programmes it legitimates and promotes (Heusinkveld, Gabbionetta, Werr and Sturdy 2018; Wedel 2011, 2014; Spence, Voulgaris and Maclean 2017; Burns 2019; Saks 2021). In this regard, finance specialists and economists have been particularly prominent to the extent they have provided the intellectual, analytical and technical resources whereby neoliberal political elites can justify the dominance of financial markets, services and products within our political economy no matter how spectacularly they fail and generate economic crises with long-term consequences for those most exposed to their ravages (Davis 2009; Davies 2014; Lapavitsas 2013; Ho 2009; Morgan et al. 2015; Christophers 2020). Expertise in financial management, whether for the corporation, household, agency or utility, becomes the sine qua non of survival under neoliberal governmentality in which market discipline comes to exercise a pervasive rule over all aspects of economic, political and social life.

However, these studies also reveal growing inequalities and divisions between different expert occupational groups and organizations which have proved so central to the rise of neoliberal governmentality. They also document the deleterious impact these factionalizing and fragmenting tendencies have exerted upon the integrity and credibility of the orthodox model of 'expert authority' as the institutional repository of 'objective knowledge' and 'passive trust'.

Evidence of growing inequality and division within those 'expert cadres' who have been so significant in enabling the rise of neoliberal governmentality and the policy regimes it has initiated and legitimated can be seen across a range of dimensions. First, there is the geographic dimension as entailed in the growing divide between those experts who function at a global/transnational level and those who are defined primarily by their local/national location and sphere of influence (Ban 2016). Second, comes the sectoral dimension as expressed in a clear hierarchy of functional domains in which finance/economics is the dominant area of expertise to which everything else comes a very 'poor second' (Christensen 2017; Davies

2017; Brooks 2018). Third, there is the employment reward and security dimension referring to widening inequalities between a relatively small elite cadre of 'corporate professionals' who enjoy levels of remuneration and protection unheard of by much larger groupings of middle and lower grade 'technicians' designing and running the information and communication technologies on which the former relies but rarely acknowledges (Kirkpatrick and Noordegraaf 2015; Sturdy, Wright and Wylie 2016; Crouch 2016; Sturdy and Mahoney 2018; Johannessen 2019). Finally, the further away – spatially, organizationally and politically – expert groups are from the core networks of power and control which emerge within neoliberal governmentality, then their capacity to access and influence national-level policy making networks is severely diminished to the point where they are downgraded to the status of 'roll out drones' (Wedel 2011, 2014; Peck and Theodore 2015; Ban 2016).

These fissures within the heterogeneous coalitions of expert groups who 'oil the wheels' of neoliberal governmentality through the mediating and brokering processes which they enable, makes an inherently complex governance system even more prone to fragment and implode in on itself. Yet, the capacity of the latter to adapt successfully in the face of these internal challenges should not be underestimated as it continues to sustain the momentum of its political strategy of 'franchising' core state functions such as justice, education, welfare and health (Bowman et al. 2014, 2015), reinforcing the move towards a 'corporate welfare state' (Farnsworth 2014; Wilks 2013) in which vast amounts of public money are transferred to private corporations, and 'financializing' personal and corporate life by making credit-based expansion the main driver of economic growth so that financial institutions and organizations come to occupy a dominant position and role within neoliberal governmentality (Gamble 2009; Willmott 2011; Lapavitsas 2013; Davies 2017).

Within each of these key policy areas, elite expert occupations and organizations, as well as their 'supporting cast' of designers and technicians, have deployed their expertise to construct, operate and normalize a complex intellectual and technological infrastructure through which dominant political ideologies and discourses can be translated into policy ideas and programmatic initiatives that remains 'loyal to the neoliberal theoretical core' (Ban 2016: 19) while facilitating all sorts of local 'hybrid trade offs' better adapted to their key constituencies and conditions. As Peck and Theodore (2015: 24) suggest, 'expert and technocratic networks have been instrumental in the propagation of neoliberal reason, practice and rule' because they provide the specialized knowledge, models and techniques through which governmental policies and programmes such as privatization, marketization and outsourcing can be mobilized and transferred within and across a wide range of institutional environments. They design, service and repair the 'travelling technologies' of government which neo-liberalization depends upon to ach-

ieve sufficient and lasting acceptance and diffusion so that they, eventually, become stabilized as dominant policy paradigms or 'prisms' through which elite 'policy makers read, interpret, and act on the world' (Peck and Theodore 2015: 19).

But the question remains as to the longer-term impact of this 'chameleon-like'
act performed by increasing numbers of, factionalized but well-rewarded, expert
groups and organizations on their established claims to authority and the legitimacy it routinely bestows. Significant shifts in the locus, coherence, resilience and stability of 'expert authority' are very likely to occur as experts become increasingly
co-opted and embedded in new configurations of power relations entailing emerging asymmetries in legitimacy and control. Indeed, the inherent dynamism, mobility and 'transformational potential' of neo-liberalization and neoliberal governmentality destabilizes established expert hierarchies and divisions in all sorts of
ways, making them more exposed and vulnerable to the dislocating impact of
'technocratic/political modernization' as it unevenly rationalizes certain expert
groups out of existence and generates opportunities for others to emerge. This
also exacerbates prevailing political tensions and conflicts within expert power
networks as they struggle to prove their worth to neoliberal governmental elites
desperate to demonstrate that the new policy paradigm is working and unforgiving of any, actual or perceived, failure on the part of 'their experts' to deliver the
technologies whereby 'success' can be documented and failure eradicated, or at
least obscured and hidden from public view.

In general terms, the rise of biopolitics, disciplinary power, and neoliberal governmentality has burnished the 'technocratic' credentials of experts but at the expense of substantially weakening their authority as 'public servants' legitimated by
their dedicated commitment to a social democratic state in which the safety and
security of its citizens is the overriding policy imperative. They are increasingly
viewed as a remote and self-serving elite disengaged from the everyday lives
and concerns of ordinary citizens as they struggle to survive under the unrelenting
pressures exerted by market-driven economies and societies in which regulative
constraints have been progressively dismantled and delegitimated. In turn, this
has ideologically and politically exposed expert occupational groups to 'populist
critique' – often mounted by elite politicians within ruling neoliberal regimes determined to secure electoral advantage from 'culture war' campaigns – which further erodes whatever shreds of institutionalized trust and legitimacy they have
managed to retain. Indeed, several researchers (Davies 2018; Bickerton and Accetti
2021; Vormann and Weinman 2021) have identified the emergence of a new political rationality or logic in which selected elements of authoritarian populism
and technocratic expertise are fused together in support of political movements
and parties hostile to the restraining influence of liberal democratic values and
norms. However, this emerging populist/technocratic political rationality requires

experts to surrender whatever independence and autonomy they may have legitimately accrued under the latter in the service of a wider ideological discourse and political project where they are forced to subordinate their collective interests to its dictates. Their 'authority' as purveyors of specialist knowledge and skills is now completely subordinated to populist causes and programmes which threaten to undermine whatever credibility they may have left as independent public servants supposedly acting on behalf of a liberal democratic state constrained by the norms and conventions of representative parliamentary government.

Analysed in these terms, expert authority 'sups with' neoliberal governmentality and its authoritarian populist inclinations at its peril; although the latter provides a socio-political context and apparatus in which the technocratic side of expert authority may flourish, it also poses an existential threat to its viability and survivability as a credible source of disinterested specialist knowledge vital to maintaining the safety and security of a democracy's citizens in the face of major threats to their health and wellbeing. Experts dealing with neoliberal governmentality is rather like children 'playing with fire' – it has its attractions and excitements but at the risk of becoming trapped in the flames of a political wildfire that will inevitably engulf them and destroy their credibility and viability as necessary and authoritative sources of knowledge and advice in high stakes, high risk environments.

5 Structural and Cultural Changes

Unsurprisingly, the structural and cultural changes which the demystification narrative identifies as being generated as a result of the shift to biopolitics, disciplinary power, and neoliberal governmentality are very different from those highlighted by the de-legitimation narrative. While the latter predicts a system-wide breakdown in the institutionalized trust relations through which expert authority had been legitimated, the former anticipates a much more complex and contradictory dynamic in which the 'technocratic' components of expert authority are strengthened but at the expense of fundamentally weakening any claims it may try to make concerning its independence, autonomy or objectivity.

To return to Miller and Rose (2008: 24), neoliberal governmentality 'seeks to de-governmentalize the state and de-statize practices of government' by drastically circumscribing what the state is expected to do and redefining how those remaining core functions are to be performed and organized. At one level, this entails the state withdrawing from many of the responsibilities and tasks which were previously taken-for-granted as being within its strategic vision and operational purview, such as 'full employment' or 'universal health and social care' or 'poverty reduction' or 'social mobility' or 'industrial planning' or 'public health' or 'climate change'. In turn, in line with the growth of rentier capitalism, these policy concerns are incrementally transferred to non-state agencies, particularly private sector corporations, who now operate as 'state surrogates' regulating and managing areas of social and economic life once regarded as central to the conduct of government.

This drastically downgrades, in theory and practice, the power and authority of 'the centre' to engage directly in the micro-management of its citizens daily lives and to take responsibility for protecting them from the threats and risks they face from recurring economic, social and environmental crises. Indeed, under neoliberal governmentality the onus is very much on 'individuals' and 'families' becoming sufficiently robust and resilient to navigate their way through the threats and challenges which market-driven economies and societies will inevitably throw at them. It also downgrades the significance and status of experts as 'public servants' who provide vital assistance to the general public, particularly in crisis situations when their expertise can make the difference between life or death, or at least between success or failure. At best, they are placed in a secondary or subordinate position and role to the newly empowered cadre of private sector technocrats, managers and consultants who take on the unenviable task of providing whatever protection and support can be mobilized for the general populace by the 'outsourced state'.

However, the other side of Miller and Rose's neoliberal governmentality requires experts to take on enhanced responsibilities and powers legitimating the elevation of 'market-based principles and techniques of evaluation to the level of state-endorsed norms' (Davies 2014: 6). A swathe of institutions, organizations, groups and practices previously regarded as being outside the discipline of market logic must now be reconstituted in such a way that they, at the very least 'resemble markets, if not entirely conforming to the latter's theoretical principles and operational requirements' (Davies 2014: 38). Thus, the technocrats, managers and consultants newly empowered by neoliberal governmentality and the political rationalities and technologies which it legitimates become the key actors in ensuring the marketization of all social relations encompassing 'the whole ensemble of social institutions, organizations, networks and norms of conduct which regularize economic relations' (Jessop 1994: 30). They are given the task of ensuring that as much as possible of non-economic life is brought under the domination and control of market discipline – even if this is a simulacrum of the latter rather than its reality – so that it conforms to the norms and rules of market competition which are the only guarantors of efficiency and effectiveness. By designing and operating the technologies through which non-market relations are transformed into market relations, experts under neoliberal governmentality become the carriers of a political rationality which putatively transforms whole ways of existing and living so that they conform to these newly state-endorsed norms of market determined exchanges.

But, of course, there are 'winners' and 'losers' under neoliberal governmentality which exposes its 'expert carriers' to criticism from an ever-expanding set of stakeholders that they can no longer sustain any kind of claim or legitimacy to be acting on behalf of the 'general good' because they are increasingly remote to and disengaged from ordinary people leading ordinary lives. Once the vested interests and norms which these 'neoliberal technocrats' serve are fully revealed by the political rationalities and technologies which they impose as they go about their business of marketizing non-market relations, then any discursive strategy aimed at defending their role and status as 'public servants' is denuded of its legitimacy. This is even more the case when we look at the mediating mechanisms through which their 'mission' under neoliberal governmentality is carried forward.

6 Mediating Mechanisms

Previous discussion suggests that a wide range of expert groups have played a central role under neoliberal governmentality in reconstructing and repurposing 'the state' in order to ensure that it becomes strategically focussed on transforming 'society' in ways which are consistent with the supremacy of 'market forces' in all aspects of its operation and organization. They have become the primary agents, operating within and across state/non-state boundaries which have become increasingly deregulated and porous, ensuring that market competition and its disciplinary impact is progressively 'rolled out' across all spheres of economic, social and political life. This is to be realized, however imperfectly and messily in practice, through a form of 'statecraft' directed to the production of 'neoliberal subjects' who conform to whatever state-endorsed norms and routines are required under neoliberal governmentality.

As a result, 'expert authority' becomes entangled in extended networks of material and discursive relations in which the systemic contradictions between its 'technocratic' and 'public service' components are exacerbated and more fully exposed to critique, whether this comes 'from above' or 'from below' in the guise of elitist distancing or populist rejection. Experts are now key actors within these networks because they assemble and operate the political rationalities and technologies through which the supremacy of 'the market' in all aspects of our lives is to be made possible. They are the major carriers of a political rationality whereby all social relations are to be subjected to the disciplining power of market forces and its liberating impact on all aspects of neoliberal subjects' identities and lives. Also, they're expected, by ruling neoliberal elites, to design and run the technologies through which this transformational project can be enacted in ways that conceal, or at least obscure, its inevitable negative consequences for those who refuse to accept its domination.

While this enhances the status and influence of experts as 'technical specialists', it simultaneously weakens whatever remains of their moral authority as 'public service professionals' dedicated to the protection of the body politic and the social bonds on which it depends for its legitimacy and stability. On the one hand, expert groups are charged with being 'remote', 'uncaring', 'self-interested' and 'duplicitous'; on the other, they begin to lose their mystique as 'guardians of the public good' as they are reduced to the status of just another vested interest desperately trying to bolster their advantages in an increasingly fragmented and 'dog-eat-dog' world. They can no longer hide behind a 'veil of ignorance' in which their clients and customers passively trust them to do their best for them and for the rest of society as their key role in unleashing the forces of 'creative destruction' which neo-liberalization inevitably releases becomes more evident. Neoliberal governmentality and the statecraft on which it relies to ensure its reproduction, exposes experts to the full blast of public resentment and political criticism because they are charged with 'making the system work' as it inevitably fails to deliver on its promises. If neoliberal governmentality and the political project it's meant to deliver can be seen as 'consistently failing forward' because they have 'always been about the capture and re-use of the state in the interests of pro-corporate, free-trading market order' (Peck 2010: 9) – this inevitably means there are likely to be many more 'losers' than 'winners' under its rule. Consequently, experts are the most obvious and convenient 'fall guys' for these deleterious outcomes. Their authority and status as disinterested public servants dispensing their expertise on behalf of society can no longer be sustained in a world where their culpability in producing so many of the ills which now confronts its members is so evident and undefendable.

However, several interrelated mechanisms have emerged under neoliberal governmentality geared to mediating and moderating these systemic tensions and their destructive impact on expert authority.

First, a whole panoply of advanced surveillance and control systems have been developed over time as neoliberal governmentality has learned from its own mistakes and striven to at least contain, if not eradicate, escalating structural tensions and conflicts within and between the expert groups who make its rule possible. Second, various creative 'discursive imaginaries' have been promulgated as a way of rationalizing mistakes and failures as necessary 'learning experiments' which must, however unfortunately, be experienced if the full advantages of neo-liberalization are to be realized. Third, a seemingly never-ending stream of innovative organizational forms and practices have been promoted under neoliberal governmentality as potential 'shock absorbers' of the risks, dislocations and polarizations which the neoliberal 'stealth revolution' (Brown 2019) inevitably produces.

Surveillance and control systems are central to neoliberal governmentality because they enable governmentality to achieve the simultaneous 'double movement' of mobility and co-ordination which would be impossible under traditional state forms and the highly centralized and formalized administrative systems through which they rule (Dean 1999; Jessop 2010; Mau 2019). The evolution of digital technologies and their capability for surveillance capitalism (Zuboff 2019) and the transformation of social life to big data (Dencik 2020), play a key role here. It allows technocracy to dominate (Sylvia and Andrejevic 2016), but also ensnares experts into to propagating more innovative modes of governmentality through more technically advanced, organizationally pervasive, and socially ubiquitous surveillance regimes (Kellogg et al. 2020; Visser et al. 2018) whilst also entrapping them with those same regimes as well. Therefore, expert authority and status are considerably enhanced through the benefits which these systems deliver – particularly in crisis situations requiring highly specialized risk management technologies – and the reality that they would be theoretically unrealizable and practically impossible without the technical expertise which their architects and operators provide. This serves to moderate the criticism and suspicion which 'experts' increasingly attract, but it also reminds us that much of the trust we place in them is manufactured rather than bestowed and consequently inherently more fragile in the face of 'evidence' which undermines their credibility as indispensable navigators through 'troubled times'.

Creative discursive imaginaries (Fairclough 2010: 444) tell us stories about how obstacles and difficulties may be overcome by representing 'how things are' and 'how they might be' if we would 'only do better next time'. Experts shape and disseminate these narratives in ways that are subject to certain 'conditions of possibility', 'including what we might call *practical adequacy* – the world must be such that the imagined reality is possible, the agents imagined as bringing it into being have the power to so, and so forth – and *conviction* – imaginaries and the strategies they are part of have to be convincing for the people who need to be convinced' (Fairclough 2010: 480 emphasis in original). Neo-liberalization has exhibited a very high degree of discursive flexibility and creativity, particularly in the face of spectacular failures to deliver on its promises in economic policy, health and welfare policy, education policy or international policy. Yet, expert neoliberal story tellers have, with unnerving consistency, managed to redefine 'failure' as requiring more of the same, or indeed stronger, treatment from the neoliberal governmentality playbook and this has further cemented their positions within its power networks. But how much longer this expert capacity to generate strategic narratives through creative discursive imaginaries which are both practically adequate and convincing to an increasingly disenchanted and sceptical public audience can be sustained is highly questionable – particularly in the face of multiple crises which seem to undermine the credibility of the neoliberal project and its governmentality.

Finally, neoliberal governmentality has supported a rush of experimentation in new organizational forms and practices which experts have promoted as sustaining, or at least reigniting, the transformation of sclerotic bureaucratic dinosaurs into dynamic entrepreneurial systems (Burrell 2022). Much of this development can be traced back to the 'post-bureaucratic' literature of the 1990s and the academic legitimacy it provided for wider organizational changes in western political economies which seemed to herald the transition to a more flexible and creative organizational future in the twenty-first century (Reed 2005). However, as Burrell (2022) documents in some detail, over the last decade or so the burgeoning literature on organizational experimentation seems to have been driven by the political drive to camouflage the realities of neo-liberalization in positive, upbeat 'change narratives' which elide the damage done by the latter to the socio-political fabric of the Anglo-American economies in which its remit has run largest. Once again, experts find themselves caught in the cross hairs of neo-liberalization as they twist and turn in the face of the opportunities and threats which it presents to them.

7 Substantive Outcomes

The major substantive outcome which the demystification narrative identifies is the transition to a neoliberal governmentality in which a 'strategic/relational state' emerges as 'an ensemble of power centres that offer unequal chances to different forces within and outside the state to act for different purposes ... the state does not exercise power; its powers are activated through the agency of definite political forces in specific conjunctures' (Jessop 2008: 37). It very strongly suggests that the sovereign power of the central state, as envisaged by Hobbes or Weber, can no longer hold under these conditions because a plurality of power centres and their supporting political rationalities and technologies have emerged that eat away at the former's structural integrity and organizational capacity. This doesn't mean to say that under neoliberal governmentality the state disappears or is so fundamentally weakened that it can no longer play any part in the political organization and management of socio-economic life. Indeed, in its more streamlined and strategically focussed form, the state under neoliberal governmentality becomes redesigned and repurposed in ways which are more consistent with the project of creating and sustaining 'market societies'.

Under this reconfigured and refocused neoliberal state, experts come to play a very different role than that envisaged in the de-legitimation or decomposition narratives as outlined in chapters two and four of this book. They become the technocratic cadres who equip the neoliberal state and its governing apparatus with the political rationalities and technologies it requires to think and act more strategically, while also providing the discursive imaginaries that are needed when its policy initiatives and programmes hit cold reality and the inevitable recalibrations and recalculations which this will call for if the neoliberal 'stealth revolution' is to survive these encounters in any kind of coherent shape. As such, experts under neoliberal governmentality are condemned to 'life on the edge' of a regime from which they derive much benefit, but in which they are forced to absorb the incessant instabilities and uncertainties that this inevitably reproduces.

8 Conclusion

Perhaps rather surprisingly, the demystification narrative proffers a somewhat more positive and upbeat evaluation of expert authority than that articulated by the de-legitimation narrative. At the very least, it sees a future for experts in which their power, status and legitimacy are reframed by the emergence of neoliberal governmentality in which they become key actors in the relational networks through which this can be enacted and reproduced. It may be their fate under this regime to have to endure the ineradicable instabilities and uncertainties which this generates and thrives on as it works its way through the institutional infrastructure of the social democratic state so pivotal to the legitimation of expert power for the de-legitimation narrative. But at least they have a future – indeed a central position and role – within neoliberal governmentality as it becomes more prominent across an increasing number of societies and economies. However, they have been reduced in status to 'technocratic fixers' for a neo-liberal governmentality regime that they simultaneously operate and are subject to – they are both architects and slaves of the latter insofar as it can't do without them but will also dispose of them in the blinking of an eye if this is deemed politically expedient by the ruling political elite.

In the next chapter we consider the third narrative account of 'the crisis in expert authority' – that is, the decomposition narrative which sees expert authority being broken down into its separate, constituent elements and being reconstituted in a form that puts it in a better position to cope with and overcome threats and challenges to its survival.

Chapter 4: Decomposition

1 Introduction

Each of the narratives reviewed in this book accepts that the restructuring of the expert division of labour which has been occurring in Anglo-American political economies over more than four decades has substantially changed the nature of expert work and the way it is organized. However, they differ considerably in how they gauge the long-term impact of this restructuring and reconfiguring process in relation to how expert authority is to be legitimated in the future.

As we have already seen, the de-legitimation narrative proffers the most pessimistic reading of these developments to the extent that it insists on seeing the latter as indicative of an unrepairable erosion of expert authority generated by a 'fatal conjunction' between ever more concentrated economic and political power and an irreversible fragmenting and factionalizing of expert jurisdictional work domains. Expert authority is damaged beyond redemption to the extent that the institutionalized trust relation between experts, publics, and states has been progressively dismantled by unaccountable concentrations of elite economic and political power at 'the centre' determined to take control of expert work and growing disenchantment with and distrust of remote and uncaring technocratic experts within 'the periphery' of civil society and local communities.

For the demystification narrative, these developments signal a socio-political process whereby 'expert authority' has been progressively stripped of its cultural and symbolic secretiveness and remoteness to be revealed for what it really is – that is, a key component within more complex and labyrinthine-like power networks in which 'experts' design and operate the surveillance technologies through which 'new subjectivities' are constructed and controlled. Considered in this way, experts and the work they perform remains of vital importance for the new governance regimes emerging in modern states and societies. But their aura of objective rationality and political disinterestedness has been dissipated by their subordination to a much more rapacious and unforgiving neoliberal governmentality pervading advanced capitalist societies. Hardt and Negri (2019: 125–138) suggest this is leading to a crisis of the modern administrative state or 'Weber in reverse'. Weber's dream of 'a rational, just, and transparent bureaucracy' run by cadres of enlightened experts, and Kafka's nightmare of 'obscure and alienating forms of modern bureaucratic power', are both superseded by 'digital Taylorism'. Within the latter, the production of 'machine subjectivities' emerges as the dominant political and administrative imperative where 'a complex mixture of legal reasoning, compassion, fear and callousness in play in governmental decisions' (Hardt and

https://doi.org/10.1515/9783110734911-005

Negri 2019: 130) shapes the organizational context in which expert knowledge is generated and consumed.

For the decomposition narrative, both the de-legitimation and demystification narratives overestimate the destructive power and impact of the restructuring and reconfiguring of expert work which has been dynamically working away since the 1980s. It offers an alternative mapping and interpretation of these changes in which the 'adaptive capacity' of the system of expert work is emphasized, so that the emergence of a more contested and complex ecology of expertise is viewed in a much more positive light because in enables the latter to grow and develop in ways which meet the new challenges posed by 21st century economic and social change. Far from witnessing the dismantling of expert authority, we are experiencing its renewal and realignment within an evolving ecology of expertise in which flexibility of response and connectiveness with wider society are the keys to future expansion and legitimacy. While the 'old order' of elite professionalization, based on epistemological exclusivity and jurisdictional control, may, no longer, be the dominant exemplar to follow, new and more innovative forms of expertise are emerging which redefine the normative frameworks and social forms through which the latter can be legitimated and stabilized. As the established system of expert accreditation decomposes, it simultaneously recomposes itself into a more complex institutional form which self-adjusts and self-corrects in order to absorb threats to its equilibrium and long-term survival.

Accepting that expert authority, particularly in its more institutionalized and formalized forms, has been exposed to the fragmenting and fracturing dynamic of rapid socio-technical innovation and change, supporters of the decomposition narrative reject the innate pessimism and fatalism of the de-legitimation and demystification narratives. They believe in the inherent organizational adaptability and resilience of the system of expert occupations to absorb threats to its existence and to retain control over the structural and cultural mechanisms through which it is reproduced and develops. Kirkpatrick, Aulakh and Muzio (2021: 3–4) express this underlying confidence in the innate organizational capacity of the system of expert occupations to absorb and transcend all threats to its existence in the following terms:

> While professionalism has adjusted partly in response to the changing political and ideological climate, overall, there has been no wholesale reshaping of the turn-of-the-millennium institution … to a greater or lesser extent, in developed capitalist economies, professionalism has been (and arguably remains) the dominant approach to organizing and regulating expert labour.

Their confident reassertion of the continued dominance of professionalism as the primary institutional mechanism for regulating expert work and of the 'minimal impact of neoliberal ideas inspired policies on professionalism' (Kirkpatrick, Aulakh and Muzio 2021: 13–14), rests on the argument that – particularly in the US but in other market-based capitalist political economies as well – *a sophisticated 'certification ecosystem' remains firmly in place* to ensure 'the robustness and embedded nature of professional regulation'. For them, the latter reinforces and reproduces the institutional architecture through which professionalism, as a formal mode of occupational regulation, retains its legitimacy and continuity even in the face of destabilizing structural and cultural changes ostensibly pushing in the direction of de-professionalized modes of organizing and controlling expert work. Far from witnessing 'Weber in reverse' – that is, a long-term decline in professionalized modes of expert authorization and regulation based on 'epistemological exclusion' and 'jurisdictional closure' as outlined in chapter one of this book – we must recognize the underlying institutional resilience of professionalism in the face of, supposedly, existential threats to its survival.

Kirkpatrick, Aulakh and Muzio's (2021) rejection of, what they label, 'grand narrative' theories of professional de-legitimation and demystification, lies at the more optimistic end of the spectrum of analyses and views reviewed in this chapter. Like other analysts associated with the decomposition narrative, they accept that the expert division of labour has become more differentiated, fragmented and contested in recent decades under the combined pressures exerted by political, economic, technological and cultural change. But they remain confident that 'professionalism', even in something like its Weberian/ideal-typical form, has the required innate institutional resilience and organizational flexibility to withstand any threats to its continuance because it provides the most reliable and robust systems for licensing and accrediting 'expert labour'. We will return to their analysis and the conclusions they draw from it later in this chapter as we review and assess the full range of arguments and evidence advanced in support of the decomposition narrative. Suffice to say at this point that they put a great deal of emphasis on 'occupational licensing' and analytically equate it with 'professional accreditation'. This conceptual elision between a relatively low-level, routine exercise in bureaucratic or 'paper checking' processing and a high-level, extended process of selective admittance and socialization into an esoteric and exclusive expert occupational association may be particularly relevant if increasing reliance on the former is seen as a key indicator of waning authority and diluted status rather than its obverse.

Kirkpatrick, Aulakh and Muzio (2021) also rely heavily, as do many contributors to the decomposition narrative discussed in this chapter, on a 'neo-evolutionary institutionalism' as their major explanatory theory of how a more complex expert ecosystem self-adjusts and self-corrects to a more threatening institutional environment in order to generate hybridized systems of expert working.

In resorting to a complexity-theory based conception of self-correcting and stabilizing expert ecosystems possessing the innate capacity to re-establish equilibrium even in the face of extreme environmental turbulence and dislocation, *exponents of the decomposition narrative risk marginalizing, if not excluding, the pivotal role of power relations and processes in shaping the legitimacy struggles through which expert authority is won and lost.* By treating the latter as the official organizational outcome of regulatory mechanisms and 'certification ecosystems' that continue to function according to their own institutional logic irrespective of escalating threats to their cultural meaning and political relevance, some decomposition analysts may be again guilty of perpetrating a recurring confusion between 'formal' and 'substantive' rationality. Just because the incidence of occupational licensing or any other form of work-related certification is empirically increasing doesn't entail that it can be 'read off' as a prime substantive indicator of the continuing, or indeed increasing, power, authority and status of those occupations to which it relates. Indeed, the proliferation of those occupational groups claiming, 'expert status and identity', through whatever licensing, accrediting and regulating mechanisms they chose to utilize, is to be expected as one of the defining features of 'reflexive modernization' as discussed in previous chapters of this book. But this differentiation dynamic is likely to generate increasing segmentation, fragmentation and factionalism as more occupational groups struggle to occupy and police jurisdictional work domains as they become more open to conflicting claims of authority-granting competence and control. In this respect, expert authority becomes even more contested, diluted and unstable the more it comes to rely on strategies of exclusion and closure dependent on formalized licensing and accreditation. Documentation containing formalized and standardized licensing agreements, even if backed by national occupational associations or local government agencies, will be less effective during intensifying jurisdictional conflicts in which securing wider public legitimacy and support, often mediated through national media and state organizations, remains the key to securing and retaining expert authority at a societal level. Indeed, an increasing emphasis on occupational licensing, rather than pursuing an expansive strategy focused on securing and retaining wider social and political legitimation through 'epistemological exclusion', can be interpreted as a key indicator of a partial de-coupling of the twin-track approach (epistemological exclusion **and** jurisdictional closure) to institutionalizing expert authority as outlined in chapter one of this book. This is a theme we will return to later in this chapter.

Occupational licensing may be part of the story but it retains a minor role in the continuing struggle to legitimate expertise within a 21st century socio-historical context which has moved on somewhat from the mid/late nineteenth/early twentieth century timelines in which 'professionalizing projects' really began to attract political momentum and support from central government elites on which professional associations were so dependent for their power and authority (Larson 2013; Burns 2019; Sacks 2021).

Our exposition and evaluation of the decomposition narrative will follow the pattern established in previous chapters. First, we will discuss the key **'structural and cultural changes'** which exponents of this approach have identified as impacting on the nature, organization and control of expert labour since the late 1970/early 1980s, primarily but not exclusively in Anglo-American political economies. Second, we will look at the **'mediating mechanisms'** through which these impacts have been filtered and interpreted to generate the potential for consequential transformations in the ways expert work is authorized and legitimated. Third, we examine the **'substantive outcomes'** that have occurred in order to assess how and why this potential has either been realized or nullified within complex socio-historical contexts in which 'patterns' are always difficult to discern and to explain amongst a wide range of contrasting and competing developments.

2 Structural and Cultural Changes

Drawing on classic studies of inter-occupational and intra-organizational jurisdictional conflicts between expert groups and the exclusion/closure strategies they engage in to establish and control jurisdictional domains within the expert division of labour (Freidson 1994, 2001; Abbott 1988, 2005; Larson 1977/2013, 1990), exponents of the decomposition narrative have highlighted four interrelated structural changes which have exerted a major impact on how these conflicts are conducted and shape emerging patterns of expert work.

First, series of **complex institutional and technical changes** entailed in the rise of neoliberal/platform capitalism and new public management which, separately and cumulatively, have transformed the structural context in which a wide range of occupational groups vie for recognition and status as 'experts' and the material/symbolic rewards that it bestows on them.

Second, the **proliferation of new managerial, technical and scientific occupations** contesting and challenging the successful legitimation and closure strategies through which the established professions have established themselves in the top echelons of the hierarchy of expert work roles and relations.

Third, the **increasingly fragmented and fractured expert division of labour** which this proliferation and intensification of expert jurisdictional competitions and conflicts has generated and reproduced.

Fourth, **intensified 'ontological insecurity'** on the part of those performing expert work as they find themselves operating in working environments characterized by increasing levels of precarity, instability and uncertainty concerning their roles and status as specialists who can deal effectively with highly complex or 'wicked' problems and the unpredictable risks they present.

2.1 Institutional and Technical Changes

A complex combination of institutional, organizational and technological changes structurally embedded in the transition to neoliberal/platform capitalism and new public management are taken as the starting point for the decomposition narrative.

At the global level, these changes embody 'the collapse of the Bretton Woods system paving the way for a new international financial and economic order built on strong ideological faith in in the inherent efficiency and stability of markets, which opened-up new profit-making opportunities for an increasingly unregulated financial sector and highly concentrated forms of footloose capital' (Gallagher and Kozul-Wright 2021: 42). This wider international economic transformation generates a series of interrelated institutional changes at the national level further destabilizing the environmental fields and organizational settings in which expert occupational groups operate. It entails a twin-track evolutionary dynamic in which nation states and their governments find themselves in a much weaker position to regulate and control the legal and administrative context in which expert occupations are accredited and monitored as a result of the transference of these functions to international bodies and agencies which play an increasingly prominent role in governing them. As Boussebaa and Morgan (2017: 77, emphasis in original) argue, in the context of the internationalization of professional service firms (PSF) and the international legal/administrative architecture through which they are regulated and governed, 'professional service firms have to balance efforts to achieve global integration against the necessity to maintain not only local responsiveness but also *professional autonomy*'. They go on to suggest that this delicate balancing act between legitimation strategies focused on global regulation and jurisdictional strategies geared to protecting local professional autonomy is fundamentally about changing power relations and the much more unstable, shifting and uncertain institutional environments in which professional service firms operate. If this is the case for knowledge-based and highly specialized expert occupations and organizations such as PSFs, located at the summit of the 'expert hierarchy', then the increasing complexity and escalating risks for others – even if they face relatively less immediate pressure from international bodies and agencies than PSFs – are likely to be considerable in their scale and intensity.

In its emphasis on the institutional destabilization and dislocation generated by the globalization of different forms of neoliberal capitalism (Swarts 2013; Cahill 2014; Ban 2016; Cahill and Konings 2017), the decomposition narrative is drawing attention to the destructive dynamic which the latter has released and its impact on the organization and governance of expert work. Although there has been considerable national and sectoral variation in the extent to which neo-liberalization has promoted a dismantling of the formal legal, administrative and political infrastructure through which a wide range of expert occupations and organizations have been regulated (Suddaby and Muzio 2015; Davis and Williams 2017; Spence, Voulgaris and Maclean 2017; Adams 2017; Boussard 2018; Davis 2018; Saks and Brock 2018), there has been an underlying movement towards market-based, self-regulation and control in which external checks and balances are minimized in the name of 'liberalization' and 'competition'. This is consistent with the ways in which neo-liberalization has reconfigured the administrative and governance apparatus through which modern capitalist states govern by 'creating new forms of regulation with new market-oriented rules and policies to facilitate the development of the "new" capitalism. Society is transformed in the image of the market and the state is now itself "marketized" [in the form of] "the competition state"' (Munck 2005: 63).

Expert occupations and organizations now find themselves in a situation where 'the neoliberal project primarily *reregulates* and institutes an alternative set of infrastructural arrangements: it never wipes the slate clean so that it gets closer to the tabula rasa of laissez faire' (Mirowski 2013: 16, emphasis in original). This infrastructure of 'reregulation' is presented, by apologists for neo-liberalization', as a 'spontaneous order' that evolves according to the logic of market competition and the self-discipline it imposes on all actors irrespective of their choices and tactics when engaged in market behaviour. However, behind this ideological and discursive façade lies a brutal social reality in which privatized and marketized reregulation, dominated by the financial and economic interests of powerful private corporations, determines the conventions, norms, and rules through which everyday organizational life is ordered and sustained. Thus, Cahill and Konings (2017: 135–137) analyse reregulation as a long-term strategy of 'regulatory capture in reverse' whereby control over state-driven public policy and the regulative programmes and regimes it produces are handed back to private corporate interests under the guise of a deregulatory rhetoric extolling untrammelled 'market rationality' as its motivating ethic.

For expert occupations and organizations, this neoliberal-driven strategy of reregulation is most clearly seen in the ways it putatively empowers individual consumers and clients to a level at which 'user sovereignty' and 'client capture' come to threaten their independence and autonomy (Saks 2021: 87–94). Expert knowledge and skill are commodified in ways that equate them with any other commodity subject to market competition and exchange and their overriding need to be responsive to changing consumer wants and demands. A new bureaucratic surveillance and control technology emerges under neoliberal reregulation geared to managers ensuring that experts meet the consumer driven performance targets and metrics which now become the quantitative proxy for market competition and quality standards (Hibou 2016; Eyal 2019; Mau 2019). The latter find themselves set-free by market liberalization and regulatory dismantling but only to be recaptured, or at least recolonized, by a neoliberal bureaucracy. The latter is dedicated to a hybrid form of administrative rule which creates new tensions, splits and divisions between occupational groups who must be forcibly socialized into a managerial culture and system in which 'market indifference' blurs the boundaries between 'public' and 'private' to a degree where they become almost meaningless (Hibou 2016). Whether it be in the field of internationalizing the International Organization for Standardization (ISO) standards with the intensification of World Trade Organization (WTO) negotiations or devolving the 'responsibilization and personalization' of healthcare pathways to individual clients, neoliberal bureaucracy constructs and legitimates a reregulation regime in which experts are subjected to more intrusive and detailed managerial surveillance and control.

Neoliberal reregulation in the private sector has been mirrored by in the public sector where new variants of New Public Management (NPM) have come to play an increasingly important role in shaping the performance and organization of expert work. We have already discussed the rise of a distinctive neoliberal form of NPM in chapter two but in the context of a long-term decline in the public sector/service as embodying an institutional logic and organizational practice based on collective values and social equity rather than private interests and market rationality. This weakening of the public service ethic and the professionally led modes of service delivery which it legitimated was seen to be reinforced by the increasing power and authority of 'calculative experts' or 'corporate professionals' who were progressively taking over the jurisdictional domains previously controlled, if not dominated, by established public service professionals (Raco 2013; Sturdy, Wright and Wylie 2016; Eyal 2019; Reed 2019; Malin 2021).

Thus, the increasing impact of a neoliberal variant of NPM over the last decade or so has been expressed through the implementation of governance regimes and organizational technologies geared to subjugating public provision to the scrutiny of markets as demanded by neoliberal economic and political theory (Peck 2010; Peck and Theodore 2015; Dardot and Laval 2013; Davies 2014). A rolling programme of policies and initiatives have been implemented over the last decade or so aimed at completing the neoliberal (Thatcherite/Reaganite) 'stealth revolution' begun in the 1980s (Blyth 2013; Brown 2015; Bowman et al. 2014; Bowman et al. 2015; Styhre

2014). The strategic role of the former is aimed at ensuring that market rationality permeates all areas of public and social life through the imposition of privatization and marketization technologies such as the private finance initiative and its successors (Pollock 2004; Gamble 2014) competitive tendering, outsourcing, franchising and benchmarking, all legitimated through the mantra of 'value for money' and 'consumer choice'. Across swathes of government activity encompassing housing and construction, justice, health and social care, education, security and defence, combinations of austerity-driven funding cuts, outsourcing to private sector corporations, such as Serco and Carillion, whose multinational expansion and power has been almost entirely dependent on this 'hollowing out' of the public sector (Wilks 2013; Crouch 2016), and the increasing political influence of finance capital over public policy formulation and implementation (Crouch 2017; White 2016; Morgan et al. 2015; Vogl 2017) have transformed the institutional landscape in which expert groups and organizations operate.

From the perspective of the decomposition narrative, this incremental colonization of public sector institutional positions and organizational jurisdictions by calculative experts/corporate professionals – facilitated and legitimated by the rise of a much more ideologically aggressive and politically motivated neoliberal form of NPM – has been reinforced by various technological and cultural changes entailing the diffusion of digitally-based surveillance and performance technologies and the shift towards an 'entrepreneurial' managerial culture.

Mau (2019: 111–129) argues that this involves a 'double movement' whereby calculative experts, such as business and management consultants, accountancy and finance specialists, information management technologists, and communications/public relations professionals, are brought into the public sector to design and implement the new organizational technologies and performance systems whereby the latter can be remade as a simulacrum of private sector business. These technologies and systems have the 'nominative power' – that is, the capacity to name, quantify and objectify inherently complex and multi-faceted social phenomena – required by neoliberal NPM to represent the market-driven reregulation which they entail as neutral, disinterested, and objective outcomes of an impersonal, deterministic process akin to the ways in which selection mechanisms operate under the laws of spontaneous natural evolution. But they also, simultaneously, have 'displacement', as well as 'nominative', power in that they break-up established public sector occupational hierarchies and the knowledge systems which they privilege by undermining the concentrations of epistemological authority and jurisdictional closure on which the latter are based. They do this, Mau contends, by challenging the centralized nominative powers traditionally exercised by established public sector professionals such as civil servants, medical and scientific specialists, and other senior public officials. These expert groups are increasingly pushed on to the margins of strategic decision making as the power vacuums opened-up by the fragmenting dynamic generated by 'reregulation displacement' are filled by networks of calculative experts/corporate professionals who are now free to roam across a wide range of jurisdictional domains unencumbered by 'bureau-professional hierarchies.' It is they who are now the carriers of an innovative and entrepreneurial management culture transforming the public sector from a bureaucratically moribund and professionally stultified institution devouring taxpayers' money with little or no regard as to its deleterious impact on public expenditure into an accessible and open marketplace for the services which it, or more likely its private sector corporate surrogates, must provide within a reinvigorated competitive environment.

2.2 Proliferation of New Managerial, Technical and Scientific Occupations

As Crouch (2016: 69) notes, the rise of neoliberal NPM is not only associated with the transference of managerial authority and organizational control from established public service professionals to private sector technocrats, but also 'stripping away ethical inhibitions in the cause of increased profitability.' Of course, he recognizes that this process of authority transference and ethical simplification will be contested in various ways, both by established public service professionals and by other occupational groups and their representative organizations. He also sees that the organizational technologies, such as target-based performance indicator regimes, through which market discipline is imposed on public services and the professionals who they employ will only, at best, partially succeed in their mission to subjugate public services to market scrutiny.

This continuing push-back and resistance against the surveillance and performance technologies to which public service professionals and other public sector workers are now routinely subjected has been highlighted by several research studies into public sector workplace behaviour in recent years (Currie et al. 2010; Currie and White 2012; Newman 2013; Reed and Wallace 2015; Gorman and Vallas 2020). Nevertheless, these studies also support Crouch's wider argument that the increasing fragmentation of the expert occupational division of labour across the public sector has generated an intensification of inter-occupational conflict and organizational gameplaying indicative of the long-term movement towards a 'low trust/high control' working environment. As the power, if not the authority, of calculative experts/corporate professionals has grown, partly as a result of their increasing numbers but more crucially as they have breached the boundaries of jurisdictional domains once dominated by established public service professionals and begun to threaten their control – by enhancing the latter's dependence on the technologies which they design and operate – then, corporate and workplace power struggles tend to get nastier and more brutish.

It might be argued that the proliferation of expert positions and roles is an outcome of external structural changes which are unrelated to any wider ideological, political and ethical struggles because they simply reflect the movement towards higher levels of environmental complexity and uncertainty demanding a transition towards more highly differentiated organizational designs and structures. Indeed, this core argument about the deterministic, causal relationship between 'environment and organization' has been pursued by generations of contingency theorists (Lawrence and Lorsch 1967) and more recently by those who draw on complexity theory as offering a more conceptually sophisticated analysis of the ecological determinants of the emergence of organizations and markets (Padgett and Powell 2012). As we have already seen, there are very strong intellectual echoes of this ecological determinism in the analysis of professional licensing and accreditation advanced by Kirkpatrick et al. (2021).

However, over four decades ago, organization theorists such as Child (1973, 2019), Perrow (1986, 2008) and Silverman (1970) effectively demolished the intellectual foundations of this approach because of its abject failure to incorporate the power of agency, particularly collective or corporate agency, to shape the structural conditions and strategic context under and in which occupational and organizational change must be understood and explained.

This is as true today as it was over forty years ago. Increasing complexity in the expert divisions of labour in Anglo-American political economies and welfare systems over this time has been driven by the material concerns and ideological beliefs of elite groups – who are also embedded in more complex power networks within government and economy (Reed 2018) – striving to reshape both the public and private sectors in the light of those interests and values. Expert groups, occupations and organizations in both the public and private sectors are struggling to protect and enhance their authority and the material/symbolic rewards that it delivers within institutional environments and organizational settings which make it increasingly difficult for them to assume any degree of stability and predictability in the conditions under which they operate and the challenges which they will face now and in the future.

Illustrations of this heightened awareness of chronic insecurity amongst expert groups can be seen in research on the intensified workplace power struggles occurring between them as the pressures to do whatever needs to be done – irrespective of its morality or ethical implications – to hit performance targets, increase turnover and profits, downsize or 'right size' employment levels, and to placate often disgruntled and vociferous customers/clients reaches new levels. While these pressures often lead to a proliferation of expert roles and an expansion of their scope and improvement in status, it can also generate a blurring, if not collapsing, of pre-existing jurisdictional boundaries and intensified conflicts around who has the right or authority to determine where they begin and end or what the 'content' of the work contained within them should (ought to?) be. This 'destabilization of expert knowledge [work] from within' (Gorman and Vallas 2020: 3) – through the fracturing and fragmenting of expert, epistemic and work, communities generated by new informational, spatial and organizational technologies and the neoliberal political ideologies driving them – has weakened the authoritativeness of expert knowledge, particularly for established professional groups who now find themselves forced to compete for control over jurisdictional domains which have become more crowded, heterogeneous and disrupted.

Recent research and investigative studies on intensifying jurisdictional struggles between expert groups generated by the continuous, if at times staccato, movement to dominant modes of market-based reregulation disrupting institutionalized forms of expert authority can be grouped in to three categories: first, ethnographic studies of the everyday organizational processes through which these conflicts are conducted (Ho 2009; Courpasson, Younes and Reed 2021; Gendrot 2021); second, historical and comparative research focused on inter-occupational power struggles between corporate and liberal professions (Sturdy, Wright and Wylie 2015; Sturdy and O'Mahoney 2018); thirdly, sector specific studies focussed on 'professional service firms' and their increasing transnational significance as the dominant organizational form through which professional services are coordinated and controlled (Empson et al. 2015).

Ho's (2009) ethnographic study of the 'white collar sweat shop' in which elite Wall Street bankers face the everyday organizational realities of 'free market capitalism in action' intricately documents the highly contested and fragmented occupational arenas in which they are embedded. Her uncovering of the 'organizational politics of hard work' in which these elite occupations are routinely engaged demonstrates that 'the pinnacle of meritocracy is necessarily precarious: it is shot through with class, race, and gender hierarchies; with the conscious and anxious performance of smartness; and with a prestigious branding so dependent on the singularity of the apex that it cannot help but degrade' (Ho 2009: 58). Thus, investment analysts, associates, and client managers vie with each other to legitimate their organizational existence as being vital to placating the gods of market position, profit-making and shareholder values. In so doing, they reproduce the material conditions and social relations under and through which an aggressive free-market capitalism which 'takes no prisoners' and is as unforgiving of its progeny as it is of its subjects.

Gendrot's (2021) investigative journalist study, involving an 'undercover journey' in a Parisian police station, reveals the organizational lives of police personnel in the French capital as they precariously navigate between the institutionalized power of the state and 'on the ground realities' they routinely encounter as they struggle to maintain everyday public order in a class divided and racially segregated urban community and society. As in the case of Ho's (2009) study, he dramatically illuminates the wider tensions and conflicts between different administrative/legal sections and intra-occupational groups within the Parisian gendarmerie as they attempt to impose some sort of control within an inherently chaotic and unmanageable situation in which 'police professionalism' is rent with the very same racial, ethnic, economic, and gendered conflicts its' meant to contain.

Courpasson, Reed and Younes's (2021) ethnographically based study of middle management and professional resistance to neoliberal corporate power and control highlights the complex social processes entailed in building and sustaining the communities and solidarities which can become a vital source of opposition to the policies and programmes corporate elites impose. Thus, it highlights how work-related and friendship-related community building, within and without the neoliberal workplace, can generate locations and spaces in which an alternative moral order to that imposed by the latter can flourish. But it also suggests that this managerial/professional resistance to neo-liberalization can have contradictory effects in generating belief systems simultaneously opposing and reflecting the core assumptions about human agency on which the latter depends. By facilitating the construction and legitimation of occupational and organizational 'enclaves of resistance', professionals and managers embedded in neoliberal corporate hierarchies unavoidably reflect and reproduce the segmented and divided loyalties on which the latter depends for its continued existence.

Historical and comparative research focused on inter-occupational and intra-organizational power struggles between calculative/corporate professionals and liberal/independent professionals (Sturdy, Wright and Wylie 2015; Sturdy and O'Mahoney 2018) shows how the transition to market dominated modes of reregulation and increasing dependence on digital control technologies has transformed the institutional landscape in which expert occupational groups now operate. They trace the rise of the neo-bureaucratic organizational form generated by the changing modes of regulation occurring under neoliberal/investor capitalism as a new site 'within which new discourses around leadership, networks, new public management, knowledge work and enterprise reside' (Sturdy, Wright and Wylie 2015: 3). As a structural hybrid recombining selected elements of 'bureaucratic' and 'post bureaucratic' organizing logics, the neo-bureaucratic form creates a context in which occupational restructuring, blurring and redrawing the boundaries between an expanding array of expert jurisdictional domains and the groups contending to occupy and control them, becomes commonplace. In particular, the divisions and distinctions between 'managerial' roles as opposed to 'consultancy' roles and the working practices which they separately embody become increasingly difficult to identify as 'management consultancy' comes to dominate an ever-expanding spectrum of co-ordinating and controlling tasks within the neo-bureaucratic hybrid organization. This, highly contested and impactful, simultaneous deconstruction and reconstruction of corporate managerial and professional consultancy roles, entailing the separation and reintegration of 'internal' and 'external' jurisdictional domains, results in a reframing of the wider institutional context within which 'specialist knowledge and expertise' are identified and legitimated. Overall, the latter becomes defined by much higher levels of personal and emotional insecurity where job tenure, career prospects and development opportunities are increasingly dependent on organizational power politics and the constantly shifting relations and precarious positionings which they entail.

Putting this study of inter-occupational and intra-organizational expert work fragmentation into a wider historical and comparative context, (Sturdy and O'Mahoney 2018) suggest that national variations in the take-up of management consulting, as constituting a distinctive body of externally sourced ideas, innovations and practices geared to enhancing the performance of both private and public sector corporations, can be accounted for primarily in relation to different forms of political economy. Thus, in Anglo-Saxon political economies much more extensive use of external management consultancy has been 'naturalized' as a universally preferred source of legitimate management knowledge and expertise because of the formers' historical, cultural, and political adherence to neoliberal market rationality and the relatively weak legal and administrative regulative regimes to which they have been subjected.

Finally, the burgeoning literature on professional service firms (PSFs) (Empson et al. 2015) also illustrates the wider ramifications of an increasingly crowded and competitive marketplace for expert knowledge and skills and its long-term impact on an expert division of labour in which a fragmenting and fracturing change dynamic has been working away over the last three decades or more. Insofar as they have become organizational vehicles for the generation and diffusion of innovative managerial practices across the economic, political, and cultural spheres of contemporary societies, so PSFs can be seen to generate new configurations of expert services and roles characterized by occupational heterogeneity and the more complex regulatory forms which they require once power and control begin to move from a national to international level. As Quack and Schüßler (2015: 62) contend, the regulation of PSFs and the expert groups employed by them become a much more complex affair in which states, firms, agencies, and international organizations negotiate and bargain to frame the organizational settings in which expert occupations operate. The relatively cosy and paternalistic regulatory modes characteristic of the 1970s and 1980s in which professionals and states, mediated by established national professional associations, bargained over the rules which would govern them is gone in a world where the proliferation of internationalized PSFs necessarily means cross border regulative regimes. While country specific occupational licensing may continue to happen, its significance is much diminished in a world where expert work and the ways in which it is organized and regulated are now embedded within national and transnational contexts in which the power dynamics of governance and management are no longer containable in national bureaucratic systems.

2.3 Increasingly Fragmented and Fractured Expert Division of Labour

Heusinkveld et al. (2018) argue that emerging patterns of workplace contestation between different expert occupational groups over jurisdictional control are structured around various temporal, spatial and organizational 'settlements' reflecting the recent expansion of management and related 'knowledge-based' occupations into what were previously 'professionalized task domains.' Consequently, they see new domains of 'competition', 'colonization' and 'control' opening-up in which there is a broadening and blending of inter-occupational jurisdictional domains characterized by increased fluidity, porosity and informality of weakly regulated national and transnational spaces. This constant 'striving for expert-based authority and jurisdictional control over organizational and field levels' (Heusinkveld at al. 2018: 250) revolves around control struggles over knowledge domains and the strength and durability of their linkages with workplace domains. Thus, the collective capacity of any expert occupational group to forge strong and enduring relations between the 'knowledge' and 'work' domains which they occupy will critically determine their legitimacy within the wider institutional fields in which they operate and the socio-economic orders in which the latter are embedded.

They also conclude with the key point that this ongoing and intensifying struggle to secure exclusive access and control over specialized expert knowledge and to translate this into indeterminate and autonomous work domains subject to minimal interference from either 'organization-level' competitors or 'institutional/societal-level' regulators inevitably generate a much more fragmented and factionalized expert division of labour. The latter becomes characterized by much higher levels of complexity, instability and hybridity when compared to a more stable situation in which a once dominant mode of professionalism comes to terms with a social democratic state and its governing elites through forms of bureaucratic credentialism and regulation which recognize the political trade-offs that must be made in order to meet the legitimate demands of both. As a result of this fragmenting and factionalizing dynamic, enhanced inter-occupational boundary contestation, weaker governance structures and management practices, as well as the increasing importance of transnational spaces and international governance all become key structural features of an expert division of labour in which the institutionalization of new expert occupational groups is inherently unstable and uncertain.

Once you factor in the increasing power of the consumer of expert services to shape how the latter are delivered, organized and regulated, as well as the 'digital empowerment' of the consumer/client highlighted in previous sections of this book, you begin to see an emerging expert division of labour that has moved way beyond the confines of a 'bureau-professionalized' system in which a social democratic state and its governing elites take collective responsibility for ensuring stable order through formalized regulation and managed consensus. The technocratic dream (or Weberian/Kafkaesque nightmare, depending on your point of view) of elite human and machine-based expertise replacing inherently 'messy' and 'wasteful' democratic processes – that is, some political hybrid of technocracy and autocracy or what Runciman (2019: 180 – 191) labels 'epistocracy' or 'rule by the people who know best' – seems likely to remain just a dream if those groups supposed to realise it remain so divided and segmented. Other scenarios involving the selective recombination of ideological, political and organizational elements of populism, authoritarianism, neoliberalism and technocracy (Bickerton and Accetti 2021) seem much more realistic options in a socio-historical context in which legitimacy struggles around claims to 'expert authority' have become more intensely contested.

Also, as we shall see in chapters six and seven of this book, alternative 'expert futures' are possible in which the legitimacy of expert authority emerges from much more reflexive, participative and inclusive forms of societal and organizational politics which reject the anti-democratic sensibilities that seem to be dominant now.

2.4 Intensified Ontological Insecurity

Giddens (1984, 1987, 2000) argues that 'ontological insecurity' has become endemic within modern societies and corporations to the extent that the latter are routinely failing to provide the everyday social relations and organizational routines through which relatively stable and resilient self-identities can be constructed and sustained. Indeed, 'reflexive modernization' has undermined the processes and relations through which individual and collective security were established by subjecting them to the ruthless imposition of disruptive expert systems and organizational technologies radically destabilizing the negotiated settlements on which bureaucratically managed order and control depended. While 'ontological insecurity' can be seen in its most 'extreme' form in 'total institutions' (Goffman 1961; Pick 2022), such as concentration camps, prisons and asylums which systematically 'strip' individuals of their pre-existing identities and subject them to pervasive surveillance regimes, contemporary corporate organizations mimic these totalizing organizational practices and relations by selectively reimposing them through widespread employment precarity, performance regimes and managerial cultures in which 'organized irresponsibility' are the dominant realities (Jackall 1998/2010; Vaughan 1996; Styhre 2014).

So, while some level of ontological insecurity has characterised the working lives of managers, experts and professionals for many years, its level of intensity and pervasiveness has grown exponentially as they have been forced to accept major disruptions to their core expectations about employment security, career trajectories and performance requirements. They find themselves operating in corporate hierarchies and cultures which seem to lack any kind of bureaucratic consistency or normative cohesion and are increasingly driven by unaccountable and random opportunism where the only thing which matters is meeting whatever targets your superiors, however temporarily and grudgingly, favour. Experts are by no means immune to this pervasive corporate culture and practice of 'organized irresponsibility' because 'professional training is not a control against the imposition of particularistic world views' (Vaughan 1996: 63) – especially in institutional environments and organizational settings where amoral and deviant corporate behaviour has become normalized as what is routinely expected if one is to survive, much less prosper, within a Darwinian struggle for existence.

Expert occupational groups are both architects and victims of this deepening sense of 'ontological insecurity' throughout private and public sector corporations in that they play a key role in designing and operating the expert systems and organizational technologies through which 'low trust/high control' regimes and relations are institutionalized, while finding themselves increasingly subjected to the very same governance and surveillance systems ostensibly directed at others. Fletcher (1973: 156) provided, over four decades ago, a somewhat apocalyptic but nonetheless powerful vision of what corporate life would look like in a world where 'ontological insecurity/organized irresponsibility' has become so culturally pervasive and structurally embedded:

> ... within the company, the intricate and delicate management structure will disappear and be replaced by a managerial atmosphere in which highly paid experts execute precise control, observation, and distraction tasks for their masters' using machines which also control themselves. By attrition, redundancy, unionization, or revolution managers will be finished, and managers themselves are facilitating their own end.

Allowing for a degree of poetic license, what Fletcher is evoking here is a sense of expert groups right across the occupational spectrum encompassing managers, professionals, technicians, scientists, engineers, designers and administrators becoming architects of their own demise because they 'have now turned upon themselves, and the professions, those last citadels of independence and humanity, are now subject to continuous erosion' (Anthony 1977: 299). As Mizruchi (2013) and others (Snyder 2016) have argued, by the mid-1980s the socio-political contract between the state, organized labour, and the banks which had constrained American corporate elites in the post-1945 era was no longer providing an effective form of countervailing power. Similar developments occurred in other Anglo-American political economies and welfare states in which the political coalitions and economic deals that shaped post-1945 societies became weaker to the extent that they had effectively collapsed by the 1980s.

Professions and other expert occupations were very much part of this post-1945 socio-political contract and alignment which held more aggressive and authoritarian ideologies and movements in check and enabled them to construct and sustain a viable legitimation strategy by effectively linking together 'knowledge exclusion' and 'jurisdictional closure'. But the demise of this political consensus and the social contract it legitimated released a powerful set of ideological, economic and cultural forces in which experts would be forced to 'supp with the devil' in order to ensure the endemic instability and insecurity it entailed would not overwhelm them, but at a price – that is, at the price of compromising their independence, autonomy and authority in the furtherance of more short term, tactical goals related to resilience and survivability.

Paying this price seems even more of a political necessity when the capacity of experts to deal effectively with the 'wicked problems' (Ferlie et al. 2013) and 'unpredictable risks' (Beck 1999) modern societies face is increasingly open to question by ruling elites and the public at large. What we might call a 'political performance' – that is, the ability to mount a show which outwardly demonstrates problem-solving expertise without necessarily delivering on the practical and measurable outcomes which the latter promises – seems to the best that experts can do when the dominant corporate culture is one in which business requires no wider moral or political justification beyond demonstrating high level shareholder value to which any notion of 'professional ethics or judgement' must be subordinated (Grace 2014).

Yet, to whom or what are we to turn except to 'the experts' when we find ourselves faced by existential challenges and threats that remind us of the inherently precarious and perilous lives which most of the people live? Rebuilding the cognitive and epistemological consensus around which expert knowledge and skill can be socially accepted, if not institutionally legitimated, seems more vital than ever

(Young and Muller 2014; Collins et al. 2020). However, this can only be possible if based on a socially and politically realistic understanding of how this might be achieved in the light of the ways in which both the context and content of expertise has been transformed by the changes documented in this and other chapters of this book.

Living with deepening 'ontological insecurity' is now an existential reality for growing numbers of expert occupational groups as they struggle to come to terms with the deleterious impact of the structural changes documented in previous sections of this chapter. However, how they attempt to mediate and moderate these deleterious impacts is considered in the following section.

3 Mediating Mechanisms

Three mediating mechanisms through which the decomposition of established expert authority has been interpreted and moderated are discussed below.

First, the emergence of more **opportunistic strategies** entailing the partial decoupling and dilution of 'epistemological exclusion' and 'jurisdictional closure' examined in previous chapters. Second, a more sustained **organizational focus** on tactical brokering combining both collaborative and competitive behaviours rather than looking for dominant positioning within selected jurisdictional domains. Third, a more concentrated collective effort around **boundary management** processes and practices entailing the acceptance of lower levels of institutional legitimation and organizational control.

Overall, these mediating mechanisms seem to involve collective adjustments on the part of contemporary occupational groups engaged in the struggle to achieve social recognition as 'experts' to the very different cultural and political realities which they now face as a result of the structural changes generating the decomposition of the expert division of labour reviewed in the previous section of this chapter.

3.1 Opportunistic Strategies

One way in which expert occupational groups have responded to the decomposition of the expert division of labour and the decay in institutionalized forms of expert authority which the latter has produced is by undertaking a series of incremental, pragmatic shifts towards closure strategies aimed at partial control through limited incursion rather than monopoly control through dominant colonization. Indeed, the increasing emphasis on occupational licensing, rather than formalized professional accreditation, which Kirkpatrick et al. (2021) detect can be read as a key empirical indicator of this shift towards less ambitious and more restrained expert closure strategies, as well as a tacit acknowledgement of the more fragmented institutional fields in which they are located.

Although developed, conceptually, with a macro-level focus on the modern state in mind, Fligstein and McAdam's (2012) 'theory of fields' offers a way of interpreting this underlying trajectory towards opportunistic and limited expert closure strategies as a collective response to the relatively unstable political context in which they are operating. Within the latter, inter-occupational power dynamics become more complex as expert occupational groups jockey for position and advantage more aggressively but within a more unsettled and open-ended political environment in which outcomes are even more uncertain and temporary. As a result, the 'strategic action field' which the contemporary expert division of labour constitutes is likely to become less dependent upon domination structures formally legitimating the power and control of elite occupational groups, like the established or independent professions, and more reflective of shifting balances of power and control between 'usurper' or 'challenger' groups engaged in a smorgasbord of competitive and cooperative behaviours.

In his original work on professionalization as an ongoing process through which occupations compete to control areas of organizational work, Abbott (1988) conceptualizes 'jurisdictional domains' as linking abstract specialist knowledge and everyday work practices. The latter emerge out of the strategies and tactics which different occupational groups engage in to open, occupy, contain and supervise areas of work activity within organizational settings by making effective performance of the latter dependant on the expertise which they provide. But he is very keen to stress that 'jurisdictional boundaries are perpetually in dispute, both in local practice and national claims. It is the history of jurisdictional disputes that is the real, determining history of the professions' (Abbott 1988: 2). He also reminds us that:

> ... any occupation can obtain licensure (e. g., beauticians) or develop abstract codes (e. g., real estate). But only a knowledge system governed by abstractions can redefine its problems and tasks, defend them from interlopers, and seize new problems – as medicine has recently seized alcoholism, mental illness, hyperactivity in children, obesity, and numerous other things. Abstraction enables survival in the competitive system of professions (Abbott 1988: 9).

Thus, to stand any chance in the struggle to establish effective control over the jurisdictional domains through which 'expert' authority, and particularly 'professional' authority, are accomplished and reproduced, occupational groups must possess abstract knowledge and technical skills which are organizationally relevant within constantly changing socio-historical contexts. Through this process of translating abstract, esoteric knowledge into organizationally usable and adaptable 'intervention packages' through which 'problems' can be identified, diagnosed and treated, expert occupational groups place themselves in a better position to secure and retain jurisdictional closure over areas of work on which their power and authority depends.

While professional association and regulation can be seen as the most developed form of jurisdictional closure and control – in terms of the formal institutionalization it achieves – all expert groups can be seen as being engaged in the competitive struggle to link 'knowledge' and 'work' through organizational strategies and tactics which effectively translate abstract, codified understanding into flexible, situationally-relevant practices. However, if they are to succeed, and continue to succeed, within the ongoing struggle to construct domains of work activity through which 'expertise' can be recognized and authorized, occupational groups must ensure 'they' retain effective control over the 'translation process' whereby the political potential inherent in abstract, specialized knowledge is turned into actual, 'on the ground' organizational power and influence. Indeed, success in the ongoing struggle to secure and retain control over jurisdictional domains by maximizing the organizational power potential contained in abstract knowledge systems and technologies is vital in a socio-historical context in which the expert division of labour has become even more fragmented and political and economic elites, egged-on by populist sentiments and movements, have become more openly suspicious of and hostile to the 'professionalized state'. In Fligstein and McAdam's (2012) terms, both 'established', and 'challenger' occupational groups are now operating within strategic action fields in which much lower levels of formal institutional structuring and regulative governance are generating more unstable contexts in which tactical jockeying for position and influence within and over jurisdictional domains are becoming more pragmatic and opportunistic.

Several research studies, broadly undertaken within the remit of a 'decomposition narrative', illustrate the emergence and growing significance of more short-term, opportunistic closure strategies focused on occupational control over jurisdictional domains within work organizations and their partial decoupling from long term legitimation strategies in which 'epistemological exclusion' through state-supported professional accreditation and association has played the central role.

Abbott's (1988) analytical focus on jurisdictional struggles over areas of workplace practice and relations in which knowledge-led competency and effectiveness claims by competing occupational groups are the primary determinants of how successful control strategies are likely to be is reflected in recent field level and organizational level research by Newman (2013), Noordegraaf (2015), Sturdy, Wright and Wylie (2017), Liu (2020), and VanHeuvlen (2020).

Newman's (2013) research on the political and organizational realignments that UK public service professionals, managers and technocrats are being forced to make as a result of the tighter imposition of neoliberal-type NPM regimes illustrates the increasing importance of reconciling competing institutional logics based on market competition, administrative regulation and occupational differentiation. Her work also documents the growing complexity and porosity of occupationally based jurisdictional boundaries within UK public services as the need to meet, or at least placate, state-imposed policy imperatives and the heightened organizational tensions this generates work their way through governance and management systems striving to absorb the escalating demands made upon them.

In a similar vein, Noordegraaf's (2015) research documents the increasing hybridization of 'organizational' and 'occupational' forms of professionalism and the increasingly dominant role played by the former as greater numbers of professionals and experts, across both the public and private sectors, find themselves subject to corporate governance and managerial regimes hostile to institutional logics grounded in conceptions of self-regulation and autonomous working practices. He also sees this hybridizing dynamic as diluting and weakening the jurisdictional boundaries and barriers between expert occupational groups as they struggle to contain the organizational pressures and managerial demands for internal rationalization and realignment which the former necessarily contains. While significant elements of 'occupational professionalism' will remain, such as collegiate work cultures and identities, these will be much more highly constrained by corporate level determined surveillance and control regimes in which the power of expert groups to resist them will indelibly shape the overall organization of jurisdictional domains which emerges from these ongoing struggles.

Sturdy, Wright and Wylie's (2017) comparative research study focuses on the emergence of 'consultant managers' out of the jurisdictional struggles between various expert occupational groups embedded within increasingly constraining and demanding 'neo-bureaucratic' corporations in which the political and administrative drive to 'de-differentiate' existing occupational specializations and silos is paramount. Their research reveals how difficult it can be for knowledge-based occupational groups to sustain jurisdictional boundaries within institutional fields and organizational settings which are relatively 'open' and 'fuzzy' in relation to the emphasis given to commercial application and the inherent vulnerability of established work domains to competitor incursion. Thus, consultant managers were able to engage in various opportunistic strategies and tactics to take advantage of the shifting occupational boundaries which neo-bureaucratic organizational forms encouraged in their emphasis on multi-functional project teams geared to the development and implementation of commercially successful products and services and the eradication, or at least dilution, of functional divisions and specialization.

But the very same openness and fuzziness of occupational jurisdictions under neo-bureaucracy meant that the challenges which emerging 'consultant manager teams' were able to mount against the jurisdictions of established expert management groups in engineering, accounting, finance and human resources, putatively lacking their 'consultancy knowledge and skills', only resulted in temporary 'jurisdictional realignments' exposed to reappropriation by the latter.

Overall, Sturdy, Wright and Wylie's (2017) study reveals a very high level of expert occupational instability and intra-organizational political tensions in which control over jurisdictional domains and the 'identity-building' opportunities that it offered were vulnerable to counterattack within the hybridity of neo-bureaucracy. Yet, as the latter becomes increasingly prevalent, if not dominant, as the underlying organizational logic on which contemporary private and public sector corporations are structured, then the best that expert occupations can hope for within the ongoing struggle to close and control jurisdictional domains is a form of 'corporate professionalism' lacking the close integration between 'legitimation' and 'closure' strategies characteristic of the independent or established professions.

Liu (2020) and VanHeuvelen's (2020) research case studies on inter-occupational jurisdictional competition in healthcare organizations involving managers and professionals illustrate the increasing importance of workplace-level closure and control where the increasing complexity and tensions generated through the imposition of private sector business logics must be accommodated some way or another.

Liu (2020) focuses on the ways in which professionals manage the threat of 'impurities' in the performance of their roles as a way of protecting their expertise from dilution and a corresponding challenge to their autonomy. Whether from clients, other professionals, organizational managers, or political agencies, professionals face the constant threat of their 'purity' being compromised or sullied by the increasing dominance of market-based and bureaucratically based institutional logics that potentially undermine their autonomy and control. He advocates a much more pragmatic approach to the understanding of the social and organizational realities of professional task performance in which boundaries must be continually policed and repaired if autonomy and self-management is to be preserved, even in a highly attenuated form.

VanHeuvelen's (2020) research documents the ways in which shifts in working practices within healthcare organizations, with specific reference to professional roles and relationships in neonatal intensive care, impacted on professional autonomy based upon jurisdictional closure and control. By focusing on the 'articulation work' in which professionals, and other expert occupations, are routinely involved – that is, identifying and mapping the co-ordination work which is needed to bring together the diverse and often complex tasks that are required to deliver plans and projects – she highlights the vital role of 'articulation work practices' in shaping the jurisdictional claims and domains on which expert groups rely to establish and defend their internal autonomy against external control. This articulation work and the relative expert autonomy which it makes possible are continually under threat from wider structural movements in policy and employment regimes because they have a major blurring effect on the established divisions and boundaries within existing hierarches of tasks through which co-ordination is achieved and legitimated.

3.2 Organizational Focus

Each of the research studies reviewed in the previous section highlight the growing emphasis on organizational level gains and loses within the competitive struggle to create, close and control expert jurisdictional domains combining collaborative and conflictual strategies and tactics. They document a shift in analytical focus away from societal level legitimation strategies built on formal accreditation and trust building and towards the field and organizational level politics in which expert occupational groups are now routinely engaged as they strive to establish and protect jurisdictional domains increasingly exposed and vulnerable to external shits in policy, governance and opinion.

In this way, they trace the trajectory of an underlying move towards much greater political realism and opportunistic pragmatism on the part of occupational groups living in a world where 'hanging on to what you've got' by the way of corporate recognition and organizational status as 'experts' becomes more pressing than the aggressive search for new jurisdictional domains through the legitimation strategies previously followed by mature or elite professions such as medicine and law. This is particularly the case if the latter are finding themselves increasingly exposed to political, economic, technological and cultural pressures challenging the relatively high levels of autonomy and control they have enjoyed for much of the preceding century. As Heusinkveld et al. (2018: 259) conclude, intra-organizational level research has demonstrated the intensification of the jurisdictional struggles through which expert occupational boundaries are 'delineated, contested and repaired and how they connect to different organizational processes and outcomes.' It has also helped us to better understand 'how new forms of expertise evolve and vary across different social groups [and provided] critical insight into the extent to which new occupations are (de) institutionalized' (Heusinkveld et al. 2018: 259).

However, it is vitally important to remember that this marked shift of emphasis towards intra-organizational jurisdictional struggles signals a *partial decou-*

pling of legitimation strategies focused on epistemological exclusion and cognitive monopoly within 'labour market shelters' (Freidson 2001) *from closure tactics geared to organizational control over the interrelated task domains through which 'organizational work gets done'.* As the extant expert division of labour has become more differentiated and fragmented, so the ongoing workplace level jurisdictional conflicts between an ever-increasing number of occupational groups claiming expert status and authority have intensified to an extent where winning or losing intra-organizational domain struggles is more important (at least for now!) than external societal recognition.

This is not an 'either or' situation, but more of 'Hobson's choice' prioritizing between equally unpalatable options within an increasingly complex and unstable institutional environment in which challenges and threats come along more often than buses. It's about the changing balance between external regulative recognition and legitimation as opposed to internal competitive success and the relatively advantageous 'jurisdictional settlements' it bestows on certain expert occupational groups. As Abbott (1988: 59) continually reminds us, 'in order to claim jurisdiction a profession must ask society to recognize its cognitive structure through exclusive rights' over the work domains in which it practices and to seek further support for these labour market privileges in relation to the legal system, government regulation and the 'court of public appeal'. But in a world in which market competition, technological rationalization, state supported 'reregulation' and populist revolt has come to dominate the political and institutional landscape on which jurisdictional struggles must be fought out, *then winning the intra-organizational battles to control the work domains through which expert status is achieved and sustained assumes political primacy over incremental successes in occupational licensing and related forms of administrative regulation.*

3.3 Boundary Management

Marking and setting demarcation lines between different forms of work practice and the potential control over work activities lying within their boundaries which they bestow has been central to the decomposition narrative as it has unfolded in this chapter. Treating this demarcating work as 'boundary management', offers further insight into the organizational processes through which occupational groups strive to claim specialist expertise and the advantages and rewards that it conveys to those groups who are successful in establishing and maintaining recognition and identification as 'experts.' Effective boundary management emerges as an essential prerequisite for success in the competitive struggle to achieve and sustain expert status, especially when the latter has become even more 'Darwinian' in its scope and intensity. Degradation of long established 'mature' or 'elite' expert jurisdictional domains, never mind of more emergent and embryonic domains, seems an ever-present possibility within an institutional environment characterized by Darwinian struggles for survival in which previous settlements over jurisdictional rights and privileges are no guarantee that your occupational group is safe from incursion and erosion from competitors.

Constructing and policing jurisdictional boundaries between different areas of work activity, within a more splintered and porous expert division of labour where boundary disputes are likely to be a more regular occurrence and boundary settlements less formal and stable, becomes a critical factor in determining the success or failure of 'expert mobility projects.' By fabricating and monitoring boundaries around work domains and the technologies through which the activities contained within them are made possible, occupational groups can mount and defend 'expert mobility projects' with a relatively high chance of succeeding. This is particularly true if these technologies and the practices they make possible are of critical importance to long-term organizational survival and growth within institutional fields and environments in which competitively generated complexity and uncertainty are preeminent.

A considerable body of organizational and occupational research dating back to the 1950s/60s supports this argument that effective boundary management at workplace and labour market levels, particularly if they are well-integrated through interlinked external regulative strategies and internal organizational politics, are pivotal in creating jurisdictional domains from which 'real' occupational power and control can emerge (Blau 1955; Crozier 1964; Selznick 1949/1966; Child 1973, 2019; Peck 1996; Reed 2011). While the formal regulation of these jurisdictional domains through occupational licensing and/or professional accreditation can help stabilize the patterns of occupational power and control which they confer, bureaucratic formalization and standardization are not essential preconditions for mobilizing effective 'expert mobility projects' in which political support from governing elites and civil society is more important to long-term success (Larson 2013; Saks 2021).

More recent research and analysis has focused on what Abbott (1988) and, as we have previously mentioned, Liu (2020) conceptualize as the relative 'purity' of different jurisdictional domains and how successful the expert occupational groups occupying and controlling them have been in managing boundaries to minimize the presence and impact of 'impurities.'

Building on Abbott's (1988) analysis of the forms of 'impurity' evident in professional work, Liu (2020) argues that taking the latter seriously helps us to develop a more socially realistic understanding of how important jurisdictional boundary management is to sustain the status and identity of expert occupational groups as 'professionals.' Abbott (1988) identifies five different forms of 'impurity' in relation to the content of the expertise claimed by an occupational group, the strength of its jurisdictional boundaries, the nature of its client base, the degree of organizational constraints to which its work performance is subjected, and the extent to which societal and institutional politics impinge on its capacity to engage in behaviours moving beyond the prevailing status quo. While Abbott sees all five forms of impurity as being driven by the need for all expert occupational groups claiming professional status to minimize, if not eradicate, 'dirty work' – that is, elements in their work roles and contexts which dilute their capacity to resist and control contact with 'pollutants' such as disorderly clients or external management control – Liu (2020) argues these impurities are inherent in all types of professional/expert work. Indeed, he maintains that these impurities, even within the most prestigious and elite status forms of professional work such as medicine and law, are structurally embedded in the work roles and performances of all expert occupational groups and their retention can prove advantageous to the latter.

His analysis suggests that this is the case particularly in relation to 'expertise impurities' and 'jurisdictional impurities' because all forms of expertise depend on a hybrid combination of abstract knowledge and technical skill if they are to be effective in real-world problem-solving situations and work task boundaries depend on a range of negotiated settlements which always leave some discretionary leeway as to which occupational group has intellectual and advisory priority. As he concludes (Liu 2020: 153) in relation to the latter, all 'intellectual and advisory jurisdictions are characterized by porous boundaries and precarious control'. Contra Abbott, even elite professional jurisdictional domains have to accept and contain 'impurities' if those groups claiming this prestigious status and the authority which goes with it are to be successful in legitimating the rights and privileges associated with this kind of high-status work. This is even more the case once we move outside the relatively rarefied political contexts and cultural atmospheres in which established or mature professions and professionals operate and enter the even more contested, polluted and unstable institutional environments and organizational settings in which the majority of expert and 'expert-aspirant' occupational groups reside.

4 Substantive Outcomes

Filtered through the mediating mechanisms identified in the previous sections of this chapter, the decomposition narrative traces the emergence of much more complex 'expert ecologies' within which the escalating environmental pressures imposed on expert occupational groups has generated hybridized forms of work and authority better adapted to the instabilities and uncertainties which the latter now routinely encounter and experience in the course of their working days and lives.

While accepting elements of the analysis provided by those working within the de-legitimation and demystification narratives, decomposition theorists insist that both fundamentally *underestimate the strength of the underlying adaptive mechanisms which allow expert ecologies to self-correct and restabilize even in the face of threats that seem to challenge their very survival as viable complex systems.* Kirkpatrick et al.'s (2021) rebuttal of 'grand narrative theorizing' anticipating the demise, or at least dilution, of professionalism as the dominant mode of expert occupational regulation rests on a competing 'grand narrative' of an underlying evolutionary logic in which the continuing empirical strength of voluntary certification and licensing supportive of professional associations across the occupational spectrum in the US is accounted for by the path-dependent, endogenous and self-reinforcing nature of professional regulation and the 'certification ecosystem' that it reproduces. This self-correcting and reinforcing expert ecosystem meets the needs and interests of various employer and governmental stakeholder groups, whilst also sustaining the institutional logic through which this underlying continuity in regulative forms can be maintained. Continuity in professionalized modes of occupational regulation is guaranteed by the evolutionary-cum-functionalist theoretical logic on which its institutional reproduction is predicated. The empirical, statistical analysis evidencing the institutional reproduction of professional regulation is already anticipated by the explanatory precepts which frame the evolutionary trajectory that the latter must follow. Anything other outcome, indicative of a more dislocated, declining, or non-linear trajectory, cannot be anticipated, much less embraced, because this would contradict the theoretical 'domain assumptions' (Gouldner 1971; Reed 1985) on which evolutionary institutionalism is intellectually founded and legitimated.

Thus, the 'evolutionary institutionalism' on which much of the decomposition narrative intellectually trades is, in turn, based on a complexity theory approach to occupational and organizational analysis (Padgett and Powell 2012) in which 'agency', 'power', and 'politics' are conspicuous by their absence. Complexity theory gives overriding explanatory primacy to self-organizing dynamics within highly interactive and nonhomogeneous systems in which loops, and cycles of self-reinforcing transformation ensure organizations and occupations discover 'new purposes for old tools' (Padgett and Powell 2012: 12) – such as reworking occupational licensing as a revitalized mechanism for sustaining professional regulation (Kirkpatrick et al. 2021). This approach seems to remove 'much of the power, conflict, disruption, and social class variables from the analysis of social processes [because] it search-

es for ecological laws that transcend the hubbub that sociology should attend to'
(Perrow 1986: 213).

Within the decomposition narrative, occupational and organizational hybridization is explained as the outcome of self-correcting and reinforcing adaptive
processes driven by impersonal ecological evolution without very much, if any, reference to the wider 'structures of dominancy' (Anter 2014) in which the latter are
embedded. It tends to retreat into a form of evolutionary institutionalism based on
life science derived biological metaphors and modes of theorizing presuming that
change, innovation and transformation can be subsumed within self-organizing
complex systems subject to generic evolutionary imperatives beyond the power
and control of individual or collective agents. Analytically stripped of any serious
explanatory interest in how power struggles between individual and collective
agents shape and reshape the contested terrain which constitutes expert ecologies,
decomposition theory 'smooths out the wrinkles' in the latter to a point where they
all but disappear within an evolutionary logic in which 'all will, indeed must, be
well'.

5 Conclusion

As we have seen throughout this chapter, the decomposition narrative offers an en-
dogenously driven explanation of the evolutionary pressures which have impacted
on the expert division of labour in ways that simultaneously destabilize and restabilize expert authority to produce much more hybridized and inherently complex
expert ecologies.

In terms of the history of ideas, the intellectual roots of the decomposition narrative can be traced back to debates over 'de-professionalisation' in the 1980s and
1990s in which professionalized modes of work and regulation were deemed to be
under increasing threat from the escalating pressures exerted by technological, organizational and cultural change (Abbott 1988; Derber et al. 1990; Burns 2019; Saks
2021). On the one side, there was a group of radical theorists and analysts who
saw an unstoppable rationalizing, deskilling and routinizing dynamic at work
that would inevitably weaken, probably fatally, the material foundations and institutional supports on which 'professionalism' depended for its cogency and legitimacy as the primary mechanism for organizing and regulating expert work. On
the other side, a group of researchers and analysts who insisted, in stark contrast,
that professionalism was much more structurally and ideologically resilient than
'the radicals' were prepared to accept because they fundamentally underestimated
its capacity to change and adapt incrementally in order to absorb immediate and
longer-term threats to its survival.

As we have seen throughout this chapter, the decomposition narrative has its intellectual roots in the second, 'incremental adaptation' school of thought on the future of professionalised modes of expert work organization and regulation – even in the face of greater threats from new technologies, political ideologies and cultural shifts than those identified as potential dangers over four decades ago. While recognizing that the contemporary expert division of labour has become ever more fragmented and fractionalized over this time, the decomposition narrative is secure in its judgement that expert-based forms of authority and regulation, including hybridized modes of professionalism which depart in several crucial respects from the orthodox model (Noordegraaf 2015, 2020), are resilient enough to 'weather the storm' and to emerge even stronger out the other side.

Whether or not this underlying optimism over the medium and longer-term prospects for expert authority, in its increasingly hybridized forms, is justified is a question to which we will return in a subsequent chapter of this book. Suffice to say at this juncture in our exposition of the decomposition narrative, adaptive evolutionary processes may reach a point at which 'the system' to which they refer may become unrecognizable from that which preceded it. Expert authority may become, over time, so dispersed, diluted and degraded that its essential identifying characteristics as a distinctive social, occupational and organizational form completely decompose into an unrelated mass of scattered elements.

Chapter 5: Covid-19 – A Case Study on Expert Authority

1 Introduction

In this chapter, we assess the three narratives regarding the demise in expert authority as outlined in the preceding three chapters 'in action' in how the Covid-19 pandemic and its relationship to experts and expertise developed. Why look at the pandemic as a particular case study? Well as Tooze (2021) highlights, this constituted the first crisis of the Anthropocene era and in a lot of respects showed our inability to cope all that well. Consequently, it is an appropriate domain in which to examine the role of expert authority and its ability to operate to help manage a global crisis such as a pandemic.

Equally, 'an event such as a pandemic is revelatory, but much of what it reveals are deep lying structures and hierarchies, which are denied or obscured during periods of stability' (Davies et al. 2022: 5). Therefore, the pandemic allows us to consider what these narratives around expert authority reveal once experts are put into a crisis rather than stable context. Whilst it posed a new challenge to expert authority, how different countries reacted to the pandemic also revealed some of the issues around expert authority that were already circulating in these narratives we identify.

Finally, when it comes to experts and expertise it has also become clear that the world was quite well-equipped with information from experts on how to deal with a pandemic from an early stage. For instance, by the end of January 2020, we knew:

> ... about the clinical progression, who was most at risk, how it was spreading, what health systems should be prepared for, potential asymptomatic transmission, the incubation period, the best strategy for containing spread and estimates of R0 for the virus. Adding this information to the emerging information from WHO on China's response provided a pretty robust picture on what other countries would be facing ... (Sridhar 2022: 76)

Nevertheless, there was a lot of deviation in response from different countries, suggesting the authority and subsequent use of that expertise matters.

The chapter begins by taking each narrative on the demise of expert authority in turn and considers how that narrative has emerged in the context of the pandemic. Then, the chapter considers what these narratives 'in action' mean for experts in the future – identifying the core dilemma expert authority contended with between the potential for re-legitimation or equally politicisation. Towards the end

https://doi.org/10.1515/9783110734911-006

of the chapter, we begin to consider what the pandemic suggests for how experts and authority can be re-imagined (and the risks this still poses).

2 The Three Narratives on Expert Authority 'in Action' during the Pandemic

In this section of the chapter, we assess to what extent each of the three narratives help us to understand and explain the role which experts played in interpreting, mediating, and managing the threats which the pandemic entailed – both globally and locally. We take each narrative in turn and look at the evidence for it in action during the pandemic. Some of these narratives lend themselves to a more global focus and for others a more local focus is pertinent to show the depth and detail of how expert authority had to contend with other stakeholders that were also interpreting and managing the pandemic. At junctures, specific aspects of the pandemic come under the spotlight such as advice on masks, use of vaccines, and the notion of herd immunity. Overall, this analysis demonstrates that expert authority was at different times, in different locations, and in different ways, delegitimated, drawn into more technocratic governance structures, and fragmented/divided.

2.1 De-legitimation and Covid-19

During the pandemic, the de-legitimation of expert authority was seen in various different locations across the globe and often centred around the behaviour of political leaders and government institutions and the use of social media to provide 'alternative narratives' of events.

Whilst China eventually responded well to the pandemic, it's initial stance to the emergence of Covid was to delegitimate its own experts, publicly condemning those that observed a new illness was spreading in the country and silencing them, to try and contain the problem before the world found out. This came to the fore with the death of whistle-blower Dr Li, a 33-year-old doctor that died from Covid after being publicly admonished by the Chinese government for releasing information about this new disease with a Chinese and global outcry in the wake of his death (Sridhar 2022). Ironically, it was scientists (within China and in other geographies) working together through the scholarly publishing system that navigated the Chinese government's crackdown on information coming out of the country at the start of its pandemic (Farrar 2021) to begin to equip other countries with key information to help them contain the disease.

Beyond the initial outbreak, de-legitimation of experts was most evident in countries led by more populist right-wing governments with obvious examples being President Jair Bolsonaro in Brazil and former President Donald Trump in the US. In the US, before Covid arrived Trump had shut down several pandemic response programmes established by his predecessor President Barack Obama (Sridhar 2022). Other instances of de-legitimation would include: Trump announcing a halt in funding of the World Health Organization because he felt it had played a significant role in the poor management of the pandemic (British Broadcasting Corporation [BBC] 2020)[1], his pronouncements regarding the potential benefits of UV sunlight and disinfectant injections to combat the virus (Broad and Levin 2020), and his treatment of Dr Fauci[2] once he started to criticise the US response to the pandemic (LeBlanc 2020) as well as other health officials (Diamond and LeBlanc 2020). Trump openly, 'rejected various evidence-supported measures to combat COVID-19, including distancing, test and trace, and masking and instead encouraged people to protest against [state enforced] lockdown rules' (Sridhar 2022: 170), which eventually led to his removal from Twitter.

As well as individual expert advisers, expert institutions were also in Trump's firing line. For instance, the CDC[3] was regularly side-lined and decried by Trump for how seriously it was taking the pandemic. As Sridhar (2022: 172) points out:

> For the H1N1 (swine flu) crisis in 2009, the CDC held 32 out of 35 press conferences in the first thirteen weeks of the pandemic. By contrast, Trump led 75 per cent of the 69 press conferences held in the first thirteen weeks of COVID-19.

Therefore, Trump was key in ensuring that expert organisations could not be as vocal as him about how to manage the pandemic. In fact, former directors of the organisation took to the *Washington Post* in July 2020 to highlight how the Trump administration was undermining their guidelines and efforts in informing the nation's response to the pandemic, particularly in relation to school re-openings (Sridhar 2022).

Overall, research 'tracked more than 400 cases of the Trump administration's efforts to restrict or dismiss scientific research or evidence' (Sridhar 2022: 174). As a result, as the Editor of the medical journal *The Lancet* Richard Horton observes:

> The story of COVID-19 in the US is one of the strangest paradoxes of the whole pandemic. No other country in the world has the concentration of scientific skill, technical knowledge and productive capacity possessed by the US. It is the world's scientific superpower bar none. And

---

1 A baseless attack in terms of evidence as Sridhar (2022: 277–8) outlines in detail.
2 Director of the National Institute of Allergy and Infectious Diseases in the US.
3 CDC stands for Centers for Disease Control and Prevention.

yet this colossus of science utterly failed to bring its expertise successfully to bear on the policy and politics of the nation's response. (Horton 2020: 46 – 47)

De-legitimation of expert authority has played a significant role in these developments in the US and has only been quelled by the election of Joe Biden to the Presidency and his alternate response (Maxmen and Subbaraman 2021).

Likewise, Bolsonaro has delegitimated expertise regarding the pandemic; regularly questioning the severity of the virus, breaking his own government's rules on social distancing (Phillips et al. 2020), potentially circulating misinformation about Covid-19 (Harris 2020), firing three Health Ministers during the crisis (Phillips 2021), and facing a severe death toll from the disease. Brazil therefore witnessed a lack of leadership on account of the pandemic not being taken seriously by its President, with the country instead reliant on states, municipalities, and favelas trying their best to respond with little to no federal support (Sridhar 2022). The country's de-legitimation of experts and expertise combined with the lack of leadership and financial support for the pandemic meant that a country that had the capacity to prevent illness and death did not do so (Sridhar 2022).

The individual behaviour of political leaders and government personnel was also key in the de-legitimation of experts because their behaviour could serve to undermine the expert advice given to the public. A studied example of this is the 'Barnard Castle Effect' on account of Dominic Cummings'[4] behaviour at the height of the pandemic in the UK in April 2020. Whilst the country was on its toughest lockdown with citizens told to 'Stay at Home' and not visit family members outside the home, it was revealed that Cummings whilst unwell with Covid drove from London to Durham to stay at his parents and was then spotted with his wife (on her birthday) at Barnard Castle which he publicly insisted was to test his eyesight before the drive back to London. As Sridhar (2022: 152 – 153) explains this had far-reaching effects:

> A study in the *Lancet* tracked more than 40,000 people's views and found that, over the three weeks after the Cummings headlines, willingness to comply with restrictions dropped steeply in England. There was no similar drop in Scotland or Wales.

Likewise, populist political leaders tended to catch the illness early on and their behaviour in relation to this was also indicative of a de-legitimation of expert advice. For instance, Trump insisted on being photographed driving outside Walter Reed hospital to demonstrate that Covid was not that bad an illness (infecting everyone in the car in the process). His response to his own experience of the disease

---

4 Cummings was Chief Advisor to the UK Prime Minister.

even, '... led some critics to suggest that he had faked getting the disease in order to prove it wasn't as serious a threat as scientists had claimed' (Sridhar 2022: 173). Bolsonaro also tried to use his experience of catching the disease to play down its effects. He claimed to have 'a slight fever, muscle pain and tiredness, and said that using the drug hydroxychloroquine[5] had cured him' (Sridhar 2022: 225)

It's telling that a lot of the countries where de-legitimation of experts took place also fared the worst in their pandemic response and volume of deaths (Sridhar 2022). They were also often the locations of the emergence of 'variants of concern' – variants of the disease that would often supplant previous variants that were often more transmissible each time it mutated.

In the behaviour of these governments is evidence of the institutional breakdown in trust of expert authority that the de-legitimation narrative highlights. These populist regimes' distrust of expertise also serves to undermine rational civic debate, '... that used to go a long way towards determining our consensus reality' (Buranyi 2020: para 8). Consequently, de-legitimation in the context of Covid-19 also evolves to become a 'culture war' against measures attempting to protect public health during the pandemic where the likes of lockdown, social distancing, and wearing a mask are constructed as constraints on individuals' liberal rights designed by elite experts (Geoghegan and Fitzgerald 2020; McKelvey 2020; Sridhar 2022). Coupled with this, conspiracy theories abound including the role of 5G in the pandemic (Goodman and Carmichael 2020), anti-vaccination sentiment, dismissing the pandemic as a hoax (Buranyi 2020), or trolling medical experts (Channel 4 News 2021). This growth in the volume and distribution of conspiracy theories has also allowed others around wellness and health to flourish in the wake of the pandemic (Wiseman 2022). Combined, these have served to allow populist and far right governments or groups to reclaim the pandemic through their own ideological lens (Krzyżanowski and Krzyżanowska 2022).

The pandemic therefore also became an 'infodemic, 'when people are exposed to large quantities of both accurate and misleading information related to a health topic' (Gruzd et al. 2021: 2). In this context, large volumes of misinformation – false information shared but without the intention to mislead – and disinformation – false information shared in order to mislead (Singh and Banga 2022) – circulate globally and at speed making it hard to fact-check and dispel. Therefore, 'an infodemic makes it challenging for people to know what or whom to trust, especially when faced with conflicting claims or information' (Gruzd et al. 2021: 2). However, emerging research on audience reception of this information suggests that a 'prag-

---

5 There's no evidence this drug can cure Covid (Farrar 2021: Sridhar 2022).

matic scepticism' (Kyriakidou et al. 2022) is emerging in response which gives experts hope for the future.

Nevertheless, evidence collected so far suggests that public trust in government to deal with a health emergency is highly dependent on the state's communication with its public (Liu et al. 2022) and the infodemic, proliferation of conspiracy theories, and culture wars generated during the pandemic serve to undermine trust in both the state and experts (often seen as too aligned with them in populist ideology). However, trust is what traditional expert authority has relied upon. Instead, distrust of government and experts (and even espoused hatred of them at times – see Kupferschmidt 2021) has prevented the pandemic being managed as effectively as it could have been.

A clear example would be the propensity for vaccine refusal in the US with Dr Fauci commenting that had the spread of dis/misinformation been as prolific in previous health crises we wouldn't have been able to eradicate smallpox and polio (Sridhar 2022: 161). Doctors observed that at the core of these refusals was a general mistrust of government and questioning of authority – it was not based on evidence and fact (Karkowsky 2021). It has led to high profile experts within the media to express surprise and dismay at the general population's rejection of science (e.g., Roberts 2021) with doctors talking of experiencing 'compassion fatigue' (Karkowsky 2021), questioning why they continue to look after people that reject medical treatment and science in some respects (i.e., vaccine) but not in others (e.g., hospital treatment if got ill from Covid), often putting medical professionals at risk as a result.

In sum, whilst de-legitimation can often focus on extreme responses to expert authority, they can have some fundamental consequences in the actions some governments take and can contribute to shifting the public discourse around the pandemic and the role and authority of expertise. In contrast, demystification demonstrates how government regimes can create distrust in expert authority in a more discreet manner.

2.2 Demystification and Covid-19

To analyse demystification and the pandemic we will focus on the UK government as it serves as a classic example of the co-option of expertise into political rhetoric where 'following the science' became the buzzword phrase in daily briefings to the population (Mathers 2020) and with it the UK government attempted to rationalise 'the science' and its scientists within the neoliberal governing policy regime (Calvert and Arbuthnott 2021).

As the Director of the Wellcome Trust[6], and member of the government's advisory group SAGE[7], Jeremy Farrar (2021) provides an insightful first-hand account of the relationship between expert authority and the UK government. He highlights that in the very early stages of the pandemic it was not clear to SAGE panel members what direction the government was seeking to take and what strategy they were pursuing (that they would therefore need advice from SAGE on). As a result, questions were being asked of SAGE members that weren't in their remit (e.g., whether to call in the Army). By March 2020, Farrar (2021) depicts SAGE advisers as becoming increasingly frustrated with government and more demonstrative with them as they did not feel they were being taken seriously in terms of the scale of death they were presenting based on the current strategy the government was pursuing. Consequently, he argues scientific experts and academics[8] were key in the UK government eventually changing course and locking down.

Nevertheless, technocratic rationality was the favoured response to the pandemic initially where behavioural and mathematical modelling was influential (Farrar 2021; Simons 2020; Sridhar 2022; Sodha 2020). Furthermore, the UK government sought to focus on numbers, figures, and graphs in their daily briefings to the population – rationalising their approach and 'progress' against the pandemic (Billig 2021), which was largely accepted by the UK media (Winston and Law 2021).

'Official' experts used by the UK government also became enveloped into the political regime and its desire to control the messaging around the pandemic. Consequently, those within SAGE (e.g., Farrar 2021) and beyond (e.g., Horton 2020; Sridhar 2022) concede there was a lack of transparency as to who constituted SAGE, what discussions were had within SAGE, what advice was given by the body, and how/when/if the UK government was following any of that advice. Minutes from SAGE meetings were not made available to the public, with Farrar (2021) insisting that members of SAGE together with Chris Whitty, Chief Medical Officer for England, and Patrick Vallance, Government Chief Scientific Adviser, pressured the government to make them public. Likewise, there are indications of other areas of disconnect between experts and the UK government with Farrar (2021) noting that minutes from key meetings of SAGE in mid-March 2020 played down the urgency and anxiousness actually present in those meetings. He also highlights that the no-

---

6 Wellcome Trust is a global charitable foundation which supports science to solve urgent health challenges.
7 SAGE stands for The Scientific Advisory Group for Emergencies.
8 Particularly Prof Neil Ferguson who's work with colleagues at Imperial College London showed the scale of death and the overwhelming of the NHS that would be likely if the government continued to not pursue a national lockdown.

tion of herd immunity[9] whilst mentioned publicly, '... was not something that I recall being explicitly recommended by SAGE or even discussed at SAGE meetings as a strategy. Other advisers share this recollection' (Farrar 2021: 104).

Despite this, the claim to the public continued to be that the UK government was 'following the science' – a statement that increasingly became untenable when the UK government brought England out of lockdown measures rapidly in the Summer 2020, prevaricated on lockdown in winter 2020/1, and abandoned most measures to contain the disease in 2021/2 (Independent SAGE 2021). Farrar (2021: 153) is adamant that 'Ministers were not following the science, even if they said they were. Governments owe it to people to be clear about when they are following advice and when they are rejecting it' and later quit the advisory group in October 2021.

When it became clear that the UK government hadn't handled key aspects of the crisis well, the medical/scientific experts were then being left to handle the tough questions with concerns they were becoming scapegoats for political decisions (Farrar 2021; Matthews 2020a; Sodha 2020; Wickham and Baker 2020). This became apparent in some of the UK government's subsequent criticism of scientific experts, such as former Health Secretary, Jeremy Hunt's critique of SAGE (Payne 2020), the criticisms made of Public Health England (Campbell and Walker 2020), and the abandonment of SAGE advice as the pandemic progressed, particularly in the second wave onwards (Alwakeel and Demianyk 2021). It has also been the subject of the current Conservative party leadership contest (and next UK Prime Minister) with Rishi Sunak stating that too much power had been conceded to experts in the height of the pandemic (BBC 2022).

Horton (2020) is particularly critical regarding the transformation of experts advising the government to technocratic functionaries, arguing that, '[Scientific] advisors became the public relations wing of a government that had failed its people' (Horton 2020: 59). The emergence of Independent SAGE as opposed to SAGE is also considered by Horton (2020) as an indication of elite experts' deference to government where Independent SAGE was needed, as official SAGE had too many government employees on it and was too secretive and thus became compromised as a trusted body of expertise. This left the British Medical Journal to observe that, 'The pandemic has revealed how the medical-political complex can be manipulated in an emergency' (Abbasi 2020: para 2).

---

9 The World Health Organization (WHO) defines herd immunity as: '... the indirect protection from an infectious disease that happens when a population is immune either through vaccination or immunity developed through previous infection. WHO supports achieving 'herd immunity' through vaccination, not by allowing a disease to spread through any segment of the population, as this would result in unnecessary cases and deaths' (WHO 2020).

As well as the co-option of experts into political rhetoric and the technocratic neo-liberal regime, there has also been the reframing of what constitutes 'expertise' for the UK state. It has been observed that before the pandemic, the UK was a country with a good reputation for public health expertise and pandemic control and yet it was not prepared when Covid struck (Sridhar 2022). Cooper and Szreter (2021) indicate that this is on account of the fact that a lot of the previous expertise on disease and infection control had been 'hollowed out' due to 'rentier capitalism'. Consequently, in line with the government's approach before the pandemic, private sector consulting expertise was sought and often dominated in the Covid strategy, demonstrating, 'quite how close the relationship between the state and those para-state industries had grown, often outside of the public eye' (Davies et al. 2022: 14).

Examples of this influence include the creation of the National Institute for Health Protection comprised of largely executives from the private sector rather than public health or medical/scientific experts (West 2020). Likewise, the UK government's test and trace programme, led by former Chief Executive of TalkTalk, Dido Harding and outsourced to private sector consulting firms rather than using local authority skill and expertise in testing and tracing. This resulted in a very expensive test and trace programme (£37 billion[10]) that never performed well and yet it constitutes a key facet in the fight against disease control (Cooper and Szreter 2021). Even so, private sector consulting has still been very well financially rewarded for its pandemic efforts with the likes of Deloitte awarded £280 m of Covid related public sector contracts with 691 partners each receiving £854,000 profit share (O'Dwyer 2021). Therefore, in this context, we see neoliberal regimes rewarding those who demonstrate 'obedience to the ideology of the ruling elite' (Cohen 2020: para 8) and thus the expert as 'technocratic fixer' is favoured, as indicated by this narrative.

Ultimately, the commons inquiry into the UK government Covid response was damning of both the government but also its expert advisors, pointing to specific instances where poor decisions were made that evidence did not support (e.g., locking down late, abandoning testing early on, discharging patients back into care homes) that the inquiry felt were a significant contribution to the UK's death toll (House of Commons 2021; Sample and Walker 2021).

The example of the UK government pandemic response certainly demonstrates a more subtle relationship with expert authority, where it doesn't seek to publicly decry or denigrate it as seen in de-legitimation, but instead either draw

---

10 Source: https://committees.parliament.uk/committee/127/public-accounts-committee/news/150988/unimaginable-cost-of-test-trace-failed-to-deliver-central-promise-of-averting-another-lockdown/.

it into its neo-liberal regime or outsource authority to other privatised consulting expertise in project delivery that are often more aligned to state neoliberal interests. But this approach can still serve to question expert authority as it has been originally conceived as well as the implicit contract and bonds of trust it relies upon. It's this theme of the 'turf war' between experts that forms the crux of the decomposition narrative that can also be seen at work in the response to the pandemic across the globe.

2.3 Decomposition and Covid-19

This narrative manifests in the tensions between the authority of different forms of expertise. In relation to the pandemic, it involved an array of different forms of expertise in order to manage a challenge of this global proportion. In turn, tensions and debates emerged (sometimes at a national level and sometimes at a global level as we shall see) between different experts, particularly with respect to advice for measures to protect populations from illness, thus presenting expert authority as more contested and fragmented.

As seen in the previous section, one particular area of fragmentation and fissure in the UK, has been between 'corporate professionals' from the likes of management consultancy versus public health or medical/scientific professionals. Contracts for PPE, the production of testing kits, the testing centres and the testing labs have increasingly been outsourced to private companies in the UK (Davies 2020b; Kinder and Plimmer 2020) and with it has been operational fragmentation and huge difficulties in achieving overall strategic coordination and direction (Jones 2021). This use of corporate professionals in a public health crisis has come under greater scrutiny as the pandemic has progressed, with investigation into procurement processes for Covid contracts (Waugh 2021a) and spending on the likes of the UK test and trace system (Waugh 2021b). This test and trace system struggled to cope with demand where private management consultancies rather than public health experts on mass screening and testing have been used (Goodley and Halliday 2020). These experts have also been side-lined for management consultancy expertise in the proposed 'operation Moonshot' programme, with public health experts identifying numerous problems with the proposal (Booth 2020).

There have also been tensions between different forms of expertise specialisms that pertain to the pandemic (for example, between public health scientists, medical scientists, economists, mathematicians, psychologists, behavioural scientists – see Bourgeron 2021). This arena of fragmentation results in highlighting the endemic complexity and opacity of the development of expertise and knowledge, where the public begins to realise that 'science' does not constitute one objective homogenous entity or practice, but instead is inherently more piecemeal, contested, and fluid (Balloux 2022; Farr 2020; Smith, Blastland, and Munafò 2020). This has been seen in particular in the differing global expert opinions around key facets of how to tackle the Covid pandemic.

In the earlier stages of the pandemic, one example would be the use of masks (Gallagher 2020) and the understanding around airborne transmission which was 'one of the most heated topics within the scientific community' (Sridhar 2022: 100), with some highlighting droplet transmission as key (similar to how cold and flu is often spread) and others indicating airborne transmission was more important to consider particularly to control the spread of the disease. Scientists such as Professor Trish Greenhalgh have been critical of WHO and the CDC for being too slow to acknowledge airborne spread of Covid (Sridhar 2022). She considers how the dominance of certain scientific disciplines over others (e. g., medical versus chemical) has been behind the reticence to declare this transmission as key to understanding the disease and with it, recommending masking as a key form of protection (Greenhalgh et al. 2021). Consequently, governments often over-emphasised handwashing over ventilation (Sridhar 2022).

Likewise, herd immunity as a concept to drive government strategy in their response to the pandemic was also debated within the scientific community. Herd immunity is based on the principle that by letting the disease spread through the population (whilst shielding the most vulnerable in society), immunity will be built up through exposure. A Professor in Global Public Health, Devi Sridhar (2022: 142) considers herd immunity 'fringe among mainstream public health and infectious disease researchers, and called unethical and immoral by the head of WHO'.

Nevertheless, there were experts putting this view forward such as Anders Tegnell, chief epidemiologist for the Swedish public health authority and the 'Great Barrington Consensus' in the UK. In Sweden, this strategy was pursued and ultimately considered a failure:

> King Carl XVI Gustaf, as well as the Swedish Prime Minister, publicly acknowledged that the approach taken had failed to protect lives. The King said, 'I think we have failed. We have a large number who have died and that is terrible. It is something we all suffer with.' (Sridhar 2022: 211)

In the UK, the government sought counsel from the Great Barrington Consensus to help counter the SAGE advisory group advice to engage in a 'circuit breaker' lockdown to stem the spread of Covid in Autumn/Winter 2020 (Calvert and Arbuthnott 2021). Anti-mask and anti-lockdown groups also jumped on this idea to pursue their goals. Consequently, we see the exploitation of scientific debate for ideological means take place in relation to this specific concept.

Other features of the pandemic also resulted in debate and contestation between expert groups. For instance, the notion of 'lockdown fatigue' suggested by England Chief Medical Officer, Christ Whitty but refuted by some at SAGE (Sridhar 2022). Equally, the testing of large-scale live events as a means to see if lockdown measures could be lifted in the Netherlands had their veracity questioned by other epistemic communities such as behavioural scientists (Sridhar 2022). Similarly, different methodological tendencies in different scientific disciplines (e. g., modelling versus observation of practice) meant that travel restriction advice by the likes of WHO was opaque and of limited use (Sridhar 2022). Once vaccines were developed, doubts were seeded over the AstraZeneca (AZ) version when it emerged blood clots had featured in some people that received the vaccine (European Medicines Agency 2021). As the scientific community investigated the source of these clots and debated the advice they should give for who should now receive this vaccine, anti-vaxxers could use this instance to voice concerns over vaccines in general and governments (such as the German and Danish) retreated from the use of AZ despite the risk being small as Sridhar (2022: 120) outlines:

> The chance of a 55-year-old having a vaccine-linked blood clot was estimated to be 4 in a million, while being hit by lightning in 2021 was 1 in a million, and dying of coronavirus (which also causes blood clots) was 800 in a million.

As with masks and herd immunity, these tensions between different expert groups had real-life consequences for the action (or inaction) of governments, the public discourse surrounding expertise and the pandemic, and ultimately the success in managing the spread and death toll of the disease.

For Sridhar (2022: 118), a lot of the debate amongst the scientific community over aspects such as masks, early lockdowns versus herd immunity, and vaccines was on account of the precautionary principle not being evoked enough: 'This allows measures to be implemented in situations where scientific evidence is deficient, but inaction threatens permanent harm.' Some scientists don't think it wise to move ahead based on this principle, others say it might be necessary in unfolding situations where the science is still learning. The Czech Republic is a good example of applying the principle as an early adopter of mask policy that was made mandatory in the country by 18 March 2020:

> ... the Czech Republic just made a decision that face coverings carry little harm, and possibly huge benefits, and therefore it made sense to mandate them. This decision would pay off in letting the country stay open for longer, while containing the spread during its first wave. By

April 2020 Spain had recorded 517 deaths per million people, Italy 453, the UK 325, and the Czech Republic only 21 (Sridhar 2022: 112)

Despite the debate and contestation of expert knowledge (and therefore its authority), there were also indications that a more diverse set of expert disciplines should have been involved in tackling the pandemic. In the UK, there have been calls for broader areas of expertise from the likes of social sciences, engineering, logistics, and cultural studies to name a few to play a role as the pandemic endured (Bingham 2021; Sozudogru 2020). Certainly, reflections from experts in the UK suggest that a wider range of disciplines beyond epidemiology and modelling should have been present on the SAGE advisory group from the start and that a greater number of international experts and a wider diversity of gender and ethnicity serving on the group would have been beneficial (Costello 2021; Farrar 2021; Grundmann 2021; Horton 2020; Sridhar 2022).

In this context, debate and contestation between different expert groups is considered healthy and appropriate to cope with an emerging situation:

> The language of unanimity in the SAGE minutes is concerning, in that it reflects a lack of dissent from the consensus that complete suppression was not the right short- or long-term strategy. There seemed little reflection that buying 6–12 months' time might help science deliver solutions. This also indicates why diversity and disagreement are healthy and necessary in scientific advisory groups, especially when there is considerable uncertainty attached to the topic and no 'correct' way forward. (Sridhar 2022: 140).

Whilst the notion that knowledge is evolving and contested might not be novel to those in expert authority its effect on the perception of expertise by the public (and by extension, policy and government officials) is a cause for concern for some (Balloux 2022). For instance, Horton (2020) argues that the differing voices of a more fragmented expertise base can be used by certain governments as a plaintive excuse for why they didn't react quickly enough to the threat posed by the virus. Preliminary indications also suggested that as the pandemic developed there was greater risk to trust in experts on account of the changes in scientific advice (Matthews 2020b). Nevertheless, Horton (2020) and Sridhar (2022) also argue that self-criticism within science and academic disciplines and beyond will be needed to continue to manage society even post-Covid, leading to a wider diversity of expertise being drawn upon in the future. Therefore, in line with the slightly more positive future envisaged by this decomposition narrative, there is some room for hope here that a diverse array of expertise will be appreciated as we emerge from the pandemic.

Ultimately, whilst the pandemic constituted a fundamental new global challenge for expert authority to contend with, each narrative regarding the demise in expert authority can be found to be in operation during this period. De-legitimation of expert authority focused on the behaviour of populist right-wing political leaders and the use of mis/disinformation to breed at the very least doubt, but also culture wars and at the more extreme end of the scale, conspiracy theories regarding the measures experts recommended to contend with the spread of the disease. Meanwhile, the de-mystification of expert authority could be seen in contexts where the rhetoric suggested that expertise was being pursued and underpinned the pandemic response strategy but also where that expertise became enveloped into the technocratic neoliberal regime of that same state pursuing that response strategy. Finally, the decomposition of expert authority is evident in the various debates and controversies that emerged over how to manage the pandemic as the expertise regarding the virus developed in real-time as we all lived with the emergence and then prevalence of different variants of Covid. Expert authority appeared more contested, heterogenous, fragmented, and fluid but there was also an emerging appreciation of the need for diversity of expertise to tackle the many different challenges the pandemic posed. The fact that all three narratives are present in the various experiences of expert authority poses some fundamental questions and tensions for the expert and their authority going forward which the next section of the chapter will analyse.

3 Covid-19: The Return of the Expert?

In establishing the narratives regarding the crisis in expert authority 'in action' during the pandemic, what is left for the expert as we begin to emerge from the challenges it posed for expert authority? In this section, we identify the fundamental dilemma which experts and their authority faced during the pandemic and what this begins to indicate for the future. At the heart of the dilemma has been the degree to which the pandemic resulted in the re-legitimation of expert authority, or a growing politicisation of expert authority. In the case of re-legitimation, this is assessing whether the pandemic allowed for expert authority to reclaim some of the legitimacy and status which had been previously lost by providing the expertise through which the risks of the virus could be effectively contained. Alternatively, for politicisation, this involves considering whether in fact expert authority lost even more ground by experts allowing themselves to be co-opted by political leaders for their ideological and political purposes and in turn, exposing themselves even more to the populist critique of being merely 'servants of power masquerading as independent and autonomous agents'.

3.1 Re-legitimation

Re-legitimation envisages a revival and renewal of the public service ethic in and through which traditional forms of expertise are ideologically grounded and organisationally articulated. Elite expert groups are able to reclaim their occupational identities and organisational roles as guardians of the public interest because their position and function as public servants protecting us from collective harm, has been indelibly reinscribed through their vital contribution to navigating a way through the pandemic. As a result, they can reclaim the social capital and political legitimacy damaged, if not lost, in recent years as their recurring failure to live-up to their liberal public service ethic has been restored by their contribution to managing the pandemic in ways that have saved lives and sustained collective wellbeing (Collins, Evans, Durant and Weinel 2021).

In some vital respects the pandemic did allow for renewed claims to legitimacy for expert authority on this basis as it quickly became clear that science was going to be a key means by which the world would manage the pandemic (Tooze 2021; Sridhar 2022). In turn, we witnessed a range of experts across the globe mobilising quickly from the outbreak of the pandemic onwards to use their expertise (often voluntarily and pro-bono) and not always within formal government structures and agencies (Farrar 2021) to help mitigate, mediate, and manage the pandemic. This was borne out in the various success stories of science: the creation of PCR[11] tests, the creation of LFTs[12], the discovery of treatments to help Covid sufferers, the development of genome variant sequencing, and of course ultimately the development of vaccines.

There were also plenty of instances across the globe where governments did engage with experts and act on their advice accordingly, re-legitimating expert authority. For instance, Greece gave their expert advisory group not only the power to advise but also to enact their advice (Sridhar 2022). South Korea, learning from its experience with MERS[13] recognised expert advice on testing as key to success and based its pandemic strategy around this, also attempting to share a lot of its protocols with other countries. Sub-Saharan Africa, learning from its experiences with Ebola focused on similar preventative public health informed measures, with cases such as Senegal showing expertise and not money was the key in the fight against the pandemic (Sridhar 2022). The obvious final example would be New Zealand, who listened to public health experts and looked more internationally in terms

---

11 PCR stands for Polymerase Chain Reaction.
12 LFT stands for Lateral Flow Test.
13 MERS stands for Middle East Respiratory Syndrome.

of the evidence base to draw from, pursuing a successful elimination strategy and with it boosting public trust in the government (Sridhar 2022).

There were also global organisations that helped to co-ordinate the pandemic response in significant ways such as WHO, providing 'technical advice, normative authority and convening action on the part of its member states' (Sridhar 2022: 273); CEPI[14], which was influential in vaccine development, centralising testing and enabling comparison of immune response to different vaccines; and COVAX[15], which focused on the global distribution of vaccines, particularly to countries with less resources. Whilst each organisation has also been challenged by national self-interest (e.g., Paiva and Miguel 2022), it has demonstrated the need for global co-ordination of expertise and logistics to tackle the pandemic and potential future global grand challenges.

The success of science in manging the pandemic and the success of experts to be influential in government responses to the pandemic has also resulted in a rise in public trust for science. For instance, the Wellcome Global Monitor that surveyed more than 119,000 people in 113 countries about their attitudes towards science highlighting that: 'more than three-quarters of people said they trusted science (80 per cent) and scientists (77 per cent)' (Grove 2021: para 2). Research into news television audiences also suggests that there is in fact a public appetite to hear more from experts, and a wider range of them, particularly when navigating a crisis (Morani et al. 2022)

Consequently, there were prospects for expert authority to be re-legitimated on account of the pandemic. However, this event also thrust experts into the political spotlight, and this has left expert authority caught in the cross hairs of the potential for re-legitimation, but also for increased politicisation, particularly as the pandemic has waxed and waned in is development.

3.2 Politicisation

Politicisation suggests that rather than experts remaining independent of the state, they become ensnared within the regime, which can in turn damage the basis of their authority. This can involve either the co-option of experts or even more extreme, the colonisation of experts, to political demands. As Jeremy Farrar observes this 'brings me back to the central moral dilemma: does staying in an advisory role

---

14 CEPI stands for The Coalition for Epidemic Preparedness Innovations.
15 COVAX stands for COVID-19 Vaccines Global Access.

mean being complicit in the outcomes of bad decisions? To be honest, I still don't know the answer' (Farrar 2021: 176).

Here, we return to the particular case study of the UK to begin to examine the potential the pandemic demonstrated for expert authority to be politicised. This is on account of the fact that the UK government engaged with experts during the pandemic, but the terms of this engagement has been nuanced and insidious where at times it has appeared to pay deference to expert authority and yet at other times it has played off expert groups against one another and/or co-opted or even colonised expert representatives to policy/political positions.

3.2.1 Co-optation

'Co-optation', Selznick (1949, 1966: 14) tells us, is 'the process of absorbing new elements into the leadership or policy-determining structure of an organization as a means of averting threats to it stability or existence'. He conceptually distinguishes 'formal' from 'informal' co-optation: the former, refers to a process that is publicly visible and bureaucratically identifiable but politically insignificant in that it doesn't alter the balance of power within the host organisation; the latter, to a process which remains privately opaque and bureaucratically obscure but is politically significant because it fundamentally alters the balance of power within the host organisation.

In the context of the UK, it might be argued that both forms occurred for key expert groups, particularly those experts that operate as government advisors. This notion of co-optation posits that experts have allowed themselves to be absorbed into a governing regime in which they come to play the pivotal roles in constructing and communicating the scientific gloss which legitimates political decisions on the grounds of objective and disinterested reasoning – that is, the application of 'scientific rationality' – rather than the political logic that has effectively driven the choices ministers have made in light of them exercising their 'political rationality'. Key instances in the development of the UK government Covid strategy highlighted that the cognitive and organisational boundaries between 'scientific' and 'political' rationality had become so blurred and porous that medical and scientific expert advisors seemed to become an integral component of what Selznick (1949/ 1966) called an 'administrative constituency' and Child (1973) a 'dominant coalition' between experts and politicians which jointly manages the crisis.

The Sunday Times investigative journalists Calvert and Arbuthnott's (2021) account of the UK government's 'Battle with Cornonavirus', makes it clear that expert advisors were being used to provide scientific veneer to political decision making. For instance:

> It had been Hancock's [UK Health Secretary] idea to present government decisions to the public as if they were entirely based on scientific advice, when, in fact, they inevitably involved a huge amount of political calculation. The earnest scientists were taken from their normal habitat in the corridors of Whitehall and thrust into the limelight as an embodiment of this scientific approach in order to gain the public's trust. *It was also a way of deflecting responsibility when tough decisions had to be made*' (Calvert and Arbuthnott 2021: 157–158, emphasis added)

Likewise, Calvert and Arbuthnott (2021) provide an extensive account of how Deputy Chief Medical Officer for England Jennifer Harries, was utilised by the government to provide scientific gloss for the herd immunity approach initially preferred by UK ministers. In particular, it focuses on a video that featured Prime Minister Boris Johnson in conversation with Jennifer Harries shared by Downing Street on social media on 11 March 2020:

> The set-up was Johnson would feed earnest pre-arranged questions and she would give a scientist's view. Therefore, the government would be seen to be 'following the science'. It would start with easy topics such as questions on the well-known symptoms of coronavirus and build up to the point where she would explain why the UK was following a different path to the rest of the world with its delay strategy ... Johnson then posed what was supposed to seem like a thoughtful question on a thorny subject. 'There's obviously people under a lot of pressure. Politicians, governments around the world, need to be seen to act', he said, with little disguise that he was referring to his own predicament. 'So, they may do things that are not necessarily dictated by the science?' *It was a leading question and Harries knew the script. 'As a professional, I am absolutely delighted we are following the science', she said, – almost as if she was appearing in a shampoo advert as the bespectacled lab technician in a white coat.* She continued: 'There are other things we can do in this country and the timing is really important'. Johnson, interjected, eager to reinforce the point: 'And the timing is very important, isn't it?' Harries was keen to confirm: 'Critical, absolutely critical. If we put it in too early, we will just pop up with another epidemic peak, later on', she said. This was a further articulation of the government's intention to allow the virus to spread so that immunity could be built-up in the population to prevent a second wave (Calvert and Arbuthnott 2021: 183 emphases added)

In another incident observed by Sridhar (2022: 144) Jenny Harries negates the WHO advice on testing, masking the political impetus behind the decision:

> However, the government was reluctant to acknowledge that testing was constrained because of capacity. Instead it said this was a strategic decision. Dr Jenny Harries, England's Deputy Chief Medical Officer, defended the policy in a press briefing. 'There comes a point in the pandemic when that is not an appropriate intervention' and argued that WHO's advice to 'test, test, test' was intended for poor countries, not the UK.

Also, this 'scientific veneer' does not appear to have been particularly questioned, with recent research into TV news coverage of the pandemic highlighting that expert sources weren't a predominant feature of bulletins but when they were, they tended to be representatives from SAGE who 'were not routinely used to scrutinise the government's advice' (Morani et al. 2022: 12).

In addition, co-optation allows for the scapegoating of experts for political ends, something Farrar (2021) considers occurred with the government treatment of Public Health England and something seen in now UK Prime Minister, Rishi Sunak's comments that too much power was handed to experts to decide on Covid measures (BBC 2022). Moreover, some of the reflection on the UK government pandemic response so far have also pointed the finger at expert advisors for their culpability and compliance to political authority as well (Walker 2021; Ball 2022). This is despite the fact that others have also argued that the UK government failure to respond well to the pandemic was largely on account of ignoring advisors at key junctures (Reicher 2021).

Consequently, what this demonstrates is that there are very real risks for experts in allowing themselves to be absorbed into the governing regime in this way. They are allowed into the 'inner circle' decision-making arenas in which key policy options are formulated and complex operational choices are framed, but their newly found status as 'insiders' risks compromising whatever social capital and legitimacy which has accrued to them as a result of their playing a central part in 'saving us' from the worst ravages of the pandemic. Their status as independent and objective 'expert advisors' is now under threat from their much closer and intimate association with political decision takers who are driven by the electoral consequences of the actions they individually and collectively take during the pandemic. Whilst potential co-option raises some serious questions as to the status of the expert, potential colonization may pose an even bigger challenge.

3.2.2 Colonization

Deetz (1992) develops the concept of 'corporate colonization' to analyse the unobtrusive, but nevertheless pervasive and effective, communication processes through which the interests and values of powerful economic elites are naturalized or normalized as 'taken-for-granted, common sense' assumptions framing all aspects of corporate life. Rather than simply being 'co-opted' into a decision-making process in which opposing views and voices are filtered-out of the decision-taking agenda in order to protect the vested interests of powerful groups, 'colonization' implies a process of total absorption of oppositional groups into a dominant ideology in which they completely lose their distinctive identities and rationalities as actual or potential 'resistors'. Potentially oppositional groups can then become enrolled within a 'framing narrative' and in supporting a set of socio-political relations in which their independence and autonomy becomes so diluted that they lose all claims to a separate and distinctive voice or standing as 'outsiders' challenging the 'status quo'.

As such, experts may find themselves enrolled, if not colonized, as 'technocrats' within an emerging political logic of 'techno populism' (Bickerton and Accetti 2021). This can be construed as:

> ... an organizing logic of electoral competition based on the combination of populist and discursive tropes and modes of political organization [it is] a new structuring logic of contemporary democratic politics [in which] a contextually and historically specific set of incentives and constraints ... affects the way in which rival contenders for public office compete with one another in the electoral sphere, independently of their substantive policy goals (Bickerton and Accetti 2021: 17–21).

It claims, in different ways and in a range of socio-historical contexts, to represent the 'people as a whole' and appeals to technical expertise and competence which can be combined and recombined with one another. It emerges out of the breakdown of the post-Second World War political consensus around managed social democracy from the late 1970s/early 1980s onwards and can be seen in New Labour in the UK, the Five Star Movement in Italy, Macron and his political movement in France and more hybrid examples such as Podemos in Spain.

Bickerton and Accetti (2021) further suggest that the pandemic is likely to reinforce this techno populist political logic insofar as it strengthens the ideological appeal and political authority of 'technocrats' by relying increasingly on scientific modes of reasoning and their associated technologies to protect the health and welfare of 'the people'. Consequently, relevant experts are being rapidly incorporated, even colonized, within the discursive embrace of this political logic to the extent that they are absorbed within a political-cum-policy narrative which presumes 'one best way' or 'rational answer' to keeping the virus under control and returning society to some sort of 'normality' resembling our pre-Covid existence.

The UK government's decision to not pursue a 'circuit breaker' in September 2020 in order to prevent a further lockdown later that year, starts to indicate some of the techno-populism Bickerton and Accetti (2021) refer to in action. Calvert and Arbuthnott (2021) highlight that in mid-September 2020 Boris Johnson is trying to establish whether to pursue short period circuit breaker of restrictions to stave off a lengthier and more restricted lockdown in later months as recommended by SAGE and Independent SAGE. A secret meeting is had between Johnson, and experts in favour of the herd immunity principle – Professor Sunetra Gupta, Professor Carl Heneghan, and Anders Tegnell, Sweden's top epidemiologist. The only other expert at that meeting was Professor John Edmunds, the UK government's leading modeller, to articulate the view of his fellow members on SAGE that an immediate two-week circuit breaker lockdown was vital.

Despite this, Johnson opts to call off preparations for the circuit breaker, largely because the herd immunity science is better for his political agenda at the time in order to appease his chancellor and other more libertarian right-wing elements of the Conservative party. Nevertheless, 'The split between No. 10 and its chief medical and scientific advisers had never been more apparent' (Calvert and Arbuthnott 2021: 360). This decision is a classic incident of policy-led science, but Chris Whitty, Patrick Vallance, Jennifer Harries, and Jonathan Van Tam still had to remain the 'faces' of this verdict. The innate ideological and political complementarity or 'elective affinity' between populism and technocracy is reinforced by the pandemic because it forces experts to 'go along with' the emerging governmental 'strategy' for dealing with the substance and impact of the Covid-19 crisis, whatever their reservations and worries over its efficacy and effectiveness. Unintendedly, they may be accruing increased public legitimacy and credibility at the cost of reduced political power and diminished social status within the wider community. Whitty and Vallance at times were on 'resignation watch' by the UK government with SAGE scientists concerned they were being used as 'human shields' (Calvert and Arbuthnott 2021) for government ministers.

It is for reasons such as these that Davies (2020a: 236) concludes that, 'in spite of the brief hiatus, when public expertise and policy competence experienced a resurgence of enthusiasm from the Johnson government, the longer-term effect of the pandemic looks likely to be a hastening of the collapse of British liberalism'. And, as previously suggested, the ethic of 'public service' which underpins the notion of expert seems to have become so fragile that it is in danger of being eviscerated by a populist-cum-technocratic political logic that speaks much more viscerally and emotionally to our fears and search for security in profoundly uncertain and unstable times. As Krastev (2020: 39) suggests:

> More than any other crises, a public health emergency can induce people voluntarily to accept restrictions on their liberties in the hope of improving their personal security … [but are these restrictions] … genuinely favourable to authoritarian concentrations or seizures of power?

4 A More 'Public' Expert

The assessment so far suggests there has been a systemic tension for some experts between re-legitimation and politicisation as they strive to maintain their distance and independence whilst simultaneously being prepared to 'put their reputations on the line' by engaging directly with the roles they were asked to perform by political elites who remained the final decision makers with the power to accept or reject their expert advice. The degree to which the re-legitimation, co-option, or colonization of expert authority becomes fully realised is yet to be seen, but is there a fourth option that the experience of expert authority during the pandemic begins to suggest for the future?

Those experts that have been involved with the pandemic in some way suggest that the answer may lie in expert authority prioritising a more public facing dimension where experts are '… more open and engaging about what we do, how the scientific process works, how scientific research and analysis influences policy making and how its benefits can be shared fairly' (Farrar 2021: 230).

Nevertheless, engaging more with different publics is by no means easy and the likes of Sridhar (2022) have also been very honest about the scrutiny, abuse, and threats she has faced by pursuing this more public facing notion of expert authority. She is but one of many examples she cites of other experts in different countries across the globe that have also received political pressure and/or public abuse or even threat to life on account of being a more public facing expert.

This individual experience is in line with *Nature's* broader survey into the abuse of scientific experts indicating that 'more than two-thirds of researchers reported negative experiences as a result of their media appearances or their social media comments' (Nogrady 2021), which can also serve to make these same experts reticent to engage publicly again. Also, a *Guardian* survey of UK scientific and medical advisers also indicated the volume of abuse they (and people close to them) experience (Sample 2021). This suggests that experts can still be de-legitimated by any means possible, and it won't just be the individual but science and expertise more broadly in the firing line as well (Farrar 2021). Consequently, this suggests the alternate future of a more public facing and transparent expert is also not without its risks.

5 Conclusion

Overall, this chapter indicates that the three narratives regarding the demise of expert authority are still very salient in capturing the experience of experts and expertise even in an emerging global crisis such as the pandemic where expertise is needed but also has to contend with different government priorities (and ideologies), a global media system more open to dis/mis information, and a range of expert groups with their own conventions and norms to begin to tackle this challenge. Consequently, analysing the pandemic in relation to these narratives reveals how the arguments contained within them are still pertinent today and could go some way in explaining how the world didn't respond to the crisis as well as it could, and certainly how there was a variance of response across different countries.

In assessing what this means for experts and expert authority there appears to be a potential triple edged sword to the pandemic for experts where it serves as:

(a) A chance to reassert traditional expert authority as societies realised they were going to need experts to navigate out of this crisis
(b) The potential for co-option or colonisation of experts by policy and the state
(c) A phenomenon that has highlighted the contingent nature of knowledge and expertise

Initially, the pandemic seemed to offer expert groups of professionals, consultants, technicians, and administrators a 'golden opportunity' to regain their position and status as trustworthy specialist advisors, if not legislators, as their knowledge and technologies become even more critical to managing the risk of the virus. As political elites seemed to become ever more dependent on the analysis and assessments which their professional, technical, and managerial/administrative elites provide, so their public standing and social status revived in ways that substantially pushed back against the accusations of 'remote elitism' and 'duplicitous objectivism'.

However, the enhanced political and social capital accruing to experts as a result of their, seemingly, vital contributions to re-establishing the public health environment to a semblance of 'normal', has to be balanced against the dangers which this new, highly visible and vital, role in restoring safety and public order presents. Experts may now be standing, if it hadn't been for social distancing, 'shoulder to shoulder' with government ministers and political leaders in ways they haven't been of late, and this offers very real opportunities to re-establish their credentials and status as 'public servants' acting on behalf of society's collective values and interests. However, there is always the lurking threat that these same experts will find themselves being, once again, regarded with suspicion, if not distrust, by the public at large as they become seen for what 'they really are' – that is, technocrats totally incorporated within governing regimes which will do whatever they have to do to retain, or gain, political power.

Likewise, Covid-19 has demonstrated that 'even populists need experts' (Bickerton and Accetti 2021: 212), but experts need to be very careful as to what they let themselves – and 'us' – in for particularly when they allow themselves to be drawn into some sort of 'Faustian pact' with populist governments. At the very least, experts may find themselves enrolled into a governance regime in which they become an integral, and vital, part of the 'dominant coalition' (Child 1973) which determines government policy during the pandemic, but at the potential cost of absorbing that regime's priorities and values without necessarily knowing it.

Therefore, the pandemic perhaps doesn't suggest a return of the expert as conceived in the traditional ideal type or in Giddens' (1994) notion of institutionalised trust. Instead, the boundaries between science and medicine on the one hand and politics on the other are becoming more difficult to police. Where this leaves the expert (and the professional groups that underpin them) is where research now needs to turn. There are signs of hope in the recognition of the diversity of expertise needed to tackle global challenges such as the pandemic and in experts recognising their authority may come from a greater engagement with a variety of stakeholders, including the public. These final points are the launchpad for the next chapter where we begin to formulate how expert authority can be re-conceptualised to suggest a more 'reflexive' form going forward.

Chapter 6: Reflexive Expert Authority and Governance

1 Introduction

Over the course of the analysis developed so far in this book, several major, inter-related themes have been identified which we focus on in this chapter relating to the emergence of a distinctively 'reflexive' form of expert authority and governance which departs in several crucial respects from the established model outlined in chapter one.

First, the need for a more realistic conception of science and scientific rationality which differs from the 'crown jewels' or 'immaculate conception' of the latter that more conventional models of expert authority and governance have traditionally relied on to justify their claims about its unique epistemological foundations and form.

Second, a reappraisal of the distinctive structural and processual features of expert knowledge and skill which are analytically and substantively grounded in a proper appreciation of the inherently contested, provisional, and contextually dependent nature of the understandings and interventions that experts provide.

Third, a more rounded understanding of the scale, scope and severity of the risks which experts are now called upon to deal within an environment where multiple threats and challenges simultaneously present themselves to 'them' and 'us' in ways that may undermine previously accumulated knowledge and practice.

Fourth, a better developed analysis of the 'trust and control dynamics' which indelibly shape and reshape all forms of expert knowledge and skill in a world where the balance between them seems to have shifted decisively in favour of the latter and to the detriment of the former.

Finally, and by building on the improved understanding made possible by the previous analysis, to appreciate the key role that reflexive thought and action plays in legitimating expert authority and the modes of governance through which it is most likely to be articulated and implemented.

However, before dealing with the above themes we focus on the political philosophy roots of reflexive authority in theories of 'associative' and 'deliberative' democracy and the endemic tensions which this dual intellectual inheritance bequeathed.

https://doi.org/10.1515/9783110734911-007

2 Democratic Theory and Reflexive Expert Authority

Associative democratic theory has its intellectual roots in a communitarian/collectivist tradition of political thinking and practice (Nisbet 1969; MacIntyre 1981, 1988; Etzioni 1988, 1993; Horton and Mendus 1994; Hirst 1994; Wolin 2004; Collier 2018), while deliberative democratic theory is grounded in a rationalist/individualist tradition in which democratic decision making is seen to rest on 'agreement through argument' (Elster 1998; Cohen and Arato 1992; Forrrester 2019; O'Flynn 2022). Yet, both traditions also share an overlapping political philosophy and practice demanding the (re)empowering of civil society in which voluntary associations, social movements, and local organizations hold big business and government to account by scrutinizing and challenging the epistemological-cum-ethical grounds on which their decisions are made and the quality of the substantive outcomes they generate. This is the new socio-political context in which 'reflexive expert authority and governance' emerges as a response to the much heightened anxieties and uncertainties of a risk environment in which multiple ecological, biological, and political crises now confront us and in which our dependence on and suspicions about 'experts' are greater than ever. As Freedland (2022: para 11) reflects, 'if the public decides it can no longer trust those in authority, then when the chief medical officer stands up to warn of a new threat to public health, there is no guarantee that anybody will listen'.

Hirst (1994: 19) defines 'associative democracy' as a political philosophy premised on the claim 'that individual liberty and human welfare are both best served when as many of the affairs of society as possible are managed by voluntary and democratically self-governing associations.' This claim legitimates a theory of political practice in which voluntary self-governing associations become the primary mode of institutional and organizational governance in which power is redistributed as far as possible to lower levels of political decision-making. In turn, this necessitates 'that the state should cede functions to such associations and create the mechanisms of public finance whereby they can undertake them [thus reducing] the scale and scope of the affairs of society that are administered by state agencies overseen by representative institutions' (Hirst 1994: 21).

Moves in this direction would create a very different political and governance context to which most expert occupational groups and organizations are used to and would radically shift the balance of power and control away from them and towards the newly empowered 'citizen consumer' (Clarke at al. 2007). As we have seen repeatedly throughout this book, the increasing power and authority of expert groups and organizations in general and of elite professions such as medicine and law has depended on political elites embedded in state administrative structures being prepared to support, if not sponsor, their 'upward mobility projects' over extended periods of time. Centralization of state power has gone together with successful 'professionalization projects' which have protected and enhanced the twin-track 'epistemological exclusion' and 'jurisdictional closure' strategies expert groups have pursued in order to legitimate and stabilize their claims to 'authorized control' over particular occupational territories and organizational domains. Although there has always been tension and conflict between state elites and expert groups and associations – and particularly as we have repeatedly seen under neoliberal state elites – over how much self-governance and management the former should allow the latter to enjoy, centralized power and expert autonomy have been able to come to terms with each other under the unwritten/informal social contract between states, experts, and publics previously discussed in this book.

Insofar as a move from 'representative' to 'associative' democracy would necessarily entail some significant deconstruction of and reduction in centralized state power in favour of 'civil society' associations and movements such as regional and local governments, voluntary organizations and other non-state agencies, then this would radically change, if not transform, the institutional landscape in which expert occupational groups operate. It would require a fundamental renegotiation of the terms on which the implicit social contract between states, experts and publics have been previously agreed in order to ensure a marked shift in the balance of power and control towards 'civil society associations' in which citizens and consumers were empowered as a precondition for them ceding greater collective and individual trust to the experts supporting them. This would also require much great openness and 'connectiveness' (Noordegraaf 2020) of expert occupational groups to the values, needs and priorities of the wider communities in which they become more socially and organizationally embedded as a result of this overarching shift towards associative democracy. This would only be possible if expert occupations and the organizations regulating and protecting them become much less defensive, secretive and self-regarding in their corporate cultures and practices.

Although not quite as radical in their scope and strategy, theories of 'deliberative democracy' also have wide-ranging implications for how expert occupational groups and organizations are regarded and regulated. Elster (1998: 8, emphasis in original) defines 'deliberative democracy' as involving 'collective decision making with the participation of all who will be affected by the decision or their representatives [and including] decision making by means of arguments offered *by* and *to* participants who are committed to the values of rationality and impartiality'. While this raises the organizational and epistemological preconditions required for deliberative democracy to a relatively high level, it has the advantage of emphasizing the need for a focus on *outcomes* as well as *processes* to the extent that it depends upon a close analogy being drawn between political and scientific argumentation in which decision-making proceeds through and is legitimated by deliberation. Again, this may be held up as an ideal set of conceptual preconditions which real functioning democracies may only approximate to in varying degrees, but it has the advantage of analytically specifying the theoretical model against which various forms of criticism may be evaluated (O'Flynn 2022). It provides a set of criteria for assessing the legitimacy of decision-making in which 'public argument and reasoning among equal citizens' (O'Flynn 2022: 17) lies at its conceptual core, as well as highlighting the vital role that 'institutional support' plays in nurturing and protecting 'deliberative procedures as the source of legitimacy' (O'Flynn 2022: 18) and hence 'authority'. Legitimacy and authority of collective decisions or choices arises out of 'free and reasoned deliberations' between participants who are not constrained by pre-existing power relations and the ideological preferences and normative conventions which they embody. Thus, 'ideal deliberation aims to arrive at a rationally motivated consensus' (O'Flynn 2022: 20), but there is no guarantee that this consensus will be forthcoming or that it will last forever. Indeed, the expectation built into the theoretical model of deliberative democracy is that consensus will be time bound and open to reappraisal and renegotiation when enough participants subject to it demand that it should be revisited.

As with 'associative democracy', the theory of 'deliberative democracy' has major analytical and practical implications for expert authority and governance (Holst and Molander 2017). It refocuses attention on the accountability and scrutiny mechanisms through which the legitimacy of the latter can be reviewed and revitalized within deliberative arenas and processes such as 'citizens' juries' in Scotland (Roberts et al. 2020) or other 'mini-publics' like 'citizens' assemblies' in Ireland (O'Flynn 2022) in which critical legal and public policy issues are debated and resolved. In these fora, the role of the expert is potentially transformed from one of exclusively possessing superior knowledge and exercising jurisdictional control into one of leading the discursive processes and shaping the technical interventions through which consensus-based decision-making over complex disputes and problems can emerge and be ratified.

Theories of associative and deliberative democracy have been roundly criticized for their lack of attention to the material and structural inequalities that indelibly shape political decision-making in real world democracies and the ways in which the institutional innovations and experiments they recommend are open to cultural and political manipulation in a social media saturated world (O'Flynn 2022). While theories of associative democracy are more cognisant of corporate power and the role which it plays in framing the structural context in which deliberative processes occur and theories of deliberative democracy are more sensitive to the importance of individual reasoning in shaping the latter, the analytical tension between them provides a useful 'jumping off point' for understanding the growing significance of reflexive forms of expert authority. This underlying tension between 'structure' and 'agency' opens up possibilities for analysing the processes through which expert authority is 'legitimated through contestation' in ways that are consistent with a more reflexive model of the latter as it has emerged from 'science and technology studies' in which deliberatively generated collective epistemological consensus plays a not dissimilar role.

3 Science and Scientific Rationality

Since the 1970s 'science and technology studies' (STS) have focused on what scientists do in their everyday work in the lab, or field, or station, rather than what they 'ought to be doing' according to some idealized, 'revelatory' or 'crown jewels' model of scientific perfection (Collins et al. 2020: 76). Focusing on 'the detailed observation of scientific practice – treating it as day-to-day work rather than a set of hidden, priestly rituals – resulted in some debunking of the mystery of science' (Collins et al. 2020: 49–50). This 'debunking process' has given rise to a more socially realistic model of what science is and how it works, while raising difficult and complex questions about how extensively epistemological consensus building in science should go beyond the scientific community itself to include a potentially infinite range of non-expert stakeholder groups.

Interpreting the significance of this body of STS research very cautiously and carefully, Collins et al. (2020: 57) suggest it paves the way for a 'rough diamonds' model of scientific knowledge and practice in which 'scientific judgements are intricately related to social judgements about the priorities, preferences and behaviour of patients or users.' It also lends support to a conception of the 'scientist' or 'scientific expert' as an 'honest craftsperson doing their best, informed by noble values, but inevitably fallible' (Collins et al. 2020: 76). They also maintain that this reconceptualization of science and scientists as organizationally and occupationally grounded in 'painstaking craftwork in the context of a complex reality' (Collins 2020: 77), rather than as high priests engaged in 'revelatory epistemology', does not detract from or undermine scientific expertise or the scientific professions' claims to authority. Instead, both the profession and the legitimation of their expertise are now based upon the conception of science as 'systematic inquiry' working towards better understandings of and solutions to complex problems by expert crafts persons who try to adhere to core values around integrity, disinterestedness and evidence. They also note that the increasing ideological and political influence exerted by free market capitalism and authoritarian populism has put this craft-based, 'rough diamond' model of science and scientific practice under extreme pressure in recent years. This is the case in that they both recognize only the legitimacy of those forms of expertise which are willing to subject themselves to external domination and control in the service of profit maximization or 'the peoples' will'.

Oreskes (2019) fleshes out the implications of this rough diamond/craft-based model of science and scientific expertise for the way we might look at 'scientific rationality in practice'. She argues that the latter emerges from the 'transformative interrogation' processes embedded within 'agnostic fields' of specialization through which 'novel solutions to problems are developed, accepted, and sustained as *facts*' (Oreskes 2019: 247–248, emphasis in original). Epistemological contestation within and between communities of expert groups and organizations operating across a wide range of scientific fields – that is, disputes and disagreements as to what is to count as 'true' or 'valid' knowledge – and the communities and institutions which they serve, is now regarded as a strength rather than a weakness of scientific practice. Scientific rationality emerges from these disputes and disagreements in the form of 'sedimented epistemological consensus' over well-founded judgements accumulating over long periods of trial and error and the ongoing interrogations and scrutiny of the results that it has produced. Rational assessment of competing epistemological claims is now seen to be grounded in the accumulated, codified experiences and understandings of scientific craft persons doing their best to adjudicated between them, rather than being determined by the mechanical application of algorithms, metrics or laws.

For Oreskes (2019: 248), it is those knowledge claims that have survived sustained interrogation and critical scrutiny by those 'craft experts' who are deeply involved their production and evaluation which deserve to be regarded as valid in the sense of being well-founded and based on the 'dynamic consensus' at the epistemological core of scientific investigation and development. Science simultaneously generates continuity and novelty in the form of competing claims made by those knowledgeable and skilled in the crafting of scientific investigations and appraising the quality of the knowledge which they produce. Articulating the irredeemably 'social' character of science and the scientific expertise through which it is made possible is not an admittance of weakness but an expression of the underlying robustness and strength of the knowledge it reproduces. Indeed, science and scientific expertise can no longer rely on 'reactive' or 'passive' trust as a basis for legitimating its authority and status. They must both actively and proactively engage in processes and practices of 'trust building' within the communities in which they are embedded, confident in the view that it will provide the social and cultural foundations for justifying collective decision making in risk environments where rising levels of uncertainty and anxiety are the 'new normal' (Oreskes and Conway 2010).

4 Expert Experience and Civic Epistemology

This more socially realistic model of science and the practice-based understanding of scientific expertise which it promotes is also reflected in more recent work on 'experience-based expertise' and the critical role that it plays in the formation, legitimation and regulation of professional knowledge and skill (Collins and Evans 2009; Collins 2013; Young and Muller 2014). If STS research and scholarship has encouraged a measured reappraisal of 'crown jewels' science through the development of a more socially grounded and politically sensitive appreciation of how science works in practice and what this means for justifying scientific expertise in a wider socio-cultural context, then experienced-based approaches to expertise have simultaneously reinforced our understanding of a 'citizens or civic epistemology' and the role of professionals in generating and curating the latter (Collins et al. 2020).

In a series of landmark publications, Collins and his co-authors (Collins and Evans 2007; Collins 2013; Collins 2019; Collins et al. 2020) have develop a general analytical framework for understanding different forms of expertise within a:

> wider transformation in the way expertise has been understood [in] a move away from seeing knowledge and ability as quasi logical or mathematical and toward a more wisdom-based or competence-based model ... expertise is now seen more and more as something practical – something based in what you can *do* rather than what you can calculate or learn (Collins and Evans 2009: 23 emphasis in original).

Specialist knowledge is now seen as being practice dependent, and requiring, above all else, 'mastering a tacit knowledge-laden specialism to a high level of expertise' (Collins and Evans 2009: 23).

Conceptually relocated within this 'practice turn' to the study and understanding of expertise, 'contributory expertise' is of greatest relevance to the analysis we have developed in this book because it redirects our analytical attention to the fact that it 'enables those who have acquired it to contribute to the domain to which the expertise pertains; contributory experts have the ability to do things within the domain of expertise' (Collins and Evans 2009: 24). A five-stage model of 'contributory expertise' is subsequently developed, entailing a move through from 'stage 1 the novice' through to 'stage 5 the expert', as consisting of the unselfconscious recognition of 'complete contexts' in which high level performance of domain specific expertise relies, primarily, on tacit knowledge and understanding that often doesn't correspond, or even contradicts, rules acquired at the novitiate stage. It also highlights the critical importance of 'interactional expertise' to the successful performance of 'contributory expertise' as entailed in mastering domain specific language and enculturation within a linguistic community's values and practices.

Without high level 'interactional expertise', contributory experts are ill-equipped and unable to bridge the gaps and fissures that often open-up and fester between expert groups and the communities which they serve. In addition, they need high level reflective ability and skill because of its critical role in building interactional expertise on the part of contributory experts who, if they are to be successful in gaining the attention and sympathy of the wider communities in which they are embedded, must cross 'social boundaries and [spend] a long time in alien social environments to which there is restricted access' (Collins and Evans 2009: 37). Only in this, relatively open, implicit, interactional and reflexive way can expert groups effectively exercise their domain-specific 'contributory expertise' in ways that build and enable our citizens to develop a more inclusive and participatory 'civic epistemology' that can counteract the severe damage which authoritarian populism would inflict on pluralist democracy (Collins et al. 2020: 84). This consensus building and pluralistically based 'civic epistemology' recognises that science, or for that matter any other 'contributory expertise' such as medicine, architecture, engineering, or sociology, can never be 'pure' in the sense of completely disengaging from society and the social relations and practices through which they are all made possible as sustainable institutional ensembles. Yet, it does insist that 'expertise must be given its due' by recognizing that the authority on which experts depend for their position and trust within the communities in which they operate presumes they will do their level best to build epistemological consensus through 'organized scepticism' – that is, through constructing, critiquing and curating the best available shared specialist knowledge and skills pertaining to society's problems and crises, whether poverty or pandemics – and that they will do this by consistently engaging with the communities in which the latter occur.

This 'experience or practice turn' in STS is also reflected in the 'sociology of professional expertise' in which reflexivity on the part of professional practitioners as they go about their daily business assumes rather more analytical importance and explanatory relevance than the institutionalized and formalized regulatory processes given so much prominence in orthodox, mainstream research focused on licensing, accreditation and closure (Young and Muller 2014; Burns 2019; Gorman and Vallas 2020; Saks 2021). Drawing on the concept of Schön's (1990) 'epistemology of practice' and Bernstein's (2000) concept of 'regional knowledges', Young and Muller (2014: 13) develop a conceptualization of professional knowledge that:

> is both "theoretical" (that is, general and unvarying) and "practical" (that is, purposive and contextual). Contemporary professions are about doing things but doing complex things

that cannot rely on experience alone, like crafts could for their expertise ... professional knowledge is always sectoral, not general, like the traditional disciplines; it relates to specific occupational sectors such as health, transport and education.

Within this practice-based conceptual framework, the concept of 'a professional or expert practitioner' cannot be reduced to merely functional technical expertise but must embrace the tacit, reflexive judgements which they are called upon to make as they confront the inevitable ethical, moral and political dilemmas the latter entails (Grace 2014).

By refocusing analytical attention on the centrality of the reflexive – that is, the 'creative/interpretive' rather than 'rational/technical' (Saks 2021) – aspects of professional expertise, the 'experience/practice based' approach to the study of professional work also reminds us of the critical importance of the wider socio-political context in which professionals operate as it shapes and reshapes the challenges they face (Leicht 2016; Reed 2018; Burns 2019; Saks 2021). Once we begin to see the full analytical significance of what Collins and Evans (2009) conceptualize as the 'contributory expertise' lying at the core of professional-cum-expert work, as it is communicated and justified through their interpretive discursive practices, shifting role identities and dynamic knowledge regimes (Burns 2019: 209–216), then we begin to appreciate how 'contextual challenges' and 'reflexive practices' are becoming intimately interconnected in a world where traditional defences of epistemological exclusivity and jurisdictional closure no longer guarantee the legitimacy and protection they once delivered.

Leicht (2016) and Saks (2021) suggest that in this 'brave new expert world' – where the institutionalized defences which established professionals once relied on to legitimate and protect them are no longer, structurally or ideologically, robust enough to guarantee or underwrite their authority and status – professionals will need to redefine their roles, practices and identities. If, for example, the 'sophisticated certificate ecosystem' on which Kirkpatrick et al. (2021) place so much reliance in defending the regulatory regimes through which professional 'labour market shelters' (Freidson 2001) and 'jurisdictional work domains' (Abbott 1988) are protected and policed are no longer able to offer the degree of 'expert insulation' they once did due to their inherent lack of administrative discrimination ('everybody has one') and declining political impact ('nobody really cares'), then this would imply the need for a radical reworking of the working practices and discursive regimes through which all forms of professional/expert authority is reflexively communicated and legitimated. Indeed, this will be even more the case for expert groups who never enjoyed the degree of institutionalized protection afforded to established professionals and who are even more reliant on 'active', rather than 'passive', trust building to garner whatever social recognition and political support they can for legitimating their knowledge claims and the authority flowing from it.

Thus, the turn from a largely 'technical/rational' conception of professional/expert knowledge and practice towards a much deeper recognition of their 'reflexive/interpretive' dimensions, as well as of the critical role the latter will play in re-adjusting and realigning contemporary professionals to a very different socio-political and economic-technical context, allows us to see the emergent nature of contemporary professionalism in a new analytical light. Between them, Leicht (2016), Burns (2019) and Saks (2021), collectively suggest that the highly specialized and esoteric 'theoretical-cum-technocratic' discursive regime which has dominated our conventional understanding of professional/expert authority is giving way to a much more inclusive 'practical-cum-mediative' discourse in which 'managing risk', 'knowledge integrity' and 'innovative change' become the new communicative signifiers. Burns (2019) summarizes this discursive-cum-practice shift in our understanding of professional/expert authority as entailing an 'unbundling' of 'professional' and 'expertise' such that the latter is cut from its umbilical institutional cord to 'professionalism' and indiscriminately reproduces across a wide range of pre-existing occupational domains and organizational boundaries. No wonder Kirkpatrick's et al. (2021) 'certificate ecosystem' remains so fecund, even if it does so at the cultural and political cost of severely diluting, if not denuding, its claims to 'sophistication' as it lends its formal legitimacy to anybody prepared to pay the certification fee required. The larger the number of occupational groups the 'certification ecosystem' recognizes, the less potent it becomes as a regulatory mechanism offering meaningful administrative differentiation between distinctive levels of occupational expertise and the political legitimation this confers on those ranked more highly within the expert hierarchy it reproduces.

We will return to the longer-term implications of the increasing political and cultural influence of 'reflexive expert authority' in the next chapter of this book. For now, we turn to its significance for our understanding of the critical role which 'contributory expertise' plays in contemporary risk management.

5 Reflexivity and Risk

As Hoogenboom and Ossewaarde (2005: 612) suggest, Beck, Giddens and Lash's (1994) original conceptualization of 'reflexive modernization' is grounded in the argument that 'late modern society is a society in a continuous legitimation crisis.' Because they can no longer lay claim to universal, rational, and objective knowledge as a basis for legitimating decision-making in government, business, public services and civic organizations, late modern societies have become much more dependent on the temporary, negotiated agreements arising out of political and economic struggles between major institutional actors as a basis for 'moving forward' in relation to longer term policy formulation and implementation. Thus, the 'epistemological consensus' taken-for-granted under rationalist modes of decision-making typical of earlier phases of modernization can no longer be relied upon because it has been seriously eroded and compromised by an increasingly disputatious, fissured and relativistic polity and culture. Rational authority has to give way to some other form of legitimation and authorization which is more 'in tune with the times' and recognizes the need for much more pluralistic, inclusive and reflective modes of collective decision-making under conditions of multiplying risks and uncertainties, and the deep-seated generalized sense of anxiety they produce.

Under reflexive modernization, 'for the reflexive organization the point is how to integrate members in the context of extreme uncertainty' (Hoogenboom and Ossenwarde 2005: 616), while also having to depend upon more informal, ad hoc and renegotiable integrative mechanisms lacking the stability and continuity associated with formal bureaucracy based on rational-legal authority. Within these reflexive organizational forms, experts play a very different role to that specified under rational bureaucratic organization. They must build and sustain 'active trust' because they can no longer rely on 'reactive or passive trust' to legitimate their authoritative role in complex collective decision-making contexts in which competing expert knowledges vie for attention and reinforce the uncertainties and anxieties embedded within the latter. 'Active trust' must be sought by 'opening out' institutions to a much broader and more inclusive range of 'voices' and 'values' in situations where 'we have no choice but to make choices, filtering these through the active reception of shifting forms of expert knowledge; in such circumstances, new forms of organizational solidarity replace the old' (Beck, Giddens, Lash 1994: 187). In this way, 'institutional reflexivity' becomes a self-reinforcing process whereby expert knowledge disputes proliferate, dividing rather than uniting and integrating organizational members, under decision-making situations already characterized by extreme uncertainties in relation to the risks that communities face and the most appropriate ways of coping with them. As they become more reflexive – that is, open to and dependent on the very expert knowledges which they generate and reproduce in their search for 'active trust' and 'contested integration' – institutions and organizations become permeated by circulating 'modes of knowing and doing' which cannot be formalized and codified as they were under legal rational bureaucracy. Older forms of organizational solidarity – such as hierarchy, function, occupation and rules – remain in place but they become more fragile as decision-making is 'opened out' to a much wider range of interests, movements and technologies which, directly and indirectly, challenge the formal authority which experts have accumulated through their monopoly control over specialized knowledge and the claims to expertise it passively justified.

This conceptualization of institutional/organizational reflexivity and the modes of governance and administration which it authorizes is logically and empirically tied to an analysis of the changing forms of 'risk' emerging under late modernity and the escalating scale and scope of the threats and challenges they pose to communities in the 21st century. Both within the sociology of organizations/professions and the sociology of science/technology, an overlapping body of knowledge has emerged that moves us away from a somewhat narrowly focused rationalistic/engineering approach to 'risk' towards a discursive/political approach in which institutional and organizational reflexivity play a central role (Turner 1976, 1978; Perrow 1984; Vaughan 1996; Beck 1992, 1997, 1999).

Within the sociology of organizations/professions research literature, there has been increasing emphasis on the political and cultural processes through which 'risks' are normalized as 'natural', or at least 'acceptable if regrettable' routine features of organizational life in highly competitive economic environments. Dominant corporate cultures and expert systems ensure that achieving targets, deadlines and profitability override any concern with the threats that risk-taking poses to human safety and well-being. As Vaughan's (1996: 387–422) case study of the Challenger disaster concludes 'contextual rationality' – that is, the rationality embedded in recurring organizational/expert routines and the corporate hierarchies and cultures justifying them – played a critical role in 'normalizing deviance' from established safety rules and permitting, indeed encouraging, unsafe, high-risk behaviour to occur on a regular basis.

In a complementary manner, recent developments in the sociology of science/technology highlights both the threats and opportunities presented by 'risks [as] *man-made hybrids*'(sic) (Beck 1999: 146 emphases in original) which combine natural and human processes in complex, unintended ways that do not lend themselves to easy scientific prediction or technical control. As 'man-made hybrids', contemporary risks require much higher levels of institutional and organizational reflexivity in order to encourage and support experts to think and act in responsible ways and not to be dominated by political and economic elites who control the 'risk assessment bureaucracies' (Beck 1999: 150). For Beck (1999: 143), 'risks are at the same time "real" and constituted by social perception and construction'. They have real world impacts on our lives and the ways in which we live them but our knowledge about them and their actual and potential influence is mediated by a complex configuration of historical, cultural and political factors which must be openly debated and sensitively calibrated as we 'go along' dealing with them as best we can.

If 'reflexive experts' are to be effective managers of hybrid risks in which natural phenomena and human processes are so intimately intertwined, then they will need the cultural sensitivities and political skills required to understand and communicate the complexities and challenges which these configurations of threats and opportunities present to 'us' as communities of pluralistically diverse and often conflicting values and interests. The 'bureaucratic-cum-technocratic' vision of expertise and the authority it conveys can no longer equip 'them' or 'us' to deal with the multiple hazards that now confront us in an era when the conventional divisions between 'nature' and 'society' are breaking down under the escalating pressures generated by ecological deterioration, social dislocation and political polarization.

What Beck (1999: 91–108) conceptualizes as 'sub politics' – that is, sub-state/national level politics which can encompass a range of institutional levels and organizational forms from regional/local governments to civic associations and voluntary organizations – cannot presume that the formal, rational legal authority represented by state-sanctioned experts and professionals will be able to sort out the disputes and conflicts crystalizing around the identification, calibration and containment of 'risks' in highly uncertain environments. Simply waiting for government sponsored and legitimated 'expert research, and more expert research' to solve the problem of effective risk management for you won't work under conditions where the complex combination of ecological and technological hazards means 'trust becomes central; a trust capital that can be wasted by continuing to act out the old industrial scenario' (Beck 1999: 101). Instead, effective risk management under these conditions demands a new form of 'sub politics' in which innovative intraorganizational and interorganizational modes of expert action are legitimated through 'much better-informed publics and socially aware firms, all brought face to face with the consequences of their actions from which they are at present largely divorced ... we have to find ways to deal democratically with the ambivalences of modern life and decide democratically which risks we want to take' (Beck 1999: 108).

Under 'sub politics', the role of the expert becomes one of facilitating this 'face-to-face' confrontation with the consequences, both intended and unintended, of our individual and collective actions through the reflexive monitoring and communicating of the complex realities which living in world where large-scale hazards, risks and manufactured uncertainties unavoidably entails. The latter are 'no longer the preserve of scientists and experts, the nature of hazards is demonstrated everywhere and for everyone willing and interested to see' (Beck 1999: 151). This means that the scientists and experts' primary responsibility is to accrue and disseminate the more collaborative and coproduced forms of expertise through which this 'seeing' can be achieved. Their authority is legitimated through their willingness and success in engaging in this process of reflexively 'opening-up' their specialized knowledge and understanding in ways which better equip the communities of which they are an integral part to see the complex realities they face and to find ways of dealing with them more honestly and collectively.

We have clearly come a long way, analytically and normatively, from the conventional, neo-Weberian model of expert authority legitimated through monopoly control over specialized knowledge and the workplace occupational closures it makes possible. Under 'reflexive expert authority', the 'trust and control dynamics' shift ineluctably towards a much more open, participatory and negotiated governance system in which experts willingly admit a far broader range of values and interests into the decision-making process. In so doing, they also must be prepared to enable these newly empowered stakeholders to access the specialized knowledges and technologies through which risks are evaluated and the actions they require undertaken.

Such a substantial shift in trust and control dynamics will inevitably encounter obstacles and resistances along the way in relation to both the political strategy which drives it and the outcomes the latter envisages. These are considered in the following section.

6 Trust/Control Dynamics

The changing balance between trust and control relations under relatively unstable and uncertain contextual conditions has been a central theme in the sociology of organizations and professions over several decades as political economies and societies began to experience escalating levels of threat posed by interrelated ecological, technological and ideological transformation (Courpasson 2000, 2006; Reed 2001; Clegg, Harris and Höpfl 2011; Courpasson, Golsorkhi and Sallaz 2012; Burns 2019; Saks 2021). Within the sociology of organizations, much of the debate centred around the putative emergence of 'post-bureaucratic' or 'network' organizational forms signalling a shift towards 'softer, trust-based' modes of governing and managing and away from 'harder, control-based' systems in which formalized hierarchies and rules had played the central role in ensuring compliance with authorized instructions 'from above'. In the case of the sociology of professions, there was a parallel debate over the extent to which the traditional defensiveness and exclusivity of established professionalism was giving way to a more inclusive occupational culture and ideology under the mounting pressures generated by the internationalization of the market for professional services, as well as by the rationalizing dynamic inherent in technological change and mounting political and public hostility to 'expert closed shops.'

Both fields were analytically and substantively converging around a shared focus on the pressures undermining established organizational and occupational forms primarily reliant on combinations of bureaucratic and professional control to legitimate their power and the emergence of alternative systems and cultures in which building and sustaining 'high trust' relations becomes the key to securing longer term stability and success. However, while there is an emerging shared recognition that trust and control are essential features of organizational life, there is also a joint realization that one is not dealing with an 'either/or' situation here but with a complex interplay between both factors as they shape and reshape the processes and structures through which the construction and coordination of organizational and occupational relations occurs. An increasing awareness of an over-reliance and dependence on control-based governance regimes in no way guarantees a successful move towards trust-based cultures and systems in which legitimation struggles are 'consigned to the dust bin of history'.

Beck, Giddens and Lash's (1994) analysis of 'reflexive modernization' and the greatly enhanced 'institutional and organizational reflexivity' which it implies – that is, the capacity to self-monitor and reproduce or modify the ability of its constituent systems and technologies to adjust to changing conditions and threats – comes at a price. On the one hand, trust in relatively abstract and remote expert systems to perform these critical monitoring and adjusting tasks becomes even more crucial to their capacity to cope with extreme risks and the hazards they entail. On the other, this also means that the 'creation of stable abstract [expert] systems are a fraught endeavour' (Beck, Giddens, Lash 1994: 89–90) when expertise itself becomes more contested and divided than ever and is open to reappropriation and redirection by anyone with the resources to do so. This is especially the case when expert systems become increasingly spatially, organizationally and experientially 'remote' as they breakdown and traverse existing jurisdictional domains in the very act of compressing time/space barriers and the political-cum-cultural protection and stability they once provided.

But there is clearly a more positive side to this analysis insofar as it anticipates the pro-active, trust-building work in which experts must engage if any kind of acceptability and stability in the systems which they design and operate is to be realized. In parallel, this would also require much greater accessibility and influence on the wide range of stakeholders increasingly dependent on the protection that expert systems provide and a move towards 'distributed control' systems in which their voice is heard more loudly and effectively than ever before. So, trade unions, local governments, civic associations, voluntary organizations, social movements and citizens assemblies would need to be empowered, not just with the formal knowledge but also the 'practical know-how', to enable them to participate in collective decision-making arenas in which critical choices over risk management are to be made.

There are a range of decision-making levels which need to be considered in relation to the move towards pro-active, trust building expert systems in which more shared/participatory modes of deliberation over the evaluation of 'risks' and of the collective response which they require can flourish and become embedded in organizational designs and routines. Experts play a vital role in ensuring various checks and balances exist within representative pluralist democracies by providing the expertise through which various 'authorities' can be challenged and 'held to account' for what they have or have not done. But they can also be seen, under certain conditions, as evolving into an unaccountable 'technocratic elite' so that, rather than be identified as an undeniable asset to the maintenance of pluralistic decision-making they become something of a liability, if not a direct threat, to building and curating both the informal conventions and formal rules on which the latter depends for its legitimacy and fairness (Taylor 2019: 210 – 233). So, as we have seen throughout previous discussion in this book, experts and their expertise are needed in all modern societies – and particularly those in which 'institutional reflexivity under extreme uncertainty' has emerged as a dominant feature of their risk management architecture – yet the expert systems they provide can be also become enmeshed in forms of private corporate power and public administrative authority which undermine the very pluralism and openness they are meant to protect.

At the level of the expert group – whether embedded in large, multinational corporate organizations or more nationally/regionally-based professional bodies and occupational associations – various regulatory and governmental mechanisms provide some degree of formal transparency and accountability to the wider communities in which they operate. However, the need to strengthen the latter in the light of growing concerns over the inherent limitations of established regulatory machinery in the face of escalating accusations over political/cultural elitism and technocratic rule has been recognized. As we have already seen, a robust 'civic epistemology that guides what is expected by way of evidence in public decision-making and identifies who is to be recognized as able to provide that evidence' (Collins et al. 2020: 79 – 80) is an essential structural prerequisite for achieving a better balance between public trust and expert control in pluralistic democracies. This needs to be supplemented by other 'checks and balances' mechanisms building public trust in specialist expertise but also ensuring that it remains open to democratic scrutiny and accountability to the wider society that both depends on it and defends it against unwarranted political interference or indifference. These additional 'checks and balances' mechanisms would be focused on opening-up expert decision-making to broader social and political debates around how complex problems and the risks they present needs to draw on a diversity of specialist and lay expertise if they are to be collectively overcome. Breaking down barriers between 'experts' and 'non-experts' in ways that facilitate building more robust and lasting consensus within and between them over 'what should be done' when dealing with high-risk situations would seem to offer a preferable way forward to the hierarchically driven and exclusionary strategies dominant under the orthodox model of expert authority as outlined in the first chapter of this book.

Yet, when moving beyond the level of expert groups to the 'corporate behemoths' in which an increasing number of them – particularly those working in private and public sector corporations with the organizational capacity and reach to make fateful decisions impacting on all our lives – are employed, then the 'trust/control dynamics' become especially challenging. Of course, there is, in one sense, nothing new about the multiple ways in which large scale, powerful corporations have come to dominate contemporary economic, social and political life as revealed in Freeman's (2018) historical analysis of the growth of the 'factory system' in late eighteenth/early nineteenth century England to early twenty-first century 'Foxconn City' in China and Vietnam. But the early twenty-first century high tech corporate giants through which 'surveillance capitalism' (Zuboff 2019) and the 'surveillance state' (Striitmatter 2019) have become institutional realities seem to present configurations of expert power and control way beyond the reach of any form of democratic scrutiny or accountability (Pasquale 2015; Taylor 2019; Daub 2020). In many ways, they – and the financial corporate giants which now operate alongside them (Lapavitsas 2013; Wilks 2013; Vogl 2017) – have come to exemplify what Wolin (2004: 605) defines as the structural essence of twenty-first century corporate power in the form of 'a permanent revolution instigated and perpetuated by elites [as] represented in what I have called the hybrid of the corporate state'. For him, the central political and ethical challenge which this 'permanent revolution from above' presents are that of 'nurturing a discordant democracy [which] in being rooted in the ordinary, it affirms the value of limits ... the task is to nurture the civic conscience of society' (Wolin 2004: 606).

A much more reflexive form of expert authority and governance, we contend, has a vital role to play in 'nurturing a discordant democracy and civic conscience' by assisting challenges to closed corporate decision-making in ways which expose it to political, legal and ethical scrutiny in its darkest corners and recesses.

Zuboff's (2019) dissection of the structural mechanisms on which 'surveillance capitalism' depends for its cycle of exploitation to function effectively (see chapter two of this book for a more detailed discussion) also includes some analysis of how it might be challenged and resisted. In this context, she emphasizes the crucial importance of 'decision rights', and the various ways in which 'we', the public, can proactively reclaim control over the knowledge and information from big tech companies which enable them to exploit our everyday lives and needs by 'monetizing' them into saleable services and products accruing vast profits in the process. In addition, these surveillance systems and control technologies can be turned towards political, rather than economic, strategies aimed at manipulating voting behaviour and other forms of democratic participation to ensure outcomes favouring the powerful and wealthy elites who benefit most from their operation. Both in regard of reclaiming economic and political 'decision rights', Zuboff sees a critical role for a wide range of experts in challenging and correcting the 'knowledge asymmetries' embedded in the highly concentrated forms of corporate power and control surveillance capitalism depends on for its functioning and reproduction. She identifies three, interrelated arenas in which the 'trust/control' dynamics inherent in surveillance capitalism can be changed in favour of citizens and communities reclaiming their economic and political decision rights: first, by repurposing expert knowledge and skill to make the public much more self-aware as to what surveillance capitalism is taking from them by way of re-asserting self-possession of our digital lives; second, by assisting individuals, groups, organizations and movements demanding the strengthening of the legal and non-statutory regulation of the mechanisms and processes through which digital exploitation routinely occurs; thirdly, by experts putting their knowledge and skill at the disposal of various private and public sector interventions aimed at enhancing competitive forces and weakening the dominant monopoly control of the high tech corporate behemoths.

Zuboff's overall strategy for 'democratizing knowledge' through reclaiming decision rights over our economic, political and social selves as 'digital agents' is paralleled by other researchers and writers who seek to nurture citizens' trust and participation in a 'discordant democracy and civil conscience 'in the face of the over weaning power and control of high tech/finance corporations. Pasquale's (2015) analysis of the 'black box society' focuses on the need to critique and refute the 'techno-libertarianism' which ideologically and politically underpins the power of the high-tech giants and the strategic institutional nexus emerging between them and the high finance giants. He further suggests that this will only be realized when there is a substantial political and cultural shift against the high tech/finance power corporate networks so that the once popular mantra of 'leaving it to the tech/fin experts' is challenged by other experts in law enforcements agencies, public service bureaucracies and civil society movements determined to 'open up the black box of surveillance and secrecy' to interrogation by a 'countervailing power' (Galbraith 1952, 1967) moving against a digital aristocracy. This analysis is echoed in Daub's (2020) deconstruction of what he calls 'Silicon Valley thinking' in which an unrestrained libertarian ideology is discursively fused with a political theory denying the legitimacy of any form of expert authority grounded in 'any large collective group having an accumulated sense of how best to do certain things' (Daub 2020: 64). Although professing a belief in 'heroic individualism' and untrammelled market competition, the corporate elite of Silicon Valley collectively think and act in ways which ensure their monopoly control is maintained in the face of all threats to its preservation. They see themselves as 'disrupters of tradition' undermining any attempts made by experts acting in the name of counter movements to challenge their status as 'keepers of an esoteric knowledge few others possess' (Daub 2020: 111) and the inalienable rights this gives them to protect others who may be led astray by countervailing sources of expertise.

All these studies cumulatively demonstrate the need for a 'countervailing theory of expert authority and governance' analytically grounded in reflexive modes of collective agency and drawing on the specialist knowledge and skills provided by expert groups and organizations prepared to put their epistemological resources and technical 'know how' to work for the benefit of a 'discordant democracy and civic conscience'. As Galbraith (1952, 1967) repeatedly emphasizes, the major source of countervailing power in modern capitalism must come from within the 'technostructure' or 'internal planning systems' of private corporations, public sector organizations and third sector agencies as their constituent expert groups collectively learn how to challenge the legitimacy of unrestrained neoliberal capitalism and the elite interests it protects. Adler's (2019) analysis of the '99 percent economy' provides a contemporary theoretical and empirical expression of the critical importance of 'expert countervailing power' in describing the very different kinds of roles experts play under the collaborative forms of working and learning made possible by democratized modes of knowledge accumulation and participative forms of strategic planning and management. As such, experts will necessarily play a pivotal role in ensuring a better balance between centralization and participation in large, complex organizations because they provide the specialist knowledge and technical skills through which functional silos and departmental fiefdoms can be broken down and replaced by more powerful 'knowledge networks and repositories' facilitating more shared and collaborative decision-making. He also provides examples of this process 'in action' within corporations such as Kaiser Permanente, IBM and Toyota in which staff experts have played a major role in reshaping real organizational conditions through building and maintaining the collaborative forms of collective working and democratic learning in which strategic needs and operational realities can be more finely adjusted and balanced.

While these more participative and reflexive organizational innovations often decay and 'run out of innovative steam', they demonstrate the possibilities that more high trust, collaborative knowledge systems and team-based working open-up for complex private and public sector organizations and the wider communities and societies in which they are located. Expert groups perform a vital role in managing the endemic tensions between 'trusting participation' and 'controlling centralization' in ways that generate more sustainable modes of reflexive collaboration, organization and governance.

7 Reflexive Expert Authority and Governance

In chapter 1, figure 1 of this book we set out the key features of the ideal typical model of 'legal rational expert authority and governance'. The latter, in summary form, has five, interrelated structural components defining its analytical distinctiveness and their explanatory implications: first, 'epistemological exclusion'; second, 'jurisdictional closure'; third, 'autonomous self-regulation'; fourth, 'elite state sponsorship'; and finally, 'institutionalized passive trust'.

We now set out, in the penultimate section of this chapter, the key features of the ideal typical model of 'reflexive expert authority and governance' and their explanatory implications for emerging forms of the latter under current and foreseeable conditions.

The legal rational model of expert authority and governance starts from the axiomatic assumption of an 'exclusionary epistemology' in which specialist knowledge and skills are systematically accumulated and protected from external influences through the construction of various cognitive and institutional 'barriers to entry' of both an informal and formal kind. While the former relates to occupational socialization and acculturation, the latter are more a matter of legal and administrative regulatory processes embedded in professional and quasi-professional accreditation or licensing in which an underlying 'meritocratic ideology' plays a central legitimating role (Taylor 2019; Sandel 2020).

However, the ideal typical model of reflexive authority and governance, in stark contrast, is analytically anchored in an **'inclusionary epistemology'** in which specialist knowledge and skills are opened-up and made much more widely available to the lay public for their edification and scrutiny. Cognitive and institutional barriers to meaningful 'civic participation' in the epistemological processes through which specialist knowledge and skills are generated, learnt and assessed are gradually diluted in favour of more collegiate, collaborative and coproduced modes of knowledge acquisition and application (Clarke et al. 2007; Ferlie et al. 2013; Newman 2013; Crouch 2016; Eyal 2019). This also logically implies that the presumption of a clear and consistent dividing line between 'science' and 'politics' or 'expert' and 'lay' understanding can no longer be made as the axiomatic starting point for theorizing contemporary forms of expert authority and governance.

Yet, as Eyal (2019:145) reminds us, this 'conceptual bottom-line commitment' to 'participatory science and "hybrid forums" composed of experts and lay people, who put their trust in the foregrounding of uncertainty [must] reckon with the inconvenient fact that openness, inclusion, transparency, and participation do not, by themselves, secure legitimacy'. Any substantial and significant movement towards the inclusionary epistemology which is the conceptual loadstone for the ideal type of model of reflexive authority and governance must recognize that a 'new consensus' around expert knowledge and its legitimate application must be constructed and that the latter is likely to be fraught with all sorts of seemingly intractable issues and disputes. Again, as Eyal (2019:145–146) concludes 'legitimacy depends on the ability to bring reasoned debate to an end, or at least a temporary halt (while keeping its potential continuation in sight). The inconvenient fact is that participatory and inclusive hybrid forums lack mechanisms for doing so, or they are extremely vulnerable to strategies which exploit the weaknesses of whatever mechanism they possess'.

This takes us to the second conceptual component of reflexive expert authority and governance in its ideal typical form – that is, the shift form 'jurisdictional closure' to **'jurisdictional consensus'.** Here we are focusing on the work task domains in which the specialist knowledge and skills of experts is deployed and the organizational structures and technologies which link them together to form integrated work units equipped to carry out complex projects and problem-solving. Moves towards civic or participatory epistemologies logically demand more 'trans domain' modes of working in which experts pool and share their knowledge and skills, both between themselves and with the lay communities in which they operate, as a precursor to achieving enhanced collective learning and understanding in highly uncertain decision-making situations (Blowers, Boersema and Martin 2005; Fischer 2003; Elstub and McLaverty 2014). Of course, organizational and institutional politics will continue to shape and reshape the actual hybrid modes of expert working that will empirically emerge 'on the ground' and the processes through which expert inter-domain jurisdictions are negotiated and justified. But the model of reflexive authority and governance insists that the role and legitimacy of 'experts and 'expertise' can no longer be defined and realized through the 'politics of jurisdictional closure' but now crucially depends on a continuing quest to achieve a workable consensus around overlapping and shared modes of specialist working that will inevitably change as the context in which they are located changes. However, this requirement for consensus-based jurisdictional work organization must also accept the much higher levels of contestability and instability which they necessarily entail as the world of defensive jurisdictional closure gives way to one in which the latter is both unacceptable and unattainable because it cannot deal with the nature and scale of the challenges, we face in the twenty-first century.

Analytically combining 'epistemological inclusion' and 'jurisdictional consensus' gives the third conceptual component of the ideal type of reflexive expert authority and governance – that is, **'embedded management and regulation'** which rejects the logic of autonomous self-management and regulation dominant under the legal rational model outlined in chapter one. Embedded management and regulation insist that the legitimacy of expert knowledge and the interventionist strategies and technologies which they facilitate can no longer depend upon 'experts policing themselves'. Instead of expert occupational groups, organizations and associations being the sole, or at least primary, arbiter of their performance in an ethical, technical or legal sense, embedded forms of expert governance and regulation give a much-expanded role to external, community-based modes of scrutiny and evaluation which often critique and reject the insularity and narrowness of performance review mechanisms where the expert remains 'on top'. No longer prepared to accept, passively and paternalistically, the 'immaculate conception' or 'crown jewels' model of expert authority in which claims to expertise and its performance-enhancing properties can be accepted with little by way of 'external checks and balances', these guarantees are now subjected to interrogation by the stakeholder communities they are meant to serve. What Oreskes (2019: 247–248) calls 'transformative interrogation within agnostic fields' goes significantly beyond expert domains of specialist knowledge and skill to encompass, intellectually and institutionally, much wider spheres of communal activity and practice in which stakeholder values and interests are taken much more seriously into account. Embedded expert management and regulation moves beyond the corridors of elite power and control to include collective voices and opinions often drowned out, or at least marginalized, within established expert governance structures and the proprietary interests which they protect.

Yet, there is no getting away from the fact that a move towards embedded management and regulation is likely to prove discomforting, not to say discombobulating, for most expert occupational groups and organizations who now find themselves in a situation where they must be much more accommodating, even welcoming, to external checks and balances restricting their autonomy and control. Under the legal rational ideal type of expert authority, experts can rely on relatively abstract, remote and formalized governance structures and regulative systems in which the political and administrative practices which they necessarily entail for their practical operation are hidden from public view and challenge (Ezzamel and Reed 2006). Embedded management and regulation logically demand, as a precondition for securing and retaining 'practical expert legitimacy', regulatory mechanisms and processes which are much closer to – spatially, politically and organizationally – the civic communities in which they operate and the representative agencies through which they mobilize public opinion over issues which matter to them. Governance and regulatory arrangements under the legal rational model of expert authority are logically driven by ostensibly objective 'efficiency and effectiveness criteria' relating to how principals can control their agents within 'low trust', market-based exchanges at minimum cost and disruption (Ezzamel and Reed 2006). However, the reflexive ideal type works with an entirely different 'risk calculus' in which the instrumental rationality dominating the legal rational model gives way to a substantive rationality in which long-term, high trust relationships between all stakeholders gradually emerge from the 'transformative interrogation within agnostic fields' (Oreskes 2019: 247–248) in which the latter are continually engaged as they struggle to come to terms with high risk, complex problem solving under extreme uncertainty. Expert groups and organizations are an essential and critical component of the interrogative deliberation processes through which collective decision-making occurs, but they must be prepared to accept the additional external regulatory restraints that the latter imposes on their internal operation and governance.

This model of reflexive expert authority and governance is not premised on some utopian or idealistic premise of a 'politics free' decision-making process in which a universal ideological commitment to collective values and interests eradicates, or at least marginalizes, sectional divisions and conflicts to a point where they all but disappear. Instead, 'politics' remains at the analytical core and substantive base of the reflexive ideal type in that it actively embraces the social reality of contestation between opposing interests and values as indelibly shaping the 'trust/control dynamics' underpinning expert authority and the mechanism through which it is legitimated and regulated. It is grounded in the logical premise that the legitimacy struggles in which expert groups and organizations are necessarily engaged cannot be democratically conducted or resolved unless experts accept the need to share their expertise with others through communal dialogue and collective deliberation in which a far wider range of voices and opinions are actively welcomed into the decision-making arena than is normally the case under status quo conditions.

Prioritizing embedded modes of reflexive expert management and regulation logically leads on to the fourth analytical element of the ideal type – that is, the transition from 'elite state sponsorship' towards **'pluralistic stakeholder sponsorship'** in which governance regimes dominated by closed networks of ruling groups and the 'passive trust' they rely on gives way to proactive support and engagement on the part of multiple stakeholder groups and the experts working with them. While the former legitimates its authority through prioritizing hierarchy, meritocracy, stability and inequality, the latter contends that an embedded mode of expert management and regulation can only become a practical reality if it emerges from a fundamental shift in value commitments where collegiality, participation, engagement and equality become the guiding principles. Rather than be seen as the defenders and protectors of privilege, exclusivity and impunity, expert groups and organizations are reimagined and repurposed as collaborators in collective mobility projects aimed at translating democratic ideals into practical collective action focused on making elite political and economic decision-makers accountable to the publics they serve and the core values which any democratic polity worthy of the name should embody.

Overshadowing much of the exposition and analysis provided in this book is a growing awareness that the 'crisis in expert authority' is an integral part of a larger 'crisis in elitist managerial politics.' This conjunctural crisis in elite and expert authority can be interpreted as the cumulative outcome of successive failures on the part of both groups to deliver on the promises of economic prosperity, social mobility and cultural integration made to an increasingly sceptical and disillusioned public distrustful of its political leaders' capacity to govern on their behalf (Runciman 2013; Stiglitz 2013; Seymour 2014; Glaser 2018; Koppl 2018; Babones 2018; Applebaum 2020; Taylor 2019; Davies 2020a; Frank 2020; Bickerton and Accetti 2021). Much of what might loosely be called the 'populist critique' of elitist managerial/expert politics emerges out of and ideologically exploits this increasing public consciousness of repeated, 'across the board' failure by political elites and their technocratic advisors to deal effectively with the escalating risks and threats which the general public now routinely confronts. Rather than prompt a serious reappraisal of how elitist managerial politics operates and the results it produces, this succession of mounting failures – to, for example, reduce persistent and widening socio-economic inequality or to integrate health and social care or to deal effectively with a pandemic – has directly reinforced the retreat into even more closed and exclusive forms of political decision-making and governing in which 'the people' play little or no part. Elites and experts hide behind defensive institutional barriers and esoteric organizational enclaves that make it even more difficult for ordinary members of society and polity to access the decision-making arenas which govern their lives. Babones (2018: 38) captures the polemical core of this populist critique of elitist managerial politics when he suggests that 'the authority of experts and the money of the rich ensure that liberal points of view are always prominently aired in political debates, but liberals as a group are never numerically strong enough to win elections under universal suffrage'. He then proceeds to argue that the insidious 'new authoritarianism' of the expert class has been directly challenged by the 'populist purgative' of Trump, Brexit and the International Refugee Crisis.

One of the fundamental errors of this kind of analysis is that it ignores the simple but axiomatic truth that expert knowledge and skill are prerequisites for the survival and functioning, much less flourishing, of any modern society, economy and polity facing complex or 'wicked problems' in which the 'decision stakes' are very high indeed (Brown 2015). While the threat of technocratic rule by illegitimate and unaccountable experts is real enough, it cannot be resisted, much less assuaged, by denying 'expertise' any kind of legitimate authority or strategic role and placing collective trust in the 'will of the people' and those political leaders who purport to speak in their name without any regard to the extensive plurality and diversity of values and interests inherent to modernity.

As Brown (2014: 57) contends 'citizens must trust experts [but] their trust need not be blind. Lay citizens and their representatives need effective opportunities to hold experts to account'. Drawing on the pragmatism of Dewey, Harbermas' model of deliberative democracy, and policy studies literature, Brown outlines an analytical framework for identifying the institutional architecture, discursive norms, communicative principles and political processes through which pluralistic stakeholder sponsorship of expert authority can be mobilized and sustained. This framework specifies a 'dual track model' of deliberative democracy built on Habermas' distinction between 'track one' of formal state institutions and professional bureaucracies and 'track two' of the informal public sphere of civil society empowered organizations and movements. The critical role of the latter is to discursively and practically challenge expert authority in institutional arenas and organizational locales in which horizontal rather than vertical power is emphasized and where non-professional, 'experiential expertise' is, formally and informally, given voice and support from civil society representative groups and agencies. Thus, 'lay judgements of expert authority need to employ both epistemic and social criteria' (Brown 2014: 57) so that the legitimacy of expert authority does not depend on 'unquestioning acceptance', but the 'tacit trust' based on lay experience given so much emphasis in Collins et al. (2009, 2020).

Finally, Brown (2014) outlines a typology or roles that 'trustworthy experts' might play, particularly when dealing with the high risk/high stakes decision-making discussed earlier on in this chapter. Adapting his typology somewhat, we might analytically identify four role types: the 'pure expert', the 'expert arbiter', the 'expert advocate' and the 'expert broker'. This envisages a spectrum of possibilities beginning with epistemic expertise in the case of the 'pure expert' and moving through to a much greater emphasis on social and political expertise in the case of the 'expert broker'. However, none of the four role types can be viable without the trust-building and reinforcing practices on which any form of reflexive authority and governance depends for its legitimacy and authenticity.

Indeed, this takes us to the fifth and final analytical component of the ideal type of reflexive expert authority and governance – that is, the foundational importance of **proactive, negotiated trust** as opposed to the passive, institutionalized trust underpinning the legal rational model. Throughout the analysis developed in this chapter we have repeatedly returned to the centrality of proactive, negotiated trust to the legitimacy and viability of expert authority under the reflexive model. This emphasizes the reality of the inherently contested, provisional and contingent nature of negotiated trust in expert authority under the analytical precepts on which the reflexive model is logically constructed and justified. Insofar as experts are primarily 'mediators' – that is, their primary role is as mediators or brokers 'between established stocks of knowledge, new developments and urgent demands for action' (Stehr and Grundmann 2011: xi) – then they are only able to fulfil this generic function if their expertise is trusted by those who depend on it to make decisions ranging from highly complex strategic policy issues to everyday routine problem solving. However, this implicit public trust in explicit or tacit expertise is never unconditional or universal; by making complexity manageable experts reduce anxiety generating uncertainty for the rest of society, but they can only do this if 'trust becomes a central component of the social relationship between expert and client' (Stehr and Grundmann 2011: 43).

By establishing their credibility and reliability within society, experts reproduce legitimacy for their authority and status as trustworthy interpreters and mediators utilizing their specialist knowledge and skill to identify the options available to decision makers facing difficult and often poorly understood problems. Yet, by setting the decision-making context and agenda in this way, they inevitably become key players in the political processes that coalesce around the issues which the former frame; as such, they play a pivotal role in 'negotiating order' by delicately navigating their course through contending interests and values. Any attempt to maintain a cast iron separation between 'science' and 'politics' is likely to founder in this situation where the experts have no option but to pay the entry price for becoming the key actors in decision-making contexts likely to have profound consequences for societies and their members.

Under these kind of conditions – where trust must be negotiated, credibility won, and legitimacy fought for in an ongoing political struggle – reliance on institutionalized or 'passive trust' is no longer a viable option for reflexive forms of expert authority and governance in conditions where many of the support mechanisms shoring up the former have become corroded and weakened. As interpreters and mediators of specialist knowledges and skills, experts 'use the leeway that exists between the production of knowledge and the need for advice, between the uncertainty of scientific facts and the need to take action, between the release of scientific research and knowledge and the urgent day-to-day business' (Stehr and

Grundmann 2011: 118). They can no longer fall back on institutionalized hierarchies of trust and control because the internal dynamics and external context of the latter have moved way beyond those hierarchies' legitimacy and authority.

The five key structural features of the ideal type of reflexive expert authority are set out in Figure 2 below and offer, in a logically and conceptually extreme form, a directly opposed configuration to the ideal type of neo-Weberian or legal rational expert authority specified in chapter one, Figure 1 of this book. Any empirical form of expert authority will consist of a selective recombination of elements drawn from each of these logically contrasting types, depending on the conditions under which they operate, and the strategic choices made by powerful and influential actors facing the latter. However, the trajectory of the analysis provided in this book very strongly suggests that there is an underlying movement towards hybrid forms of expert authority in which the conceptual elements associated with the ideal type of reflexive authority are likely to become stronger and more pronounced, while those associated with the legal rational type are diluted and weakened. Nevertheless, there is no 'historical promise or guarantee' of movement in this direction because the complex interplay between 'agency' and 'structure' generates a dynamically moving socio-historical context in which several possible outcomes can emerge and find traction.

Figure 2: Reflexive Expert Authority

---

(1) An inclusionary epistemology in which as wide a range of stakeholders' technical and experiential knowledge as practically possible is taken seriously into account within the collective deliberative process

(2) A search for jurisdictional consensus in which experts operate across a range of working domains while sharing their knowledge and skills with other experts and lay personnel as they attempt to work towards agreement over decision-making agendas and options, as well as over the criteria on which judgements between the latter are to be made

(3) Embedded management and regulation in which epistemic communities working within and across jurisdictional working domains must be open to scrutiny by and made accountable to the lay communities in which they are located

(4) Pluralistic stakeholder sponsorship in which publics, states and experts are brought together within institutional forms and organizational locales dedicated to realizing the potential for collective learning and collaborative decision-making when dealing with highly complex and uncertain problems

(5) Proactive negotiated trust relations in which the core interpretive and mediating role of experts is governed by regulative conventions and norms prioritizing openness, transparency and consensus-building as precursors for effective decision-making in high-risk situations.

---

8 Conclusion

In this chapter we have set out the key conceptual features of reflexive expert authority in ideal typical terms and contrasted it with the Neo-Weberian legal rational type outlined in chapter one. Although substantive forms of expert authority will display combinations and re-combinations of elements drawn from both types, we have also argued that these are likely to exhibit stronger features of the reflexive form. We think this is the case to the extent that the latter is much better equipped to handle the competing challenges and pressures that legitimation struggles over expertise in the twenty-first century will continue to present to societies in which high risk decision-making becomes more commonplace. In turn, this will also require a shift in the 'trust/control' dynamics of reflexive expert authority in which trust-building under conditions of increasing complexity and uncertainty is a prerequisite for effectively engaging publics, experts, and states in expert practices to generate collective learning and collaborative decision-making.

However, a substantial move in the direction of reflexive expert authority doesn't solve or remove the fundamental dilemma or conundrum which lies at the core of legitimation struggles over expertise – that is, the structural tension between public acceptance of the primacy to be afforded to expert knowledge in decision-making situations and public trust that experts will not misuse their discretionary powers for their own or others' advantage. Expert authority, whatever form it takes, is about exercising power and control in decision-making contexts which, by their very nature, are open to 'multiple authorities' and the 'expert systems' that they rely on to justify and implement the decisions they take – or don't take. Expert systems and the technologies they rely on are designed and operated by specialists on behalf of elite groups to, directly and remotely, monitor and control ordinary people in their working and domestic lives. The former has a built-in tendency to favour remote control logics that disembody and decontextualize 'local experience and knowledge' in ways which make it amenable to manipulation and closure in the furtherance of other objectives such as surveillance, resocialization or profit (Beck, Giddens and Lash 1994). Yet, this dynamic of remote control fatally weakens the generalized trust it needs to cultivate and sustain the acceptance and stability it craves if its legitimacy is to be secured.

Reflexive expert authority significantly moves the trust/control dynamic more in favour of localized trust-building and away from remote control, but 'openness, inclusion, transparency, and participation do not, by themselves, secure legitimacy' (Eyal 2019: 145). As Eyal (2019) also argues, making expert decision-making processes more accessible and amenable to public participation runs all sorts of additional risks, including increasing the influence of powerful groups and organizations who gain legitimate entry to the former on an 'openness/inclusive ticket' with the aim and means of turning them in directions they favour rather than for the public good. Sectional interests and values are given extended opportunities to make their presence felt in more reflexive and participative modes of expert decision-making and they can effectively take control of the process by undermining the credibility of and trust in those who supposedly speak in the name of 'expertise'.

In this respect, support for a move towards more reflexive forms of expert authority does not expunge the dilemma which lies at the core of the neo-Weberian legal rational model – that is, how to ensure the accountability and legitimacy of expertise to the publics which it serves, while simultaneously ensuring that the latter has sufficient autonomy and capacity to do its job of "'bringing the bad news" [and] teaching others how to "recognize inconvenient facts'" (Eyal 2019: 149).

In the following chapter we consider how this core 'trust/control' dilemma might be handled under different trajectories and forms of future expert authority and governance as they take shape against the background context of contestation, instability and uncertainty emerging from our analysis so far.

Chapter 7: Expert Futures

1 Introduction

'Business as usual' for the established approach to expert authority is no longer viable, analytically or substantively, because the socio-historical context in which it was promulgated has changed dramatically in ways that severely weaken its core theoretical premises and empirical claims. In particular, the assumption that institutionalized trust could and would continue to legitimate legal rational expert authority in ways that protected it from sustained threats and challenges to its coherence and stability cannot be sustained in a world in which 'multiple authorities' have the capacity to mount extended campaigns against its authenticity and veracity. Established modes of expert authority are 'in the firing line' and will continue to be so for the foreseeable future. They can no longer hide behind an institutional carapace of taken-for-granted ideological conventions and structural protections which attempt to laminate the 'politics of expertise' in a veneer of scientism and technocracy.

Yet, even the alternative models of expert authority which have been developed in response to the perceived weaknesses of the orthodox model, such as the reflexive mode we have outlined at some length in the previous chapter of this book, will continue to struggle with the 'trust/control' dilemma or dynamic which is to be found at the centre of any theorization of such a complex phenomenon. Thus, the various scenarios of 'expert futures' which we develop in this chapter will be forced to confront the structural contradictions and dynamic tensions between 'expert control' and 'lay trust' that lies at the heart of any socio-political process striving to legitimate expert knowledge and skill in a world of multiple and competing authorities.

In this chapter, we will review four scenarios which map out rather different 'futures' for expert authority in a world in which it is widely accepted 'experts alone should not determine the purposes for which their expertise is used' (Brown 2014: 57) but also the reality that 'at some point, expertise inevitably depends not on persuasion but authority' (Brown 2014: 59). First, we will look at attempts to rehabilitate 'meritocracy' as the ideological and institutional cornerstone of a revivified conception of expert authority in which 'the aristocracy of talent' (Wooldridge 2021) is rebuilt on solid social and ethical foundations. Secondly, we examine the vision of an expert future in which 'technopopulism' has become the dominant ideological and political strategy for wining and retaining power in contemporary representative democracies (Bickerton and Accetti 2021). Thirdly, we assess the emergence of 'civic' or 'connective' professionalism as a potential hybrid strategy

https://doi.org/10.1515/9783110734911-008

for redefining and reworking the future occupational cultures and organizational architectures through which expert work is legitimated (Clarke et al. 2007; Noordegraaf 2015, 2020). Finally, we turn to the concept of 'critical elitism' as it develops a model of expert of authority in which contestation between a wide range of expert institutions, civil society organizations, and democratic movements – collectively striving to fashion a 'dynamic consensus' over how expertise should be legitimately authorized and deployed in a pluralistic democracy – emerges as the hallmark of twenty-first century expertise (Moore 2017).

2 Meritocracy Recrudescent

We have already seen that 'meritocracy' has been subject to a series of excoriating critiques and attacks of late which fundamentally challenge its intellectual coherence and institutional capacity to legitimate unequal access to and control over expert knowledge and skills through occupational and organizational mechanisms guaranteeing 'equality of opportunity' and 'fairness of outcomes' (Taylor 2019; Sandel 2020). Going much further than earlier critiques focused around the 'latent' as opposed to 'manifest' functioning of meritocratic ideology and practice – that is, their actual role in promoting and protecting structures of inequality rather than opening them up to genuine competition and increasing opportunities for social mobility (Young 1958) – recent critiques have concentrated more on meritocracy's necessary connection with 'credentialism' and its strategic role in perpetuating elite power structures closed off from any kind of democratic scrutiny and accountability. They see credentialism as an integrative mechanism through which professional elites legitimate their occupational power and social status by systemically linking educational attainment and career progression together. 'Winners' are awarded the top jobs based on their educational performance and 'losers' are justifiably denied access to these elite positions due to their failure to secure the necessary credentials which entry into elite circles and networks requires (Sandel 2020; Frank 2020). By ideologically cloaking elite professional self interest in the meritocratic discourse of 'equality of opportunity' and 'fair competition', credentialism makes the securing of high-level educational qualifications a political and moral justification for the perpetuation of socio-economic inequality and cultural division. What Sandel (2020: 104) labels 'the diploma divide' generates a 'relentless credentialism [driving] working class voters towards populist and nationalist parties and deepened the divide between those with and those without a university degree', as well as legitimating a belief in a mode of technocratic governance overriding any residual concern with democratic niceties.

Taylor (2019: 210–211) takes this critique further by insisting that 'expertise is inherently undemocratic' because it necessarily excludes most citizens from its deliberations and, over time, gives rise to an elite class based on the principle of meritocracy 'which means the rule of a class of educated or otherwise advantaged people while most citizens are frozen out'. Thus, educational attainment becomes a 'sorting mechanism' whereby 'the best' go on to the top-level elite jobs in business, government, media and communication while 'the rest' are consigned to middle and lower-level positions. But within this 'technocratic-meritocratic' approach to educational attainment and occupational allocation, 'everybody has a chance' because the performance criteria for success are clearly stipulated and potentially achievable by all those who enter the educational system. By institutionally and ideologically tying credentialism and meritocracy together in this way, expert status and authority can be legitimated on the presumption that it's an outcome of a competitive process in which there is equality of access and mobility to the extent that it transparently rewards those who perform best in a rule-based and objectively measured system of educational attainment.

Much of the analysis and critique of technocratically-meritocratically legitimated expert authority is anticipated in Collins' book The Credential Society (2019), originally published in 1979, but at a time when suspicion of, if not hostility to, expert authority was only beginning to gather political pace and cultural momentum which rapidly accelerated in the following decades. His book provides a detailed historical and sociological analysis of what he calls the 'credential system' in the US between the mid-nineteenth and mid-twentieth centuries in which the rapid expansion and institutionalization of the tertiary education sector is closely linked to the ethos or ideology of 'technocracy'. The latter, he continues, legitimates the massive 'proliferation of professional and technical degrees and their control over specialized work enclaves' (Collins 2019: 117) thus establishing a very high degree of integration between a system of educational stratification and occupational stratification which is structurally, materially, and culturally advantageous to the professional, managerial, and expert classes. In this way, Collins (2019: 120) isolates the growth of the educational credential system as the 'most direct agent' generating the expansion of professional and other related forms of expert occupational labour and the very powerful occupational associations and elite groups which have emerged to promote and protect their collective interests and values.

These professional and related expert occupational groups, he opines, have come to be regarded as 'the saviours of the modern world' (Collins 2019: 175), even if they sometimes fall somewhat short of this idealized vision through 'professional hubris' as a recurring organizational dynamic (Tourish 2019) or in the form of systemic 'professional resistance' to external scrutiny and accountability (Picard, Durocher and Gendron 2021). Nevertheless, such professional/expert bodies and organizations have deployed political and cultural power very effectively in defence of their 'monopoly and self-governing rights by getting the force of the state to license them and back up their collective authority' (Collins 2019: 177). They have also successfully engaged in a series of sophisticated 'mystification strategies' (see chapter three of this book) in which various forms of occupational secrecy, emotional manipulation, and discursive dissembling play a central role in protecting their autonomy and authority. Overall, he concludes, professionalization through meritocracy and credentialism 'is an extension of the age-old struggles of self-interested groups using refinements of traditional tactics' (Collins 2019: 180). While recognizing the reality of professional/expert altruism as embodied both in ethical codes and occupational cultures/practices, Collins' sociohistorical analysis continually emphasizes the strategic role of meritocracy and credentialism in providing the integrated stratification mechanism whereby expert groups secure the patronage of the state in licensing their monopolistic control over critical jurisdictional domains within the workplace.

Although Collins (2019: 253–270) notes that the credential system which has come to dominate American education and employment has undergone a series of rolling 'mini-crises' since the 1960s in which the 'mobility guarantees' underpinning it began to look increasingly uncertain, if not threadbare, its ideological and institutional resilience should not be underestimated. Dismantling, or even reforming, the credential system will remain a distant possibility if institutional and organizational politics around current forms of 'positional property' continue to favour the preservation of 'educational barriers to entry' – particularly for high status/reward specialist occupations and the hierarchically stratified occupational systems over which they preside.

Goodhart (2020) brings the critique of the meritocratic/credential system and the technocratic ideology legitimating it right up to date in his historical analysis of the 'rise of the cognitive class' and the various ways in which it has come to establish political and cultural domination over both education and work in post-industrial societies. He distinguishes 'meritocratic selection systems' and 'meritocratic societies' on the basis of technical/practical necessity as opposed to political/social division; while the former is a functional necessity in any post-industrial political economy, the latter remains a major source of stratified inequality in that it systemically and amorally excludes the majority of citizens from effective participation in the decision-making arenas that determine their, and their offspring's, life chances. Effectively managing the endemic tension between technocratically-driven 'inequality of esteem' and democratically driven 'equality of esteem' or between 'economic inequality' and 'political equality' is the fundamental problem for all post-industrial societies.

Identifying three types of work in post-industrial societies – 'head work', 'hand work' and 'heart work' – Goodhart (2020) explores the structural mechanisms and socio-historical processes through which 'head work' – in which specialized knowledge and cognitive skills are valorised as being more functionally critical and culturally prestigious than craft skills or emotional intelligence – has come to dominate political debate and the policies followed by successive governments. Nevertheless, recent social and economic trends clearly indicate that 'hand' and 'heart' work are becoming more necessary and relevant as revealed during the Covid-19 crisis and our increasing collective reliance on 'key workers' who often lack the meritocratic credentials prioritized by the professional classes and other expert elites who have shaped social and political debates in recent years.

His analysis of 'the rise of the cognitive class', and the mechanisms through which it's social reproduced, assigns explanatory primacy to the complex ways in which educational and occupational stratification became closely aligned in all industrial societies from the mid-nineteenth century onwards and how the latter became institutionally and culturally embedded in post-industrial societies during the twentieth century. He recognizes that the 'respective roles of professional associations, universities and the state in certifying membership of the cognitive class played out differently in different countries' (Goodhart 2020: 38). But the underlying dynamic and the trajectory it generated institutionalized the power and authority of scientific knowledge and cognitive skills over experiential knowledge and practical skills to the detriment of wide-ranging abilities, capacities, and talents which could not or would not conform to the epistemological and technical hierarchies which the former imposed. The emergence of post-industrial political economies and societies in the latter half of the twentieth century structurally reinforced the changes which had produced 'the cognitive class', to the extent that they 'hollowed out' labour markets based on 'hand' and 'heart' work while buttressing the elite status of 'knowledge work' and those qualified and smart enough to do it. By depoliticizing technocratic rule in ways which seemed to make democratic politics redundant, political elites were disengaging or withdrawing from the 'rough and tumble' of everyday political life and turning governing over to a professional/expert elite who weren't subjected to the usual checks and balances associated with representative democracy (Mair 2013: 96 – 98).

Yet, Goodhart (2020: Part 4) argues that the political tide has begun to turn decisively against this meritocratic-technocratic ideology and politics as its inherent limitations and failings become more and more apparent under the combined pressures of widespread socio-economic dislocation and cultural alienation generated by digitalized Taylorism and the rise of populism. While these developments are extremely distressing and uncomfortable for many, they provide a much more favourable socio-political context for the recalibration of 'head', 'hand'

and 'heart' work so that much broader, more inclusive and participative conceptions of 'knowledge' and 'skill' come to frame contemporary debates over the future of work in twenty-first century post-industrial societies. Only this way can the 'institutional stranglehold' of meritocratic credentialism and the technocratic ideology and politics that legitimated it be broken.

Although meritocratic credentialism has taken a lot of 'critical fire' in recent times, there are those who are more than prepared to defend it – both as a ruling ideology and a dominant regulative practice. Wooldridge (2021: 16) offers a defence of meritocracy as a global, even 'ruling', ideology which has shaped the organization of modern society since the nineteenth century in relation to its status as a 'protean idea' 'allowing people to rise as high as their talents will take them'. He distinguishes between different forms of meritocracy – 'political', 'economic', 'technocratic' and 'academic' – but insists they are all equally open to 'self-correction' in that they can prevent themselves from degenerating into closed and self-perpetuating elites through moderating counter measures based on regulation, competition and legislation. Indeed, he maintains that this is exactly what is happening currently in that the danger of the meritocratic elite 'hardening into an aristocracy which passes on its privileges to its children by investing heavily in education, and which, because of its sustained success, looks down on the rest of society' (Wooldridge 2021: 17) is being counteracted by increased emphasis on market incentives, selective state financial support, targeted affirmative action, upgrading vocational education, and 're-moralizing the meritocratic ideal' so that governing elites are reminded of their continuing responsibility to maintain merit-based accessibility. In this way, he concludes, the only viable mechanism for re-establishing the integrity of meritocracy as a universal principle of educational stratification, occupational allocation, and social mobility is to overhaul and reset 'the meritocratic machine' by making it function properly according to its founding principles and ensuring it remains responsive to wider political and social concerns over its innate tendency to degenerate into a domination structure protecting the self-interests of a self-perpetuating elite. Meritocratic renewal is a necessary precondition for meritocratic survival, and the former can only be realized if the 'machine's' innate failings are fully recognized and dealt with through corrective action that restores its moral virtues against populist, communitarian and libertarian critiques. Thus, his call for both a 'better' and 'wiser' meritocracy is intended to revivify the credentials of meritocracy as the primary organizing principle for rewarding talent and achievement in which 'the "winners" of the meritocratic competition have much more of a sense of responsibility to the wider society – and that the "losers" have alternative paths to dignity and self-fulfilment' (Wooldridge 2021: 376).

In much the same vein as Wooldridge (2021) offers a defence of a meritocracy as a ruling ideology, legitimating the organization and governance of a competitive struggle to reach the top in which genuine 'talent' can succeed – even if with a re-newed sense of 'noblesse obliges' suited to modern conditions – Kirkpatrick et al. (2021) develop a parallel case for credentialism as providing a resilient and adaptive 'regulatory ecology' grounded in formal rationality and procedural fairness. They insist that the 'certification ecosystem' on which professionalized modes of occupational regulation continue to depend has been sufficiently robust and effective – at least in the US and by empirical extension in other advanced political economies as well – to minimize the inroads made by neo-liberalization into its capacity to generate and sustain labour market shelters for occupational groups claiming a significant degree of autonomy in and control over their work performance. Thus, they see the continued combined strength of professional association formation, voluntary certification programmes and occupational licensing, supported by the state and other key stakeholders, as providing robust evidence for the continuation of a dominant pattern of expert occupational regulation in which formalized, legal and quasi-legal, credentialism plays the central role.

They explain the continuing resilience of 'certification credentialism' in terms of a complex interaction between a range of variables including path-dependency, institutional inertia, stakeholder self-interests and, echoing Wooldridge's (2021) analysis, the turn towards 'home grown talent' and the collective investment in enhanced skills training and professional development which it requires. However, they ultimately turn to a combination of 'historical legacy and switching costs' as providing an overall explanation for the continued power of occupational credentialism and the authority it bestows on occupational groups relying on specialist expertise as their primary route to jurisdictional closure and the material and symbolic rewards it conveys and protects. Neo-liberalization may have severely weakened trade unionism and collective bargaining but professional regulation, embedded within a certification ecosystem that continues to support the latter's legitimacy and efficacy, has, at least so far, proved to be a 'much tougher nut for it to crack'!

In previous discussion we have argued that Kirkpatrick at al. (2021) have a very limited, not to say restricted, analytical focus on professional/expert regulative authorization in relation to its formal accreditation and functional adaptation; any interest in the substantive rationality on which the latter depends – that is, its core values, symbols, rituals and routines – is conspicuous by its absence. However, even if we were to take their, and Wooldridge's, defence of meritocratic credentialism at face value, another fundamental problem remains – both analyses only provide support for what Turner (2014: 7–10) characterizes as a **'process-based legitimacy'** which leaves untouched the substantive, **'output-based legitimacy'** issues around which most of the controversy has raged in recent years. A defence of meritocratic credentialism relying primarily on a functional or procedural rationality – in which bureaucratic structures and systems are relied on to absorb 'trust-based' legitimacy controversies by neutralizing them through administrative norms and rules technically guaranteeing procedural equity – is unlikely to prove that effective when, for 'users of expert claims, including experts themselves, there are issues of trust [relating to] what is called output legitimacy as distinct from process legitimacy' (Turner 2014: 9). 'Output legitimacy' essentially revolves around doubts and uncertainties which users and other experts articulate concerning the specialist knowledge and skills that 'these experts' are assumed to hold and deploy when dealing with the vast array of problems which they are expected to solve. Diplomas, certificates, rules and regulations may provide some solace in the face of 'process legitimacy' challenges but they are much less likely to prove sufficiently reassuring when 'output legitimacy' controversies concerning the innate trust-worthiness of expert claims and the interventions they authorize are increasing in magnitude and intensity. Credentialism is not a functional substitute for trust-based 'outcome legitimacy'.

Indeed, the technocratic disguise which meritocratic credentialism often cloaks itself in can prove to be much more receptive to 'going into partnership' with those ideological systems and political movements, such as populism and neo-liberalism, which have been most virulently hostile and condemnatory in relation to the former's credibility and viability. We consider the implications of the emergence of these ideological-cum-political hybrids for the legitimation of expert authority in the following section.

3 Technopopulism

Bickerton and Accetti (2021) provide the most theoretically well-developed analysis of 'technopopulism', but it is anticipated in earlier publications such as Hurt and Lipschutz (2016), Davies (2018), Callison and Manfredi (2020) and Vormann and Weinman (2021). All these texts identify the emergence of hybrid ideological formations and political movements which have made significant impacts on the organization and conduct of legitimacy struggles around power, authority and status in contemporary political economies and societies over the last decade or so. These hybrid formations and movements are also seen to have major implications for the range and diversity of the legitimation strategies through which political and expert elites have come together in various networks and coalitions in order to defend or enhance their 'hard' and 'soft' power resources in the face of increasing economic and political instability. In this respect, they seem to generate a very different political, social and cultural context in which experts, both collectively and individually, must navigate with instrumentation which has to be thoroughly recalibrated in order 'to get them through' the much more threatening conditions they must cope with now and in the future.

We have briefly discussed Bickerton and Accetti's (2021) book in a previous chapter, but we now need to consider their analysis in a little more depth as we attempt to develop a scenario of an expert future which stands in stark contrast to the somewhat complacent, if not myopic, scenario of 'refurbish and reset' outlined in the previous section. For Bickerton and Accetti (2021), 'technopopulism' is an organizing logic followed by political parties seeking electoral success in representative democracies in which technocratic and populist discursive topes and political organizations are combined to form more inclusive electoral strategies encompassing a wide range of economic, political and social interests. Although it can take different forms, technopopulism is a strategy which claims to represent 'the people' as a whole and to deploy 'expertise' in the furtherance of their collective values and interests as a unified community in a highly fragmented and fissured world. Rather than *replacing* more conventional and established political logics, it *superimposes* itself on them from above and below through a combination of tactics encompassing elite-led takeover and follower-led entryism in which social media and digital technologies play a pivotal role.

As technopopulism becomes more evident across a range of European and North American representative democracies, so its medium and long-term implications for expert power and authority grow in significance and scale. Increasingly, expert occupational groups and their representative organizations find themselves drawn into an ideological embrace and political movement in which they are tied in much more explicitly and closely into 'projects' and 'causes', rather than 'policies' and 'issues', dominated by 'techniques of theatre and spectacle' (Bickerton and Accetti 2021: 148–153). Rather than providing objective technical advice based on rigorous research and analysis, experts find themselves now operating and mediating between governing elites and the electorate as they 'sell' the latter's 'offerings' to an increasingly divided and sceptical public. They are no longer seen, or can expect to be seen, as the carriers of independent specialist expertise and the autonomous role it once played in the formulation and implementation of 'policy'. Instead, they metamorphosize into technocratic fixers whose very existence, much less status, depends on their usefulness to governing elites always on the lookout for 'manufactured consent' in a world of rapidly shifting alliances and deals.

In this extremely unstable and uncertain world, the unwritten social contract on which the institutionalized trust between states, experts, and publics once depended upon to legitimate expert authority can no longer provide the surety and stability it previously delivered. Its vulnerabilities and limitations have become increasingly exposed to more extreme ideologies, organizations and movements in which a political discourse of tolerance and compromise has given way to one dominated by the discursive tropes of conflict, division, and mistrust. Techno-populism provides a logic and mode of political representation in which the latter can be subsumed and dissolved within a more encompassing unitary ideology and discourse in which reconciliation between 'trust' and 'control' becomes possible without recourse to conventional liberal democratic politics and all the messy compromises on which it relies for its legitimacy and viability. Technocratic and populist discourses merge in a hybridized melange of political ideology and practice in which collective differences are translated into 'individual problems' that require technical solutions through a depoliticized management of public affairs overriding sectional interests represented through party-based organizations and oppositional social movements (Bickerton and Accetti 2021: 178–180).

However successful a technopopulist logic and strategy may have been in recent years – as exemplified in the New Labour triumphs of the late 1990s and early/mid noughties, the Tory landslide in the 2019 election, Trump's successful presidential campaign in 2016 or Macron's election to the French presidency in 2017 – constituted as a recombinant ideological and political hybrid, it must absorb and contain some very significant internal tensions and pressures. At its core, technocracy is a politics based on 'truth' as generated and confirmed through some sort of independent epistemic process and its supporting 'knowledge-producing institutions' such that those experts who speak in the name of 'science' or 'medicine' or 'profession' do so with the legitimate authority conferred by the former. Their 'epistemic authority' is generated and validated through processes and procedures by means of which the highly esoteric and specialized knowledge they possess and profess is legitimated so that it comes with a 'gold ticket' guarantee of its independence, objectivity and relevance. Populism, on the other hand, trumps (no pun intended!) 'truth' with an appeal to 'popular sovereignty' in which expert authority must be subjected to the collective will and priorities of 'the people' as refracted through populist movements and their leadership and the political parties and elites which emerge from the latter. Its political elites and media cheerleaders are assumed to have a 'direct line' to what the people want and how they want it, unencumbered by the conventional trappings of expert knowledge and all the confusion and uncertainty which its prevarications and qualifications sow.

Consequently, ways need to be found to soften these differences, take the ideological and political edge out of them in ways that ensure a transition into power and modes of governance effectively containing what residual internal tensions and pressures remain. Here again, experts play a central role in discursively 'smoothing over' and organizationally 'co-opting' potential recalcitrant interest groups and movements into a wider configuration of political representation within which their voices and concerns can find some expression and articulation. They become the 'bridge builders' and supporting maintenance crew whereby internal ideological contradictions and policy differences can be translated into more neutral, inclusive discourses emphasizing the 'non-political' character of what the party or movement, particularly when it comes into power, wants to achieve and how it will go about achieving it.

Yet, 'the attempt to use as a political resource a form of legitimacy – expertise – usually legitimized by precisely its *non*-political character certainly has limits' (Bickerton and Accetti 2021: 198 emphases in original). As we have already seen in chapter five of this book on the Covid-19 crisis, these limits are very likely to become even more apparent and stressed under the pressures generated by the latter when high-risk, high-pressure decision-making situations become a routine sociopolitical reality in which the reconciliation between 'expertise' and 'popular will' becomes extremely difficult – if not impossible – to pull off. By reshaping the discursive frame and political means through which contemporary democratic politics is conducted, technopopulism may be rather more effective as a logic and strategy for gaining power than it is for exercising power once governmental office is secures. Once in office, a technocratic governing strategy based on discursively legitimated expert authority and politically sanctioned administrative interventions threatens to push populist ideology and leadership on to the margins of power and to exacerbate all sorts of pre-existing internal tensions and conflicts as a result. Various initiatives may be undertaken to moderate the latter's impact on the governing regime's practices and popularity – such as setting up specialized units of experts enabling technologically-driven governing at the administrative core of the government machine – but these debilitating tensions and conflicts are likely to continue to haunt governments whose paths to power depended on powerful emotional appeals to cultural identity, popular sovereignty, and national exceptionalism. Although more 'pure' forms of technopolitics – such as that practiced under Blair's New Labour administrations in the UK between the late nineties and midtwenties – are unlikely to experience these problems with the same severity as they better integrate technocracy and populism, all governing regimes following such a political logic and strategy will be exposed to the endemic tensions between the latter.

One way out of this post-election impasse for technopopulist governing regimes may lie in the direction of importing selected elements of the 'neoliberal playbook' into the strategic mix of policies and practices which they develop when coming under sustained external political pressure. Hence, the repeated tendency for most administrations pursuing a technopopulist strategy to fall back on 'managerial politics' subjecting government policy making and practice to private sector cloned methodologies and technologies in which market competition, benchmarking performance targets and corporate surveillance play an increasingly important role. In an American rather than European context, Peck and Theodore

(2015: 5) refer to the 'mobilities of neoliberal governmentality' in which 'fast poli-cies' based on 'hybrid mutations of policy techniques and practices across dynamic institutional landscapes' emerge and become discursively legitimated through an ideologically promiscuous mix of technocracy, populism, and neoliberalism in which adaptability, flexibility and 'realism' are the dominant themes. However, this tactic entails a significant shift in the locus of authority over policy making and implementation which risks 're-politicizing' expertise as it becomes re-em-broiled within disputes over 'the role of expert and technocratic networks, many of which have been instrumental in the propagation of neoliberal reason, practice and rule' (Peck and Theodore 2015: 24). This is likely to increasingly jar against populist sentiment, ever suspicious of elitist technocratic rationalism and its marked preference for globalized policy paradigms over localized senti-ments and geographies (Kennedy 2016).

Thus, the structural and ideological fault lines characteristic of technopopulist parties and movements, once they get into power, are almost certain to become more pronounced and destabilizing as they struggle with the realities of governing with a political/policy paradigm in which expert authority is simultaneously laud-ed and despised. Their dependence on experts and their expertise is a 'truth which cannot speak its name' because to do so would reveal how they cannot dispense with them and their knowledge in a highly complex and extremely uncertain world. On the other hand, the more populism and neoliberalism re-politicize' ex-pert knowledge and skill, the more damaging this can become for claims which at-tempt to legitimate the latter based on their disinterested objectivity and techno-cratic acumen. In this respect, technopopulist politics presents very real dangers as well as rewards for experts and their claims to epistemological authority and technical control; right-wing populist parties/movements and their leaders remain hostile to professional and technocratic elites no matter how much they might need them – particularly in crisis situations when their expertise is desperately required to shore-up decisions often made on 'political' rather than 'technical' grounds. Indeed, the more power and influence which experts inevitably accrue in crisis situations will be greeted by right wing populists and libertarians alike with unrestrained suspicion and derision as, for them, it smacks of a return to the social democratic 'statism' which they abhor and detest (Reed 2022).

Overall, the technopopulist scenario is, at best, a 'mixed-bag' for expert author-ity in that it promises a degree of recognition as a legitimate element of the gov-ernmental regimes and policy paradigms it's likely to generate but this remains highly conditional on the understanding that experts continue 'to know their place' in established power hierarchies. It certainly doesn't hold out any realistic promise or prospect of a return to the heady days of 'institutionalized trust' when experts could realistically count on the support of both state elites and general publics for their claims to authority and status.

In the next section of this chapter, we turn to consider a third scenario in which the return of institutionalized trust may be regarded as a realistic possibility – that is, the emergence of a new form of 'civic' or 'connective' professionalism.

4 Civic/Connective Professionalism

Within the technopopulist scenario, experts are seen as critical mediators and brokers between the technocratic and populist wings of the political logic and strategy on which the former depends for its ideological and electoral appeal. However, once in government, parties and movements which have successfully followed this political logic and strategy in their 'ascent to power' find it increasingly difficult to accommodate expert authority. Those who claim it are often seen, especially by committed populists, to exceed their allotted role and status as 'technical advisers' or 'political fixers' in their aspirations to shape, if not direct, the policies and programmes which technopopulist governments are wanting to initiate and develop. This tension between 'technocrats' and 'populists' is exacerbated if those expert groups attempting to achieve much greater influence over governmental strategy and policy come to be seen as 'professional elites' who threaten to wrench strategic control from those leadership groups regarded as the 'carriers of the populist flame'. Expert authority is an endemic source of tension and conflict within the technopopulist scenario because it constantly threatens the 'meritocratic recrudescence' so despised by populist leaders and followers committed to its demise. For them, 'professionalism', in whatever form or guise it appears, is to be regarded as an enemy to be defeated because it has become the major source and expression of the present-day elitism which populists must eradicate if popular sovereignty is to be regained and protected.

However, this scenario singularly fails to consider the possibility that 'professionalism' may mutate into an institutional form and practice which can accommodate a broader range of interests and values in connecting much more meaningfully to the wider civil societies and communities in which professions are embedded. This possibility leads us to the third scenario we consider in this section – the emergence and potential of 'civic' or 'connective professionalism' which seeks to rejuvenate selected elements of the institutionalized trust relationship so badly damaged by recent economic, political and cultural transformations.

In a series of publications, Clarke and Newman (1997, 2005, 2007) have identified the potentialities for the emergence of a 'civic professionalism' in UK public services as they respond to the imposition of market-based, consumerist policies and practices associated with various 'waves' or 'phases' of New Public Management (Reed 2019). They trace a long-term developmental process whereby 'bureau-professional' governance regimes – in which public service professionals must adapt to new modes of managerial control unsympathetic to established norms and practices of professional autonomy and self-regulation – eventually give way to more open and flexible forms of 'stakeholder governance' in which 'citizen consumers' demand more accessibility and accountability from managers and experts alike. Thus, their book 'Creating Citizen Consumers' (2007) identifies a paradigm shift from a 'bureau-professional' governance regime based on a tripartite 'economic/political, social and organizational settlement' in which managerialism and professionalism accommodated each other in an inherently uneasy and unstable ideological and institutional compromise to a more reflexive 'consumerist-citizenship' governance regime. Within the latter, 'the problem of how to manage diverse, differentiated and mobile populations [who] are also "reflexive" and becoming detached from previous forms of authority, identity, identification and attachment' (Clarke at al. 2007: 23) emerges as the key strategic issue for successive New Labour regimes responding to increasing public scepticism and cynicism over public services organized and managed by remote technocratic and professional elites.

Subsequently, the book analyses the rise of the concept of the 'citizen-consumer' in which both major UK political parties became ideologically and organizationally committed to bringing a consumerist culture much more prominently into the provision and evaluation of public services. Although they differed considerably in the policy strategies and organizational mechanisms through which the latter was to be realized – internal/manged markets and performance targets as opposed to marketization and outsourcing – both major UK political parties agreed that 'users/consumers' needed to be at the centre of a consumer-centred model of public services in which 'choice', 'equity' and 'quality' were to be the new priorities. As Clarke et al. (2007) note, the populist undertones of this paradigm shift from 'bureau-professionalism' to 'citizen-consumer' were never very far from the surface as the increasing prominence of a consumerist culture across the ideological/political spectrum gave voice to representations of government in which popular sovereignty assumed priority over vested interests and elite control. Hence, the 'authority of the consumer' became conjoined to the 'needs of the citizen' within policy hybrids that attempted to rework existing networks of ideas in which individual choice and collective security could be selectively recombined to form new, innovative 'programmes and projects' focused around reconciling the competing demands of providers and publics within marketized service sectors. Various 'evaluation methodologies', such as 'best value inspection audits' in local government (Miller 2005), were developed and utilized to assess the extent to which individual service consumers' needs and interests were being properly represented, either materially or virtually, in these new programmes and projects in which 'network governance' systems were meant to replace professionally dominated 'hierarchical governance'.

These developments have major implications for public service professionalism to the extent that they call for a radical overhaul of the occupational-organizational formations in which public service professionals operate and through which they legitimate their authority and status as 'expert staff' who play a central role in shaping the strategic direction which their services will follow. Empowering 'the citizen-consumer' under the dispensation of a new policy and governance paradigm in which users, patients, customers, and voters – rather than politicians, professionals, managers, and technocrats – become the new source of primary legitimate authority, as articulated through their choices as consumers and their votes as citizens, becomes highly problematic for established service professionals as they scramble to adapt to a changed world in which they are no longer at the epicentre of its movement and trajectory. As Clarke et al. (2007) document in some empirical detail, service sectors and the organizations which populate them become sites of increasing strain and tension between the various stakeholders who are meant to make 'the citizen-consumer' paradigm work at the level of policy implementation and service delivery. It is here that the old and the new paradigms clash most transparently and where service professionals are expected to 'keep the wheels turning' in health trusts, local government authorities, police authorities, school chains and a myriad of devolved agencies. Various organizational innovations such as 'expert patients' or 'responsible health users' are serially tried and dispensed with as they run up against the realities of widening disparities in the range and quality of provision and the continuing impact of power inequalities on the allocation and distribution of scarce resources.

Yet, it's the service professionals who must embrace the operational outcomes which the 'citizen-consumer' paradigm generates by opening themselves up to the challenges it presents and adapting their occupational cultures and organizational practices to a consumerist ethic and civic responsiveness to new laws and regulations enshrining individual and collective rights to services. In place of a policy/governance paradigm in which experts and managers are always expected, and even deferentially trusted, 'to know best', they must now regain legitimate authority in situations where the dependency relationships between providers/professionals and users/clients seem to have been permanently rebalanced in favour of the latter. Hierarchically organized professional knowledge and the authority it automatically bestows on those formally responsible for its deployment has given way to horizontally distributed expertise and the much more inclusive civic networks of relationships and demands within which it has become enmeshed. Meeting and managing an often bewilderingly complex spectrum of needs and expectations has become 'the norm' for public service professionals and managers as they struggle 'to make the hybrid happen' (Reed and Wallace 2015).

Indeed, Newman (2013) argues that, by the time a coalition government comes into power in the UK in 2010, the shift from hierarchical to network governance is well-advanced enough to ensure that a more open, adaptable and inclusive form of public service professionalism is here to stay. Professionals have always held a somewhat ambiguous position within public services in that neoliberal-led 'marketization' and 'managerialism' has become so organizationally pervasive in the UK and the US it has severely weakened whatever occupationally based resistance expert groups might have mounted in their defence. Nevertheless, she also identifies significant institutional spaces and organizational enclaves in which they create and sustain new forms of agency such as 'professional social entrepreneurs' or 'personal advocacy groups' which gives them much greater control over their work and the ways in which it is evaluated. In turn, this is likely to make more established, even 'small c-conservative', professions more aware of the need, indeed imperative, to connect-up with wider civic interest agencies and movements, while developing the new communicative, promotional and political skills required in this 'brave new world of the citizen consumer'. Even though professional and other expert jurisdictional boundaries still prevail and make a positive contribution to getting work done under pressure and with high quality care and outcomes (Currie and White 2012; Currie et al. 2012; Farchi, Dopson and Ferlie 2022), in the future professional/expert legitimacy will have to dispense with the melange of deference, passivity and proceduralism characteristic of 'bureau professionalism'. In its place must come the recognition of radically transformed institutional, organizational, and occupational realities in which professional/expert authority will have to work much harder and more transparently to establish rather different trust relationships based not on secrecy and dependency but on visibility and partnership.

Noordegraaf (2007, 2011a and b, 2013, 2020) tells a very similar story to that told by Clarke and Newman but from a Northern European rather than Anglo-American perspective in which the influence and impact of neoliberalism and populism have been much more muted and nuanced because of continuing governmental and communal support for 'professions and professionalism' from both the state and the public. His work has consistently demonstrated an awareness of the innate potential of hybridized forms of professionalism to metamorphosize into a new type of professional work organization that moves considerably beyond the established or orthodox model of expert authority which we outlined in the first chapter of this book. In particular, he has drawn attention to the multiplicity of pressures and challenges impinging on contemporary professions as they struggle to adapt to demographic shifts, high risk problems and rising public uncertainties that corrode the structural foundations and cultural frameworks on which established professionalism depended for its legitimacy and credibility. Indeed, he sees professional hybridization as a response to the manifold ways in which professional associations and work organizations are being forced to open-up to these 'externalities', and the internal restructurings and reconstructions which they require if 'professionalism' is to be able to sustain itself as a viable mode of expert work regulation in the future.

By selectively recombining elements of organizational logics and practices drawn from a range of institutional forms – including managerialism, collegiality, marketization, digitalization and communitarianism – professional hybridization generates a change dynamic in which qualitatively different modes of professionalism based on inclusion and collaboration rather than exclusion and competition become realistic possibilities (Kirkpatrick and Noordegraaf 2015). While internal structural and cultural tensions will necessarily remain in whatever modes of professionalism emerge from this change dynamic – between hierarchy and network, control and autonomy, compliance and commitment – the latter can be seen as real attempts 'to move beyond established dualisms [and] seeking new ways to become more organized to ensure legitimacy and sustainability' (Kirkpatrick and Noordegraaf (2015: 103).

This, relatively optimistic, vision of what the future of professionalism, and expert authority more generally, might look like has been outlined in some detail in Noordegraaf's (2020) theorization of 'connective professionalism' and the latter's capacity to repair much of the damage that has been wrought by growing social and political distrust. He sees the latter as constituting an ideal type of professionalism entailing a distinctive move 'beyond hybridization' in that it embodies a fundamental reconfiguration of the three core conceptual elements that define 'what professions are' – 'expertise, 'autonomy', and 'authority'. 'Protective professionalism' is configured around a series of 'protective shields' or defensive mechanisms simultaneously distancing and linking professional work to real world situations by means of interlinked external labour market shelters and internal workplace jurisdictional controls enabling professions to remain essentially inward-looking, self-regulating and self-reproducing expert occupational cartels. However, this form of professionalism has come under extreme pressure in recent years from the accumulated impact of economic, technological, political and cultural changes undermining its internal cohesion and external viability to the extent that it has been forced to adapt to the threats and challenges which the latter pose. Hence, the emergence and momentum of various hybridizing strategies in which competing organizational logics and practices – such as 'managerialism' and 'professionalism' or 'bureaucratization' and 'marketization' or 'hierarchy' and 'network' – are selectively recombined, both at the level of work organization and roles, in ways that partially move the configuration of expertise, autonomy and authority towards a more inclusive, collective, and collaborative mode of professional action.

However, Noordegraaf (2020) argues that hybridizing adaptations simply don't move far enough away from the core components of the protective model because they still retain significant residues or 'leftovers' from the latter as embodied in the continuing commitment to professional epistemic exclusivity and jurisdictional independence. Only the transition to full or complete 'connective professionalism' can realize the radical reconfiguration between expertise, autonomy, and authority which the underlying logic and dynamic of contemporary environmental transformation demands as it drives us towards a better understanding of professionalism as 'an *interactive*, living phenomenon, taking shape in real-life processes, situated in complex service ecologies, with multiple relations to stakeholders' (Noordegraaf 2020: 2011 emphasis in original). Once we conceptually and empirically grasp the ontological status and significance of 'professionalism' as a living, dynamic, relational entity – necessarily embedded in external ecologies indelibly shaping its form and content – then, and only then, will we be in a position to appreciate how 'professionalism' has to be enacted on a continuous basis through various processes and mechanisms and able to answer the $64.000 question 'how can connected professionals remain experts, autonomous and authoritative in complex webs of relations?' (Noordegraaf 2020: 2011).

Noordegraaf proves a relatively optimistic, upbeat and consensus-building answer to this key question in his specification of an ideal type of 'connective professionalism' in which 'distributed/adaptive expertise', 'collaborative autonomy' and 'performative authority' are linked together and enacted by means of proactive, trust-building mechanisms ensuring much greater internal transparency and external accountability shared between all stakeholders within this increasingly complex and dynamic expert ecology. No longer the highly secretive, exclusive and guild-like defences of traditional professionalism but the emergence of a mode of professional action and organization in which 'professional acts are not performed by "professionals" but they are part of service *processes*, in wider service *ecologies*, in which many actors and factors play a role; "professionalism", in other words, is not so much made or produced by professionals themselves and then secured, it is largely "made" by others/outsiders when they interact with professionals' (Noordegraaf 2020: 219 emphasis in original).

While recognizing a role for agency, individual and collective, in shaping the transition from 'protective' to 'connective' professionalism, Noordegraaf clearly thinks that 'history is on the side of the latter' in that change in service ecologies is seen to be driving change in service processes and forms within an overall trajectory guaranteeing a successful transition to a more connected, inclusive, and participative reconfiguration of professional/expert authority. Indeed, he sees empirical indicators of the latter's inevitability in a range of contemporary organizational experiments such as 'community judges' and 'multi-disciplinary medical health teams' and 'impactful academics' which exemplify many of the key features of connective professionalism's inherent capacity to move beyond more partial and limited hybrid forms and to embrace the logic of 'relational professionalism' in all its interactive complexity and high-risk visibility.

Putting to one side methodological reservations over Noordegraaf's use of ideal types (Adams, Clegg, Eyal, Reed and Saks 2020), very real concerns remain over the teleological/evolutionary logic which underpins his analysis of the transition from 'protective' to 'connective' professionalism. By choosing to emphasize the long run determining impact of environmental or ecological change on occupational or organizational change, Noordegraaf assumes that the inherent 'divisiveness', 'messiness', and 'incompleteness' of any change process is overridden by evolutionary dynamics and forces driving in the direction of higher-level adaptation and growth. His 'teleological optimism' – that is, the belief that there is an evolutionary logic underpinning history inevitably driving in the direction of better adapted and integrated ecological systems – underwrites his analysis of the eventual triumph of 'connective professionalism' and the distinctive form of expert authority on which it depends. It also illustrates the socio-political specificity and cultural relativity of that analysis within a 'continental/European', as opposed to an 'intercontinental/Anglo-Saxon' theoretical tradition (Collins 1990; Kirkpatrick and Noordegraaf 2015), in which central states played a more explicit and directive role in professional development and formation. Within the former, key institutional actors such as states, governments, and political parties are seen in much more benign, even positive, terms insofar as they are consistently supportive of modes of professional development and formation embedded in wider collective and communal mobility projects. Perhaps even more crucially, the unwritten, implicit social contract which underpinned the trust-building processes and mechanisms between states, experts, and publics in Anglo-Saxon political economies and welfare systems has been much more formalized, and legally and governmentally protected in their European counterparts. Thus, the latter exhibited a much higher degree of resilience and robustness in the face of economic, socio-political and technological changes which threatened its cohesion and standing, while the former became increasingly frayed and threadbare under the accumulative pressures exerted by neoliberalism, populism, and digitalization.

In this respect, Noordegraaf's confidence in the eventual transition to 'connective professionalism' may be much more historically, politically, and culturally relative than his 'teleological optimism' permits. Try telling UK academics that 'impactful academics' may be seen as a contemporary empirical illustration of 'connective professionalism in action' when the political agenda behind the former has been driven by a decade or more of central state policy in relation to higher education (and public services) reform strategies in which 'corporatization' and 'managerialism' have been, and remain, the dominant change ideologies imposed on public service professionals (Reed 2019; Wallace et al. 2022). Also, Noordegraaf's analytical commitment to an evolutionary, rather than historical, institutionalism (Campbell and Pedersen 2001; Thornton, Ocasio and Lounsbury 2012) means that he sees change, necessarily, as a linear movement towards more socially and normatively progressive social forms across a wide range of institutional fields. This linear/progressive analytical focus marginalizes, if not excludes, the possibility of a backward or return movement towards more regressive social forms because the 'direction of travel' logically built-into evolutionary institutionalism rules out the possibility of any cyclical dynamic reversing the trajectory towards higher levels of 'managed complexity'. As Hay 2001: 199) has argued, under evolutionary institutionalism, 'the process of policy evolution then tends to be characterized by successive stages or iterations of strategic learning within the broad parameters of an evolving paradigm' where crises lead to policy and practice transformations in which established configurations are succeeded by new ones extirpating any residual elements of the latter. In this respect, Noordegraaf's evolutionary logic of 'protective – hybrid – connective' configurations of professionalism underplay, if not ignore, the power struggles within and between economic/political elites, expert groups and publics which shape both the trajectory of change and the outcomes that it generates in terms of the ever-shifting 'trust/control dynamic' between these key institutional actors (Reed 2018). Instead, we are expected to accept the underlying explanatory logic and methodological protocols of a form of analysis in which a unidirectional movement towards a more democratically advanced and organizationally complex form of professionalism will necessarily be secured because it is implicit in the evolutionary mechanisms and ecological processes which determine the developmental path it must follow. If history is on our side, then there's no need to worry too much about the modes of collective and individual agency whereby it might be brought, however contingently, untidily and ambiguously, into existence. Yet, Keynes' salutary reminder that 'in the long run we are all dead' suggests that the historical possibilities and options are much broader and contested than evolutionary institutionalists might suggest.

As such, it also reminds us of 'the elephant in the room' with evolutionary institutionalist analyses of the 'rise and rise of civic/connective professionalism' – that is the inescapable reality of the fact that 'expertise necessarily involves inequality' (Moore 2017: 6) insofar as it constitutes 'a social relation among unequals, which depends on recognition by a given audience' because 'experts claim to possess knowledge, skills, information and experience that others do not'. Noorde-graaf too easily assumes that a move towards more relational forms of expertise necessarily entails a progressive shift in the direction of more open, inclusive and connected professionalism, whereas the actual 'historical out turn' is likely to be much more contested, contradictory, and ambiguous than his analysis suggests.

5 Critical Elitism

Our fourth and final scenario for 'expert futures' rejects the teleological optimism underlying the evolutionary institutionalism which seems to have become so intel-lectually influential, if not dominant (Reed and Burrell 2018), within mainstream sociology of organizations/professions over the last decade or so. It begins with the reality that relational expertise is necessarily embedded within a structure of power relations based on inequality of access to and control over scarce and val-uable resources such as knowledge, skill and experience which must be legitimat-ed if it is to be established and recognized as 'epistemic authority' (Moore 2017: 8–9). Although the innate risks to democratic accountability and control posed by the latter can be mitigated in various ways, epistemic authority is anchored in configurations of power relations that cannot be 'wished away' however inclu-sive, connected and deliberative they may become in certain circumstances (Eyal 2019). Expertise, if it is to remain 'authoritative', can never become fully 'democrat-ic' in the sense of being constituted by and subject to the rule of others who are unable to sustain any legitimate claims to the epistemic knowledge on which its authority is based. This does not mean that expert authority is beyond contestation and challenge, quite the reverse, but it does entail acceptance of the reality that the former needs to be protected from becoming 'politicized' in the way which it has under neoliberal libertarianism and populist authoritarianism. As Eyal (2019: 30–36) argues, 'expertise' entails a capacity to perform specialized tasks which cannot be carried out in its absence or are more ineffectively and ineffi-ciently carried out without its presence; in turn, experts organize themselves in corporate groups to exercise control over the knowledge which effective special-ized task performance requires and to ensure appropriate standards against which the latter can be judged. Neither of these will work if they are to be routine-ly subjected to public vote or other forms of formal, external intervention based on a political logic in which ideology or popularity are the overriding considerations.

There is a structural contradiction and systemic tension between 'expertise' and 'democracy' which must be factored into any set of proposals relating to how epistemic authority and those claiming it are to be scrutinized and made ac-countable to a set of values and priorities ranging beyond their immediate jurisdictional domains. If the 'golden era' image or vision of experts as 'objective empiricists' or 'technical nerds' can no longer be sustained under the combined pressures we have examined in this book, this does not mean to say that the endemic tensions between 'expert autonomy' and 'democratic control' have simply withered away. As Rosenfeld (2019: 89–91) insists, 'technocratic expertise can threaten the basic values of equality, pluralism, and shared decision-making on which democracy is meant to stand ... if technocracy attached to global capitalism has increasingly threatened to overpower the idea of cooperative democratic decision ... the reaction, with its characteristic anger and know-nothingness, has started to constitute its own form of risk'.

Building on the 'deliberative democracy' tradition we outlined in the previous chapter of this book, Moore (2017) develops his model of 'critical elitism' as a positive response to the crisis in expert authority in which *expertise has been politicized and politics depoliticized* as they both become caught in the crosshair of authoritarian populism and technocratic egalitarianism. For him, the fundamental problem 'is how to conceptualize and construct expert authority in a context of widespread public capacities to challenge and contest it' (Moore 2017: 4). Rising public scepticism and questioning of expert authority, reinforced by various political movements determined to take advantage of this situation and the increasing economic inequality that capitalist-led technocracy has generated, have produced a series of 'legitimation crises' which show no signs of abating even in the face of various policy responses and initiatives from governments, businesses and other key institutional actors such as universities. 'Expertise' is increasingly viewed as a major source of unaccountable power which must be 'democratized' if it is to be transformed into a legitimate form of authority subject to collective supervision and control by independent institutions and movements beyond its purview and influence.

In opposition to strategies for re-legitimating expert authority demanding its 'democratization', Moore's (2017: 6 emphases in original) offers his model of 'critical elitism' 'as a framework for understanding the ways in which expertise is *not* in itself democratic but can be integrated into a wider democratic system'. In this way, 'critical elitism' is based on three, interrelated core assumptions: first, that *expertise necessarily involves inequality* because it is integral to a complex web of social relations necessarily entailing variable degrees of dependency on the part of those needing it; second, that *some degree of exclusion and passivity* on the part of the latter are also necessary because complete or total 'public inclusion and participation' in expert decision-making would compromise its independence and effectiveness (Collins and Evans 2009); third, that *expertise must be deliberatively constituted* if it is 'not to be construed in terms of blind deference ... in order to be effective, claims need to be accepted as authoritative; it is vital that over time and across institutions there are live possibilities for contestation and challenge' (Moore 2017: 8).

This model of expert authority as combining both epistemological elitism and public scrutiny is subsequently developed in ways which demonstrate how the necessary inter-relation between expertise and critique – as it unfolds within and across different 'deliberatively participative contexts' – strengthens the former's capacity to deliver good and effective interventions reducing risks in both the social and natural world. Reconciling structural asymmetries of power and knowledge between 'experts' and 'non-experts' demands more open and inclusive modes of decision-making in which various 'publics', and their concerns are regarded a pivotal component of the deliberative processes through which the latter emerge and are legitimated. But 'the puzzle is how to have inclusion without collapsing the very concept of expertise, how to engage public judgement in expert practices in a way that does not reduce to populism' (Moore 2017: 10).

Moore's 'critical elitism' responds to this theoretical and practical conundrum by systematically focusing on the inter-connected modes of communication, representation, and contestation through which expert/public consensus over 'wicked problems' and the complex solutions they require can be generated and sustained in ways that break the self-reinforcing relationship between 'the politicization of expertise and the depoliticization of politics'. Given thar expert authority is both a 'promise' and a 'threat' to democracies – because it offers the means to cope with the complex risks which the latter face, but those very same means can become a source of unaccountable power – then ways must be discovered and implemented to strike the right balance between 'trust' and 'control' by experimenting with different modes of 'distributed deliberation'. Within the latter, authority is 'ontologically pluralised' – that is, it is a precondition for authority's existence – and is regarded as 'a sort of voucher for discursive justification advanced against a particular good' (Moore 2017: 74). Also, societal practices of contestation and critique must play the central role as 'conditions of possibility of the exercise of citizen judgement and with regard to complex, expert-mediated issues, and are thus vital to the generation of the democratic authority of expertise' (Moore 2017: 95). Only through systems of distributed deliberation based on societal practices of contestation and critique can 'active consensuses' between opposed arguments and positions be realized and the latter, by their very nature, are open to reappraisal and recalibration in the future as new evidence, analyses and evaluations emerge. Under Moore's conception of 'distributed deliberation', expert-mediated and societally scrutinized epistemological consensus and the authority it generates is never final, unconditional or closed as it's always open to the outcome of future interactions between 'expert' and 'public' deliberation.

Finally, Moore considers some of the institutional innovations which might be required to make the systems of 'distributed deliberation' on which critical elitism organizationally-depends practical possibilities. The former, he suggests, aspire to provide organizational settings in which citizens can engage with experts through deliberative modes of collective decision-making which positively embrace the need for critical public scrutiny and the challenge to generate expert/lay consensus over the policies and practices which 'ill-structured problem solving' requires. Experiments with such forms of deliberative expert/lay collective decision making have been attempted across a wide range of policy areas including technology, science, medical/health care, environment, transportation and development (Moore 2017: chapter 7) as policymakers and policy-experts respond to 'legitimation pressures' with discursive and organizational practices in which securing public trust, involvement and dialogue are their priority. They provide 'deliberative forums' which 'draw on expertise without being dominated by it' (Moore 2017: 150) and in which lay participants have genuine 'collective voice' leaving them less open to manipulation and control by governmental elites and their technocratic advisors. These types of arrangements often morph into 'hybrid deliberative bodies' such as collaborative planning processes and other forms of 'minipublics' focusing on underlying thematic issues of risk, uncertainties, and trade-offs between 'competing collective goods' in major policy domains such as abortion, electoral reform and biotechnology. Responding both to challenges to expert authority and the threats of expert hubris and domination, these experiments in institutional innovation have the potential to integrate citizen/lay engagement and expert/technocratic governance within distributed deliberative forums meetings 'the demands for communicative accountability and justification without empowering critics to veto or obstruct democratically authorized purposes and delegation' (Moore 2017: 178).

Moore's theorization of critical elitism speaks to the key issue of the 'politics of extension' highlighted by Collins (2013, 2020) and Eyal (2019) as the 'deference model of expert authority' is finally forced to give way to its democratic counterpart- that is, how far can the democratization of expert authority go in its ever-widening inclusion of lay publics until the knowledge boundaries between experts and non-experts effectively dissolve away? Given, as Eyal (2019: 31) argues, our knowledge systems are governed by expert abstractions, theories, models and methodologies which do not easily lend themselves to lay understanding and evaluation, then how far can lay participation be extended without compromising the very effectiveness and trustworthiness of expertise? This built-in 'trust/control dilemma' generates a political dynamic through which expert power must be legitimated through the publics' acceptance of its right and capacity to take decisions on their behalf because they believe that it's in their collective interest to do so. However, this acceptance and belief are not unconditional in that they can be renegotiated and even withheld in the event of expert authority failing to live up to its ethical ideals and/or failing to deliver on its performative promises. There are inherent limitations to how far expert authority can be democratized along the lines of maximum lay participation and citizen engagement which go substantially beyond the various experiments in institutional innovation outlined by Moore (2017). As Eyal (2019: 148) insists, they 'are attractive ethical ideals, but poor machineries for producing legitimacy. They possess no mechanism for bringing debate to an end, and no defences against abuse by the merchants of doubt and other determined and interested parties.'

6 Conclusion

Each of the four responses to the crisis in expert authority and the 'expert futures' which they anticipate – rejuvenated meritocracy, technocratic populism, connective professionalism, and critical elitism – reviewed in this chapter struggle with the conundrum of how democratic oversight of expertise is to be realized without damaging the 'trust rebuilding' efforts on which the latter depends or conversely pushing experts into an even more defensive repositioning in which they desperately scramble to reassert their untrammelled autonomy and control. They all speak to the 'trust/ control dilemma' we have highlighted throughout this book and attempt to provide a reconceptualization of 'expert authority' in which the balance between them shifts in the direction of rebuilding public trust through greater democratic transparency and accountability without so fatally weakening expert autonomy and control that they become bereft of any material significance or symbolic value.

Rejuvenated meritocracy aspires to overhaul the ideology and practice of 'meritocratic credentialism' in ways that make it genuinely more open and accessible to those normally excluded from effectively participating in the competition for opportunities and rewards which it entails. 'Equality of opportunity' is to be reconstructed and revitalized in ways that translate its promise into a reality through enhanced educational and social mobility, better vocational training, affirmative action and political leadership attuned to the need for 'levelling up initiatives' directed at breaking the stranglehold over positional power and wealth enjoyed by established elites.

Technopopulism envisages a new rapprochement between technical elites and political leaders around the need to develop winning electoral strategies in which the critical role of experts and expertise is fully recognized, but without ignoring the legitimate claims of 'ordinary people' to be included in and benefiting from the policies and programmes that elected populist governments deliver. Experts are re-imaged as genuine 'servants of the people' rather than 'servants of power' and their expertise is rededicated to the design and delivery of 'programmes' and 'projects' better equipping currently disadvantaged groups to compete in the struggle for material rewards and social recognition.

Connective professionalism anticipates the emergence of a form of professional work organization and association much more open to the wide range of stakeholder interests and values which must be fully taken into account when striving to solve complex problems with sensitivity, compassion and tolerance. Citizens, clients, and consumers are reimagined as partners in a collaborative endeavour to deal with seemingly intractable and recalcitrant obstacles standing in the way of achieving better forms of living for the community as a whole. Deference to expert authority gives way to relational forms of expertise socially and ethically grounded in shared understandings of 'what needs to be done and how it needs to be done' if entrenched political polarization and extreme socio-economic inequality are to be overcome 'in the quest for community' (Nisbet 1969).

Critical elitism calls for a sensible and deliverable balance to be struck between 'epistemic authority' and 'democratic accountability' through the design and construction of innovative institutions which can effectively accommodate deliberative decision making around complex social, political and economic problems inherently resistant to 'quick fixes' or 'bureaucratic massaging'. It recognizes the inherent limitations of political and administrative strategies aimed at democratizing expertise, if expert authority is to retain its legitimacy as a trustworthy and reliable source of specialist knowledge and skill vital to the management of risk in highly unstable and uncertain environments. In this respect, experts will retain significant elements of their positioning and status as cognitive or epistemic elites, but the latter will be exposed to much greater scrutiny and challenge – by other experts, government agencies, civic groups, social movements, and public interest organizations – than was routinely the case under the deferential model.

However persuasive each of these scenarios for expert futures may be, they also remain open to further interrogation and contestation – a rejuvenated meritocracy still remains a mechanism for entrenching elite power and wealth however flexible it may become; technopopulist movements and parties seem to be eternally distrustful, if not dismissive, of expert authority once they get into government; connective professionalism relies on a communitarian ethos and ethic which may prove far more difficult to sustain in the long-term when the clamour of competing sectional interests and values begins to gather political momentum; finally, critical elitism is ideologically and practically embedded in a political realism which recognizes the trade-offs and rebalances required when 'change' seems to be transitioning into 'crisis' but the question remains as to whether or not the latter can hold out against rising anti-elitist populism.

Once this wider social and political context is fully considered, then the putative collapse of the unwritten, informal social contract between states, experts, and publics through which expert authority was underwritten as a 'collective good' requiring no further legitimation or justification seems to cut the ground from underneath all four of the 'expert futures' discussed in this chapter.

It is to this pivotal issue – that is, the viability of calls for 'a new social contract' to underwrite, if not guarantee, the kind of futures for expert authority reviewed in this chapter – that we turn in the final chapter of this book.

Chapter 8: Towards a News Social Contract

1 Introduction

Battered and bruised on all sides, 'expert authority' – as a concept, relation and practice – has seen much of its accrued social capital dissipated by waning public belief in and support for its probity and effectiveness. As the 'deferential model' (Moore 2017) of expert authority has increasingly struggled to defend itself against the accumulated threats posed by political, cultural and technological change, so the emergence of a 'democratic/reflexive model' has striven to fill the intellectual void left by the former's eclipse. Yet, it too has struggled to renew the legitimacy of expert authority and replenish its accumulated social capital as the social and normative presuppositions on which it's based have come under extreme and sustained scrutiny, both 'from above' and 'from below' over the last decade or so in which 'crises come along like buses' – never on their own but in frighteningly and disturbingly quick succession.

Indeed, 'continuing crises' – or 'permacrisis' to use the most recent term used by Collins dictionary – seems to have become the default position over the last decade or so. As economic crises (financial crisis of 2008/2009 and the decade of austerity which followed) and political crises (presidential election of Trump and other authoritarian populist leaders from 2016 onwards, and political crisis around attempts to block Biden's occupancy of the White House in 2020; UK Brexit from EU in 2016) have given way to global public health (global Covid-19 pandemic from 2019/2020) and military conflict crises (Russian invasion of Ukraine in 2022 and the prospect of economic recession/stagflation) – and all the while, the climate change timebomb is ticking away, louder than ever! Moving from 'passive' to 'active' trust as a basis for repurposing, if not remaking, expert authority has proved to be rather more difficult in practice than the theorists of 'reflexive modernization' (Beck, Giddens and Lash 1994) seemed to anticipate back in the closing decade of the twentieth century. Then, globalization was in the ascendancy, both structurally and ideologically, and the overriding problem seemed to be whether liberal democracies could develop the self-reflexive technologies and cultures required to cope with whatever dislocations and disillusionments it brought with it. While this book has indicated that the general thrust of their analysis of the weakening of institutionalized trust has been confirmed in the early decades of the twenty-first century, the projections and trajectories which they formulated and anticipated in relation to rebuilding and renewing 'active trust' have proved to be overoptimistic and oversimplistic. In short, they seriously underestimated how difficult it would be to revitalize 'active trust' in core institutions and practices – such as ex-

https://doi.org/10.1515/9783110734911-009

pert authority – through the instigation of more 'reflexive governance systems' when the later were being subjected to escalating ideological, political and technological pressures to reverse the economic and social gains which globalization had supposedly produced. As the twenty-first century unfolded, it became increasingly evident that the destructive dynamic released by neoliberal globalization, digitalization, and de-industrialization would be much less easy to contain as the 'dis-embedding mechanisms 'on which it depended – particularly expertise and expert systems (Giddens, Beck and Lash 1994: 82–95) – to do its work would effectively 'rip-up' so much of the institutional infrastructure on which the post-1945 liberal/social democratic settlement had depended for its stability. Escalating strains and stresses on the latter revealed that it was much less resilient than many had assumed as they tested its capacity to absorb structural dislocations and ideological fractures which challenged its very institutional core and the conventions on which it depended for its legitimacy.

Relying on institutionalized trust as the primary structural mechanism and discursive formation through which expert authority has been legitimated is no longer viable for reasons we have identified throughout the preceding chapters of this book. The overarching rationale for 'cutting the umbilical cord' between institutionalized trust and expert authority is the increasingly threadbare condition of the unwritten and implicit social contract between states, experts, and publics which stabilized the relationship between them within a delicate mesh of informal understandings, conventions, and norms underwritten by the post-1945 liberal/social democratic settlement. Both states and publics have become increasingly suspicious of, not to say hostile to, the taken-for-granted assumption that experts are delivering on their side of the bargain which this settlement entailed. This is the case both in relation to the latter's intentions and capacities to meet their obligations under the social democratic consensus which emerged at the end of the Second World War. Since they have become key players in a technocratic elite which turns a collective deaf year to public opinion and has consistently demonstrated its capacity to circumvent 'the unwritten rules of the game' in pursuit of their vested interests, expert occupations and organizations are now seen as 'the problem' rather than 'the solution' to tackling complex, high stakes problems in high-risk environments.

Yet, this done not mean to say that the situation which expert authority is now placed in is irretrievable – that it is no longer defendable or dependable in the world we live in now and are likely to live in tomorrow. As we have also consistently documented in the previous chapters of this book, *we will remain dependent on expert authority for the foreseeable future because the knowledge, insight, and skills which experts possess remain indispensable to our, individual and collective, attempts to live safer and better lives in an increasingly threatening world. However,* on the other hand, it does mean to say that we need a fundamental rethink and revision of the liberal/social democratic social contract underpinning the interrelationships between states, publics, and experts which is now in need of a radical overhaul if it is to be up to the challenges that the 21st century presents to all three collective actors. Institutionalized expert trust, based on a passive, deferential and defensive modus vivendi between states, experts and publics has become so ossified that it can no longer provide the substantive, values-based foundations for legitimating expert authority in the twenty-first century. Even if the regulative husk of its 'certification ecosystem' formally remains in place (Kirkpatrick et al. 2021), it cannot sustain the trust-building mechanisms and relations on which a much more openly contested, transparent and accountable mode of expert authority must be legitimated.

There are several intellectual resources we can draw on to get a better understanding of what this renewed social contract in which states, experts, and publics can be re-embedded might look like, and how it may help to legitimate the much more democratic and reflexive forms of expert authority and governance required in the 21st century.

We will begin by exploring the intellectual inheritance bequeathed by the communitarian/Durkheimian tradition in social and organizational theory, highlighting its analytical focus on the 'non contractual foundations of contract' (Lukes 1975; Wolin 2004; Collier 2018; Courpasson, Younes and Reed 2021). Next, we proceed to the revival of social contract theory in contemporary political theory with its renewed emphasis on the need to reconceptualize the 'modern subject' as both 'a bearer of rights' and 'a carrier of communal obligations' (Forrester 2019; Shafik 2021). Thirdly, we focus on those analysts anticipating the revival of the social democratic/interventionist state and the 'collectivist individualism' on which it is ideologically predicated as a result of the massive increase in the scope and depth of governmental action in response to the global pandemic as it unfolded from 2019/2020 onwards (Kahl and Wright 2021; Cooper and Szreter 2021; Tooze 2021; Gerbaudo 2021). Finally, we return to the contemporary political sociology of expert work as it attempts to absorb and evaluate what this 'long decade of crises' – and the fundamental rethinking of contemporary socio-political and organization theory which it generated – means for our understanding of expert authority 'beyond contract' (Fox 1971, 1974, 1985). Here we emphasize the enduring significance, both theoretical and practical, of the complex networks of 'countervailing power' (Reed 2018; Reed and Reed 2022) in which expert authority is necessarily embedded as coalitions of governing elites, expert organizations, and public institutions come together to shape 'the politics of expertise' in twenty-first century societies (Stehr and Grundmann 2011; Turner 2014; Moore 2017; Eyal 2019).

2 Non-Contractual Foundations of Contract

Durkheimian/communitarian social and organization theory has consistently emphasized the dependency, both structurally and ideologically, of formalized contractual exchanges and relationships on the tacit, implicit and unwritten understandings and conventions on which they must rely if they are to function as protections against rule and promise breaking. As Lukes (1975: 140–160) argues, Durkheim rejects the Spencerian model of society as nothing more than a spontaneous form of social cooperation and coordination emerging automatically from the free play of individual economic interests requiring only the minimum of legal regulation to ensure that 'free exchange' can continue unencumbered by external interference. This philosophical and sociological reduction of 'society' to the multitude of atomistic contractual exchanges through which economic interests are spontaneously and temporarily coordinated – which has become the intellectual bedrock of contemporary neoliberal theory (Davies 2014) – treats society as 'a vast system of bargaining and exchange' (Lukes 1975: 143) ontologically and theoretically stripped of the complex infrastructure of conventions and norms in which the latter are embedded and on which they necessarily depend for their functioning. For Durkheim, modern societies are 'organized social structures characterized by a high degree of interdependence ... changes at one point are rapidly transmitted to others' (Lukes 1975: 154), so that the social solidarity which emerges within them cannot be reduced to the free play of individual material interests and the legal rules through which they are regulated. Indeed, the latter cannot exist, much less function, without the socially dense and ethically rich configuration of informal conventions and norms in which they are embedded and on which they depend as 'trust-building mechanisms' underpinning the formalized rules and regulations through which market exchanges are stabilized and regularized.

This Durkheimian/communitarian tradition in social and organization theory rejects the economic rationalism which has come to dominate social science since the 1980s, and its intellectual roots in a form of liberal individualism that elevates the unencumbered pursuit of self-interests to the 'fundamental essence of morality' (Wolin 2004: 362). In denying the philosophical and theoretical significance of 'organization' as a living structure constituted by and through a rich and subtle socio- political life which constantly evades the attempts of formal rules and regulations to capture it, economic rationalism and neoliberalism cannot even begin to see how and why its existence pre-empts the very ontological and methodological reductionism they rely on for their intellectual legitimacy. As Witztum (2019) has exhaustively documented in his two-volume philosophical and theoretical deconstruction of both liberal classical and modern economic theory, the continuing failure of the latter to recognize the historical roots of 'rationality' in 'sociality' means that it is constitutionally incapable of understanding the inherently dynamic relationship between individuals and society because of its innate propensity to reduce social reality to conceptual abstractions that 'freeze' the latter in fixed, timeless and context-less categories.

Communitarianism, as mediated through the writings of philosophers such as MacIntyre (1981/1985, 1988), Horton and Mendus (1994) and sociologists such as Fox (1971, 1974, 1985) and Anthony (1977, 1986), has undergone something of an intellectual renaissance of late in contemporary organization and social theory (Nielsen 2006; Collier 2018; Forrester 2019). In so doing, it has renewed and refocused attention on the vital 'obligation-building' role of communal values and norms as they nurture and expand our innate inclinations and capacities as social beings to collaborate with others in pursuit of collective projects requiring the subsuming of individual interests within wider social goals.

Fox's (1971, 1974) analysis of the complex dynamic between a 'low trust/low discretion' and 'high trust/high discretion' syndrome within modern organizations is indicative of this Durkheimian/communitarian tradition and the various ways in which it continues to speak to control relationships within 'the neoliberal organization' (Courpasson, Reed and Younes 2021). He suggests that organizational managers veer between a control strategy driven by the priority of securing worker compliance through a combination of tight disciplinary surveillance and externally imposed sanctions in which the risk of potential resistance and misbehaviour is minimized through fear and coercion, as opposed to one that radically shifts the emphasis towards securing worker commitment through 'trust building' mechanisms encouraging collective problem-solving and shared risk taking. While recognizing that this 'control/trust dynamic' is subject to considerable historical and socio-cultural variation, in true Durkheimian fashion Fox contends that the move towards a 'high trust/high discretion' strategy combining social integration and solidarity signals a shift 'beyond contract' in which the traditional conception of 'master-servant relationship' underpinning economic rationalism and liberalism is superseded by notions of social partnership and workers' democracy.

Whatever the inherent philosophical and theoretical limitations of this Durkheimian/communitarian tradition in socio-political and organizational theory, it has the undoubted intellectual and practical benefit of reminding us of the 'non-contractual foundations of contract' and the crucial role they will play in rebuilding trust in expert authority as it struggles to renew its social contract with states and publics. It shows that any attempts to develop a new social contract between publics, states and experts must be grounded in an appreciation of the structural tensions, contradictions and conflicts that are likely to continue to prevail between them, however quickly and far we move 'beyond contract' into a more 'high trust/high discretion' reflexive governance regime.

3 Social Contract Theory

By refocusing attention on the non-contractual foundations of contract, the Durkheimian/communitarian tradition in social and organization theory highlights the crucial importance of what MacIntyre (1981) sees as the necessary interdependence – functional, political and ethical – between 'institutions' and 'practices.' As Moore and Beadle (2006) reflect, as a communitarian theorist, MacIntyre also sees the systemic contradictions and tensions embodied in this 'love/hate' relationship between institutions/organizations and the values/practices through which they are generated and reproduced. While institutions/organizations and their managers are primarily concerned with achieving 'external goods' geared to long-term survival within a competitive and hostile environment, practices/values valorise 'internal goods' aligned to cooperative care and communal wellbeing which often come into conflict with managerial priorities. Managerial logics driven by the search for contractual relationships giving the institution/organization a degree of security and stability unavoidably clash with communal logics in which the nurturing and curation of collective mutuality and respect between people is the overriding obligation, irrespective of its impact on formalized legal agreements.

Recent developments in social contract theory (Forrester 2019; Shafik 2021; Hennessy 2021; Tooze 2021; Gerbaudo 2021) attempt to rework the concept of 'social contract' so that it can more effectively bridge the underlying tensions between 'rights-based' theories of protecting individual liberty and 'obligations-based' theories of sustaining collective wellbeing. Forrester's (2019) detailed conceptual deconstruction and historical reconstruction of the 'social contract tradition' in liberal egalitarian political philosophy and it's theoretical anchoring in Rawls' *A Theory of Justice* (1971), forensically identifies the exposure of the latter to a communitarian critique which refuses to accept the deracinated conception of human agency it depends on to make its arguments work. This communitarian critique also challenges the first principles on which liberal egalitarian, individual rights-based theorizations of 'justice as fairness' is based and does the philosophical groundwork on which a thorough going rejection of 'meritocratic credentialism' (as discussed in chapter 6 of this book) can be carried forward. Thus, communitarian philosophers such as MacIntyre (1981) prepared the theoretical ground for communitarian sociologists such as Nisbet (1969, 1970) and Etzioni (1993) to mount a defence of human agents as 'institution builders' who are continually engaged in social practices entailing wider communal obligations which cannot be reduced to their individual self-interests and the 'utilitarian decision-making calculus' through which they are prioritized.

Contemporary attempts to revivify the social contract tradition in socio-political and organization theory seem to have learnt the lessons of this ongoing dialogue between liberalism and communitarianism by calling for a renewal of the shared ethical frameworks and institutional relationships through which human agents can collectively thrive across the generations. In this respect, Shafik's (2021: 2) call for 'a new social contract' is predicated on the assumption that the norms and rules governing how collective institutions operate are 'the most important determinants of the kind of lives we lead. Because it is so important and because most people cannot easily leave their societies, the social contract requires the consent of the majority and periodic renegotiation as circumstances change'. Here she is explicitly recognizing the inherently dynamic character of the social contract and why its structure and content must be open to review and renewal as the balance between trust/control relationships shifts in response to the changing socio-historical context within which it is embedded. Individual self-interests and the decision-making mechanisms through which they are translated into formalized preferences subject to contractual regulation, alone, cannot provide the tools and aides which we require to navigate our way through the complex and dense networks of mutual obligations and collective relationships on which we depend to live better and more fulfilling lives. Instead, we have no choice but to rely on extended norms of reciprocity and the shared expectations which they embody as we collectively build the institutional frameworks and supportive normative infrastructures on which they rely to gain legitimacy and stability.

This 'partnership model' of the social contract in which individual and collective agents can pool their risks and routinely engage in collaborative relationships to their mutual benefit and wellbeing takes us, conceptually and substantively, considerably beyond the liberal egalitarian and utilitarian tradition in which rights-based theorizations of justice and fairness were originally formulated. It also highlights the growing disappointment and disillusionment of those individuals and groups who had been led to expect something much better from those key collective actors, such as states, political and business elites and technocratic managers, who had promised so much but had failed to deliver on their side of the social contract with the general public. As the latter becomes more fragmented and fissured through the cumulative impact of political, economic and technological changes polarizing and dividing groups and communities into mutually hostile and suspicious 'interests', so the capacity of the 'partnership model' to sustain social solidarity and collective action is seriously called into question.

Shafik's (2021) proposals for designing a new social contract are based on three core principles and a range of organizational mechanisms for translating the latter into actionable projects and programmes. First amongst the former is a call for minimum economic security for all as provided through universal basic income schemes tailored to guaranteeing a decent standard of living for all citizens relative to prevailing levels of economic prosperity within the countries in which they live. Second, there is a demand for maximum investment in citizens' capabilities allowing them to realize their full productive potential and to contribute to the common good of their countries for as long as they are able through lifetime training and personal development programmes. Thirdly, is the principle of pooled or shared risk-taking such that individuals, families and communities can be confident that if they face difficult economic and social conditions they can reply on material and moral support from the state, businesses, public agencies and civic organizations to help them navigate their way through these trying times.

These principles and their policy implications, Shafik (2021: 188) are based on the axiomatic premise that 'a more generous and inclusive social contract would recognize our interdependencies, provide minimum protections to all, share some risks collectively and ask everyone to contribute as much as the can for as long as they can'. She also insists that this new social contract does not entail the uncontrolled expansion of the welfare state and the bureaucratic apparatus required to administer it, but it does demand a much more inclusive and supportive institutional framework for collectively managing the inevitable disruption and dislocation that rapid technological, political and social change will impose on those least prepared to withstand their impact.

Such a set of general principles and their broad policy implications has garnered ideological support across the political spectrum from the centre/left (Etzioni 1993; Srnicek and Williams 2015; Hutton 2015; Reich 2016; Collier 2018; Coats 2018; Cruddas 2021) and from those sympathetic to a more progressive and inclusive populism (Seymour 2014: Mouffe 2018; Frank 2020; Sandel 2020). However, it is the Covid-19 pandemic and its implications for the possibility of a new social contract to emerge which has generated most debate about a 'post-pandemic future' in which the latter becomes a political and social necessity rather than an increasingly attractive policy option in an increasingly uncertain world.

In a UK context, Hennessy (2021) has recently insisted that the pandemic has been the biggest collective experience of the British people since the Second World War and constitutes a 'new Beveridge moment' in which the state and other collective agencies have been called upon to protect the safety and security of its population on a scale and scope unheard of since that time. In ideological and political terms, he argues, this entailed an unqualified recognition by the government and a wide range of economic, social and cultural organizations that they owed 'a duty of care' to its citizens which could only be delivered if the state, the professions and the public came together in a new social settlement geared to its overriding mission of protecting the collective wellbeing of all. This would generate 'a new, more consensual politics and a shared programme made possible by that consensus, strengthening it in a cycle of mutual reinforcement' (Hennessy 2021: 131) through a 'new Beveridge' in which a long-term programme of reform tackling injustice, inequality and economic/technical underperformance simultaneously would become a political reality. This would be focused on improved social care provision, a rapidly expanded social housing programme, enhanced technical education, gearing our economy and society up for artificial intelligence, and mitigating and combating climate change over a period stretching to 2045. It would also include specific policies relating to a universal basic income, improved welfare support for those struggling to avoid the poverty trap and a reformed justice system in which the dispensation of timely and fair justice is guaranteed to all of those who come before it.

Tooze (2021) and Gerbaudo (2021) analyse the long-term impact of the pandemic on our economy, society and politics at a more global level. Tooze (2021: 28 – 41) begins with an excoriating critique of the 'organized irresponsibility' – a theme that we have previously discussed in this book – which dominated government thinking about the threats which biomedical catastrophes pose to their citizens in which 'preparedness' and 'mitigation' rather than 'eradication' or 'overcoming' become the overriding imperatives governing state policy. As a result, 'there is no willingness to make structural changes to our food chain or transport system to reduce risk or even to invest in an adequate public health system' (Tooze 2021: 35) and, in turn, this leads to widespread state failure to protect its citizens' lives – the core normative and political foundation of the modern state's existential rationale as identified by Hobbes in the late seventeenth century (Garrard 2022). This generates not just economic and social dislocation on a massive scale but also a major political crisis fundamentally calling into question the willingness and capacity of modern states to take responsibility for their citizens' wellbeing and to engage in the forward-looking planning and interventions which the discharge of the latter requires. Indeed, too many administrations, at all levels of governing, seemed more than prepared to pursue a policy of 'trade-offs' in which legal regulations, normative conventions and ethical considerations could be, temporarily, 'put to one side' in balancing-out the, admittedly regretful, loss of human life against business interests and 'state raison'. If protecting national health care systems from being overwhelmed and collapsing eventually emerged as the driver of state policy and action during the first two years of the pandemic – as the threat which it posed to collective order and individual liberty waxed and waned with alarming unpredictability – then this would leave those individuals, groups, organizations and societies most dangerously exposed to its ravages to fend for themselves as best they could.

Yet, Tooze also goes on to argue that 'organized irresponsibility' gradually gave way to collective responses which, however piecemeal and contested they proved to be in practice, paved the way for policies, programmes and projects that took the threat posed by biomedical crises much more seriously and developed 'expert systems' of various kinds – surveillance technologies, vaccine development programmes, and economic recovery strategies – to cope with their more damaging impacts (see chapter 5 of this book for more detail). He concludes that the collective capacities of governments and societies to mobilize the massive scientific and technical resources required to mount effective responses to future pandemics and the existential threats they pose to 'our way of life' will determine whether 'organized responsibility' prevails. Without key established institutions such as central banking to provide the ultimate support for market-based financing, the technoscientific networks needed to develop effective vaccines at such a rapid pace and the resilience of health and medical systems in the face of stress-testing pressures of a scale and intensity never experienced, the, interim, outcome of the pandemic would have been very different. Nevertheless, he accepts that the evaluation of the threats posed by 'reflexive modernization', as provided Beck, Giddens and others in the 1980s and 1990s, have been vindicated by the Covid-19 pandemic insofar as it reinforced our continued dependency on governing institutions alone having the collective capacity to respond to 'systemic mega-risks' in the face of which neoliberal shibboleths such as 'free markets' or 'minimal states' simply crumbled. They remain the ultimate providers of 'organized responsibility' because only they can legitimately mobilize the vast resources which 'systemic mega-risk management' requires in ways that secure the levels of generalized public trust and compliance on which the latter depends for its authority and efficacy.

Tooze (2021: 303) concludes his analysis with a fulsome recognition of the strategic role that interdependent networks of elite and expert power will continue to play in systemic mega-risk management. Only by identifying and dissecting these elite/expert power networks can we hope to uncover 'the thickets of analysis, information, and knowledge produced day by day from inside the apparatus as its protagonists struggle to cope with the radical outcomes that their systems are producing'. It is this 'arcane expertise' which lies at the organizational core of the power-knowledge systems which simultaneously contain and intensify the existential risks we all face in a high risk, high stakes world where the pace and scale of change has accelerated in ways that seem to challenge our capacity, individually and collectively, to deal with them.

Finally, Gerbaudo (2021) provides a synoptic overview of 'the return of the state' under the cumulative pressures generated by economic recession, technological rationalization, biomedical crisis and political chaos since the financial crash of 2008/2009. Neoliberal ideology has been seriously 'found out' as these crises have come together to present it with systemic challenges requiring collectivist responses in which the central state and its supporting governing institutions are the 'only game in town' if its centuries old promise of protecting the safety and security of its citizens is to be kept. Although neoliberal ideology, policy and practice has moved closer to an authoritarian populism in which national sovereignty, economic protectionism and cultural identity have become the dominant themes, there is increasing evidence that this will not save it from deep-rooted structural transformations moving in the direction of a new post-pandemic, neo-statist politics in which 'government protectivism' emerges as the key trend and new reality. This movement has entailed the return to a more inward-looking politics – in stark contrast to the outward-looking politics which dominated the era of neoliberal globalization – in which internal order, security and safety becomes the dominant concern as we struggle to cope with the extreme uncertainty and polarization that the 'era of continuing crises' has produced.

Both right and left-leaning populist movements and parties have exploited this demand for 'taking back control' through the promotion of nationalist-based ideologies and policies that reject the dominance of an elite politics in which the capacity for collective action has been effectively outsourced to international bodies and corporations in which a clique of global 'experts' replaces the role once performed by the state. As Norris and Inglehart (2019: 66) suggest in their exhaustive review of authoritarian populism across the globe:

> populists claim legitimacy from direct popular expression reflecting the voice of the people, where majority preferences override minority interests. The authority of the voice of the people is valued even when at odds with professional experts ('Britain has had enough of experts'), legal authorities ('so called judges'), main-stream media commentators ('fake news'), scientists ('climate change is a hoax'), and elected politicians ('just in it for themselves').

However, as Gerbaudo (2021) insists, this return to 'the politics of interiority' has a progressive potential as well as a regressive drive; it reasserts the centrality of the need for collective democratic control over institutions and resources in the face of natural and social existential threats of a magnitude and complexity defying market-based and technocratic solutions. Growing appreciation of the extent to which neoliberal globalization has directly and indirectly reinforced extreme inequality and insecurity opens-up political spaces in which collective action – at a wide range of levels of political organization from the central state to civil society and across a broad swathe of organizational forms from the business corporation to the voluntary agency – is given a renewed lease of life as a mechanism and vehicle to rebalance and rebuild through democratic decision making. Only in this way can the 'hollowing out' of formal democratic institutions by neoliberal globalization and authoritarian populism be reversed so that great areas of political decision-making, either outsourced to an international cadre of brokers and experts or delegated to unelected national authorities, can be returned to their rightful location in a range of public arenas where 'expertise can be reconciled with democracy'. Within the latter, a new middle class of well-educated and relatively young 'knowledge workers' and professionals across the public and private sectors are likely to play the critical role in providing the technical expertise and cultural legitimacy for a new form of 'post-pandemic politics' in which central governments, regional/local agencies and business corporations come together to pursue a policy agenda in which sovereignty, security, sustainability and control are the overriding themes.

In their very different ways, the analysts previously reviewed in this section are searching for the renewal of the social contract between states, experts and publics which has all but been destroyed during an era in which socio-economic dislocation and political polarization have pushed it on to the margins of debate. Yet, they all realize that this process of renewal must be undertaken in very different conditions and constraints from those prevailing between the mid-1940s and early-1980s. In addition, they accept that 'reconciling expertise and democracy' is going to be particularly difficult when experts seem to have played such a significant part in ripping-up the very foundations of the social democratic settlement through their design and operation of systems and technologies which so radically disrupted and destabilized the 'shared protective expectations' on which the latter had rested. Thus, the key question remains as to how the 'disembedding mechanisms' which lie at the core of expert systems – that is, their inherent logical drive and organizational capacity to rip, stretch and codify localized knowledge, skills and routines away from their situated contexts so that they become transformed into portable and remote technologies (Beck, Giddens and Lash 1995) are to be reprogrammed and repurposed to facilitate 're-embedding strategies' in which localized control, security and stability can be revitalized.

Cooper and Szreter's (2021) historical study of the vital role that 'collectivist individualism' has played in managing existential biomedical crises in the UK since the seventeenth century gives us very real insight into how expert authority and governance have come to serve the wider community in the past and can continue to do so in the future. They contrast the way the Covid-19 crisis has been managed in the UK with the emergence of the Elizabethan Poor Law inaugurated in 1601 and the ways in which it supported England's economic growth over the next 150 years, as well as the period after the Second World War when the welfare state was constructed. By the time the Covid-19 crisis hit the UK in 2019/2020, it had experienced a series of central government administrations which had managed a decade or more of retreat into a neoliberal minimal state totally and utterly unprepared to cope with a microbial existential threat due to long-term disinvestment in the public infrastructure through which the latter could be effectively managed. This retreat from the liberal/social democratic welfare state into the neoliberal/ minimal state also entailed radically undermining the ideology of 'collectivist individualism' on which the former had rested with its historical roots deep in the

Tudor era when the institutional foundations of a modern British nation were laid down.

Cooper and Szreter (2021) also maintain that this retreat into a minimalist, disempowered neoliberal state was carried through over a number of linked historical phases – the financial deregulation of the 1980s/1990s in which corporate and finance capital became the dominant economic and political coalition within the UK as its economy completed its transition into a form of 'rentier capitalism' (Christophers 2020) where it became 'butler to the world' (Bullough 2022) which was followed by a wider deregulation of public services in which 'just in time' delivery by marketized and privatized agencies in healthcare, public health, social care, education and justice became the overriding political imperative – which ate away, locust-like, at the 'collectivist individualism' which had legitimated the liberal/social democratic welfare state. But this retreat from the post-Second World War welfare state and the implicit social contract underpinning it 'hit the buffers' as the Covid-19 crisis unfolded and widening asymmetries of wealth, power and status which the neoliberal state proactively deepened severely weakened the collective capacity of the country to respond effectively. Emerging cracks in the neoliberal order, incrementally constructed since the 1980s, started to become chasms as the neoliberal state and its incumbent political elite repeatedly failed to accept the enormity of the crisis which faced them and the scale of the collective response which it would require if it was to be contained and brought under public control.

Renewal of the 'collectivist individualism' – that is, reviving the dynamic balance and ideological fusion between 'collectivism' and 'individualism', between practices and relations which prioritize communal wellbeing and those which protect individual rights and personal freedom – which has informed public policy and practice in the UK over centuries of its history has become both a political and moral necessity according to Cooper and Szreter (2021: 286 – 317). The 'negative liberty' on which UK neoliberal/rentier capitalism depends for its ideological oxygen and political momentum has been exposed to a test which it has completely failed to pass in that it has left millions of its citizens facing the trials and tribulations of the Covid-19 crisis alone and bereft of protection from that institution which, above all others, is charged with guarding their safety and security – that is, the central state and its panoply of supporting agencies and organizations. While the success of the vaccine programme may have 'saved the political bacon' of governing elites for now, sustained reinvestment, financial, political and social, in universal public services by a newly empowered and modernised welfare state is the only way in which we are going to enhance our collective preparedness for 'crises to come'.

Cooper and Szreter (2021: 318 – 350) conclude their analysis with an outline of the core principles on which this renewal of the tradition of collectivist individualism and its legitimation of a proactive state and an empowering society are to be founded. These range widely across a spectrum of values from 'respective and inclusive support for all' to a participatory politics in which democratic and civic engagement are revitalized. Echoing the call for a new social contract between states, experts and publics repeatedly made by the analysts and researchers considered in this section of our book, they put a renewed call for a democratically accountable and publicly visible expertise – as displayed during the pandemic – at the centre of their recommendations. As Cooper and Szreter (2021: chapters 2, 3 and 13) serially demonstrate, public service expertise – in public health, healthcare, biomedical science and other critical domains of collective intervention – was consistently challenged and undermined by private sector corporate power and incumbent political elites determined to profit from the Covid-19 crisis to the greatest degree possible, even if this meant endangering the general public as a result (Calvert and Arbuthnot 2021).

Once again, this raises the question as to how a contemporary 'political sociology of expertise' might play a significant role in helping to translate these aspirations for a new social contract and a renewed collectivist individualism into reality.

4 Political Sociology of Expertise

Working within a mainstream neo-institutional approach within the sociology of organizations, Muzio, Aulakh and Kirkpatrick (2019) have recently presented a broadly reassuring – theoretically, empirically and normatively – appraisal of the continuing longevity and resilience of professionalized modes of work organization and occupational regulation. For them, the contemporary sociology of organizations remains focused on a social phenomenon that retains the institutionalized trust of the societies in which it is embedded and has continued to cope in an exemplary fashion with the technological, ideological and political disruptions it has faced so that it retains its established social legitimacy and moral authority. However, even though this, largely unqualified, reassuring narrative might be seen as somewhat complacent by some researchers – and as will be crystal clear to any readers of our book by now, this would certainly be our view – even they must admit that 'the field might also be enhanced by incorporating the sociology of the professions within a more inclusive 'sociology of expertise' (Muzio, Aulakh and Kirkpatrick 2019: 66). In this way, their relatively narrow and single-stranded focus on the institutionalized logics through which jurisdictional boundary management, task control, and formal regulation become reasonably well-integrated and stabilized can be at least complemented, if not superseded, by a much wider and inclusive analytical lens through the development of a contemporary political sociology of expertise properly attuned to the multiple threats that the established 'professional state' faces (Burns 2019; Saks 2021).

Unlike neo-institutionalist perspectives in the sociology of professions/occupations which tend to assume that 'professional authority' is necessarily embedded in and reproduced by the institutional logic from which it derives its legitimacy, a 'political sociology of expertise' must treat the latter as 'essentially contested' as an interrelated concept, relation, and practice. Neo-institutional theory (Thornton, Ocasio and Lounsbury 2012: 29) presumes that legitimacy, and hence authority, is based on the shared preference that humans and organizations have 'for certainty, predictability, and survivability [so that] much behaviour falls into the category of seeking legitimacy to garner resources which sustain existing institutions.' While later versions of the institutional logics' perspective give greater emphasis to the power politics and material interests which drive this inherent tendency towards the cyclical reproduction of legitimacy and authority through 'institutional isomorphism' – that is, the various developmental processes and trajectories through which organizations, occupations and organizations come to resemble each other – it remains an axiomatic assumption on which neo-institutionalist sociology of professions has been predicated. Underlying pressures driving towards organizational isomorphism will cyclically self-reproduce the processes and structures through which organizations and occupations secure legitimation and authority within the fields in which they operate. Thus, Muzio, Aulak and Kirkpatrick (2019) restrict their discussion of 'cultural de-legitimation and the loss of confidence in expertise' to declining cultural support for professional expertise and waning trust in professional socialization which various self-corrective mechanisms, such as tighter formal regulation and more transparent external scrutiny, will correct to enable reconfigured forms of 'hybrid professionalism' to prosper in the future. They omit to engage with the more fundamental critiques of expert authority and what Weber called the 'structures of domination' and Foucault identified as the dominant 'discursive formations' through which its legitimacy is, however contingently and temporarily, secured. Their institutionalist proclivities incline them to a social ontology in which underlying evolutionary dynamics will, eventually, self-correct the temporary instabilities, even short-term crises, which any social ecology of occupations, organizations and professions undergoes in order to ensure its long-term survivability and prosperity. Institutionalization is a guarantor of professionalized occupational forms and their underling social legitimacy because it always 'comes to the rescue' as a self-correcting mechanism repairing temporary breakdowns in public trust and reputation and restabilizing the formal organizational scaffolding around which they can be rebuilt.

Once we move away from this neo-institutionalist approach to the sociology of professions towards a political sociology of expertise in which the legitimacy and authority of experts are subject to continuing contestation and instability, then a much wider range of theoretical possibilities open-up in which the enduring socio-political realities of the latter's, collective and individual, existence can be brought into analytical focus. As an 'essentially contested' concept, relation, and practice, expert authority is made and remade out of the struggles – intellectual, social, and technical – through which it is legitimated in a sociohistorical context in which there is no underlying guarantee that it will be reproduced through the process of institutionalization and the evolutionary dynamics which determine its trajectory and outcome. To say that a concept, relation, and practice such as 'expert authority' is 'essentially contested' is to argue that it necessarily and contingently entails open-ended disputes about its meaning, status and relevance (Connolly 1983) which cannot be permanently settled or resolved because they are integral to its application and significance. In this respect, 'expert authority' is an *appraisive* concept, relation, and practice 'in that the situation it describes is a valued achievement, when the practice described is *internally complex* in that its characterization involves reference to several dimensions' (Connolly 1983: 10 emphases in original). Consensus around shared rules of interpretation and application can and do emerge, but they are always subject to challenge and revision as new and unforeseen situations arise that open them up to further interrogation and reappraisal in the light of what the latter entail.

There can be little or no doubt that we are living in times when there have been seismic shifts in the material conditions and structural contexts in which 'expert authority' is understood, organized and undertaken so that its meaning and status as an appraisive concept, relation, and practice need to be fundamentally re-evaluated and reset. This relates both to the similarities and differences between 'expert authority' when compared to other forms and modalities of authority and to its resilience and sustainability under the extreme pressures to which it has been subjected as they have been identified and assessed in previous chapters of this book.

Although 'expertise' comes in a very wide range of forms and modalities (Collins 2009, 2013, Collins et al. 2020), its contested authorization as a legitimate and trusted practice differentiates it from other types of authority even if they are all, ultimately, based on power relations and the legitimacy struggles that coalesce around them. These legitimacy struggles make and remake expert authority as a distinctive concept, relation and practice as they are shaped and reshaped by the 'trust/control dynamics' that drive the former.

Considered in this way, expert authority has a number of interrelated and defining dimensions which differentiate it from other forms and modalities of authority. First, expert authority is hierarchically structured but is increasingly required to extend its socio-political base significantly beyond those 'experts' who claim it if it is to be successful in mobilizing its 'legitimacy claims' within the societies in which it operates. Second, this structural or systemic tension between 'autonomy/control' and 'accessibility/trust' is likely to become even more complex and disruptive as experts, either through choice or necessity, reach out beyond the jurisdictional domains in which they are most comfortable to engage with wider audiences and stakeholders who are already more sceptical, even suspicious, about their 'legitimacy claims'. Third, there is the issue of how the increasing plurality and diversity of expertise might complicate attempts to bring it under more inclusive and participative governance arrangements without compromising its capacity to 'do its job properly' as it comes under ever more intrusive forms of public scrutiny and accountability. Finally, there remains the overriding problem of 'if and how' experts can continue to perform their vital role in mobilizing and mediating specialist knowledge under conditions of extreme instability and uncertainty when the political pressure to produce results that work rapidly and convincingly intensifies.

Expert authority is hierarchically structured epistemologically, institutionally, and organizationally: forms of specialist knowledge are differentially ranked in relation to the processes through which they are produced and reproduced, as well as to their reliability and relevance for problem solving; the institutional source and standing of these specialist knowledges plays a critical role in determining how they are rated both by fellow specialists and the public at large; the jurisdictional work domains which these specialist knowledges support and legitimate are also subject to wider evaluation as to their relative status and prestige so that 'reputational politics' has a major impact on the material resources and social support they receive from the societies in which they are embedded (Stehr and Grundmann 2014; Turner 2014; Moore 2017; Collins et al. 2020). This interrelated hierarchical structuring process generates a multiplicity of problems for any movement, policy or programme aimed at 'democratizing expertise' because it highlights the inherent limits of the latter and exposes the systemic tension between 'expert authority' and 'political authority' (Heazle and Kane 2016; Moore 2017; Collins et al. 2020).

Heazle and Kane (2016) maintain that 'expert authority' and 'political authority' relate to each other in highly variable and complex ways depending on the wider political regimes in which they are located and the specific socio-historical contexts in which their dynamic relationship unfolds. Nevertheless, they contend that there is a systemic tension between them to the extent that 'expertise' is legitimated through scientifically generated and validated claims to specialist knowledge and technical skill, while 'policy' is justified based on goals and priorities emerging from ideological values and the material interests they promote. This distinction has been questioned by successive waves of conceptual and empirical research over the last decade or so, but its credibility has been sustained through the development of a more nuanced and sensitive appreciation of the interplay between 'epistemological credentialism' and 'political authorization'. The 'linear rational' model of policy development and implementation in which 'science and politics are wholly autonomous and distinct' (Heazle and Kane 2016: 6) has been seen to be conceptually and empirically unsustainable. However, more recent formulations of the relationship suggest an interdependency which is 'messy, dynamic, contested and unstable' but which generates sufficient expert legitimacy and political consensus to move forward incrementally across a range of policy areas such as climate change, environmental health, nuclear power and assisted reproductive technology. While research in these, and other, policy domains reveal an in-built tendency for expert authority to become politicized as the struggle for legitimacy intensifies, the former remains robust enough to resist political domination as long as liberal/social democratic 'checks and balances' remain in place to counter the challenges posed by populism or neoliberalism.

Yet, this shift towards a more sociologically and politically realistic analysis of the tensions between 'expertise' and 'politics' leaves unresolved what Collins et al. (2020: 83) call 'the problem of extension' and its relationship to 'the problem of legitimacy'. While the former problem relates to increasing the *diversity* of expert decision-making sufficiently to include both 'experience-based' experts and 'technically-based' experts, the latter refers to the *democratization* of policy making in order to ensure that it doesn't become dominated by a narrow range of scientific experts and technocrats excluding other relevant points of view. Collins et al. (2020) suggest that both issues can be dealt with my demarcating the 'technical' from the 'political' phases of policy making and implementation such that 'participation in the technical phase is limited to those with relevant specialist expertise but participation in the political phase remains open to all citizens'. However, the question remains as how sustainable this division of labour between 'technical' and 'political' phases or domains of policy making proves to be when 'it is likely that expert authority will more often be hijacked by political interests that selectively support one expert position over another on the basis of its ability to *fit with* policy rather than its ability *to inform* policy' (Heazle and Kane 2016: 191 emphases in original). This suggests that the boundaries between 'expert' and 'political' authority have become so permeable and diluted that the former is always likely to face the prospect of being penetrated, if not dominated, by the latter as our earlier analysis of expert authority during the pandemic indicates (see chapter 5).

Yet, expert authority must retain the epistemological power and organizational capacity to challenge the political status quo whatever its ideological predilections and policy agenda because they are crucial to retaining its legitimacy and trust-building capability. As Eyal (2019: 93) consistently argues, the crisis in expert authority is recursive in the sense that it varies in scale and intensity temporally and spatially but is cyclical and persistent in its dynamics and effects insofar as it relates to 'the institutional frames and mechanisms that organize deliberation, and especially of the temporal frames that separate, in time, technical problem-solving from political decisions.' As Weber and Foucault insist (O'Neil 1986; Reed 1999), expert authority is always embedded in systems of domination which simultaneously support and threaten it; while the latter needs the former to fulfil a wide range of administrative, technical and organizational functions, there is always the danger that it will 'turn on' its functionaries in ways that threaten their legitimacy. In turn, once political and economic elites begin to 'turn on' expert authority, they will do their best to ensure that 'the people' follow their lead, particularly when wider conditions in the economy and polity encourage increasing public scepticism and suspicion over the power that experts wield within their societies.

However open, participatory, reflexive and deliberative expert authority may become, 'they do not, by themselves, secure legitimacy' (Eyal 2019: 145). Legitimacy must be secured and renewed in a continuing struggle to retain its potency and efficacy in which the power it authorizes and justifies has recognizable limits but also supportive institutions and mechanisms that generate sufficient epistemological consensus and closure required 'to move on' in any sphere of contemporary life. In short, expert authority must retain its freedom and capacity to challenge the prevailing status quo and to protect itself against threats to its integrity and credibility which cannot be guaranteed by simply widening its 'participatory reach' or enhancing its 'reflexive capacity'. As Turner (2014: 73) maintains, expert authority – if it is to reproduce its social legitimacy and public trust – must retain an institutional infrastructure and personal substructure that guarantees, however imperfectly and messily, the impersonality and integrity of expertise. It must have the collective capacity to ensure that 'the production of expert knowledge is controlled through the indirect means of professional certification and recognition, as well as the concentration and control of opinion through methods of peer review and evaluation that typically do not directly assess the truth or validity of expert claims, just their minimal professional adequacy.'

Only in this way can expert authority ensure that it retains the wider public support and trust it especially needs when those in positions of power within domination systems 'turn against it' and try to recruit the general populous to their 'ideological drumbeat'. It must constantly revivify the core institutions and mechanisms on which its legitimacy rests if it is to retain sufficient public trust and support when its integrity and relevance are under extreme ideological and political pressure. This will necessarily entail retaining limits on how participative and open it becomes to wider influences and demands.

Currently, the 'politicization of expertise' constitutes as much of a threat to the legitimacy of expert authority as the 'technologization of politics' in that it negates whatever protestations experts might make against claims that they are simply 'servants of power' with little or no regard for the communities they are expected to serve. Once expert authority is seen to be irrevocably compromised by the hierarchies and networks of political power in which it is inevitably intermeshed, then its corrosive impact on its internal integrity and external status is likely to become irreparable. Only by maintaining a flexible and shifting balance between 'trust and control' relations within a dynamic institutional landscape can expert authority expect to retain the legitimacy and trust on which its veracity and viability depends. Contestation and instability, both internal and external, are inherent within such a dynamic process and relationship; they cannot be contained and stabilized within certification ecosystems and credentialled regulations however formalized and entrenched they may seem from the inside. Ultimately, it is this endemic dynamism and flexibility which will save expert authority from the twin threats of bureaucratic ossification and political imperialism which many of its friends refuse to admit much less contemplate.

5 Conclusion

Throughout this book we have focused on how ongoing debates about expert authority have fused to form an intellectual crucible in which so many of the structural and political tensions which have defined the last half century or so have intermixed to produce all sorts of 'strange and wonderful' alloys.

Thus, the tensions between globalism and nationalism, liberalism and populism, pluralism and authoritarianism, science and tradition, meritocracy and community, and planning and markets have coursed their way through the crucible of 'expert authority' as it attempted to capture something vital about the times we are living through. These have been, indeed are, times in which crises and crisis narratives have been pervasive and somewhat overwhelming. While not underestimating the scale and significance of these crises, we have also attempted to navigate an intellectual course between dystopian visions of 'digitalised Taylorism' or 'surveillance capitalism' or 'technocratic authoritarianism' on the one hand and complacent narratives about 'resilient certification ecosystems' or 'refurbished meritocracy' on the other.

Along the way, we have also tried to make a case for a 'reflexive expert authority and governance' which recognizes the need for more open, participative and deliberative modes of policy making and implementation but also remains firm in the belief that 'expertise' must remain true to itself, and resist attempts to democratize it in ways that rob it of its own 'machineries for producing legitimacy' (Eyal 2019: 148). Expertise cannot and should not be collapsed into politics, both for its own sake and for the sake of those whom it may serve. As Eyal (2019: 149) also concludes, in sympathy with Weber, the most important role that experts serve is as 'bringers of bad news' to both political and economic elites and the wider polity. They must act with an 'ethic of responsibility' as their guiding principle where the recognition of inconvenient facts, particularly in crisis situations where states, experts, and publics have a lot of 'skin in the game', may prove very difficult for all decision-makers and stakeholders to admit. As Owen and Strong (2004: xxxi–xxxii emphasis in original) remark in their introduction to 'The Vocation Lectures', 'Weber argues that science does have an important ethical role to play within the totality of human life, namely, to provide *clarity* concerning "ultimate" problems [and] must operate against the background assumption that there is a plurality of incompatible orientations to life'. Considered in this way, expert authority – whether of the scientist, medic, academic, architect, lawyer, administrator or manager – consists in legitimate claims to specialist knowledge and skills with their own internal integrity and responsibility to be 'bringers of bad news' in a world where a plurality of incompatible values and interests bely any attempt to produce universal agreement and certainty.

Expert authority is much more than certificates, licences and regulations but it must retain its own distinctive organizational forms and regulative structures if it is to remain in a position where it can at least question and even challenge power elites based on its own internal values and the wider obligations they entail. Expert authority, at its organizational and discursive core, is about legitimating specialized knowledge and the critical role it must continue to play in our lives in general and particularly in high risk, high stakes decision-making. 'We' cannot do without it, and 'it' cannot do without us, but the relationship in which we are jointly engaged will always be prone to conflict, tension and breakdown that will require repair, compromise and consolidation.

In this final chapter, we have argued that the re-emergence of the 'interventionist state' (Tooze 2022; Cooper and Szreter 2021; Gerbaudo 2021; Garrard 2022), ideologically and politically nourished by a new 'social contract' reviving and realigning the tripartite partnership between states, experts, and publics prevailing under liberal/social democratic regimes (Shafik 2021; Hennessy 2021), constitutes a major structural change likely to transform the governmental context in which experts will operate. As a response to a series of crises, in which the global pandemic has, at least so far, played the critical role, the re-emergence of an interventionist state, ideologically driven neither by neoliberalism or populism but by a rejuvenated 'collectivist individualism' (Cooper and Szreter 2021), offers experts a very real opportunity to re-establish their high trust relationship with the general public and to renew their authority within the wider polity. Not only this, but the return of the 'interventionist state' also offers the opportunity to restate the centrality of 'the public good' in our lives and the key part that reflexive expert authority will play in making that collective concern a political reality. Expert legitimacy struggles will continue to emerge and ebb and flow around the three core purposes which the modern state fulfils, and which have become even more self-evident in the aftermath of the series of crises which the world has faced since 2008 – 'security, welfare and democratic control of both politics and the economy' (Garrard 2022: 175). Keeping its people safe, securing and promoting their social and economic wellbeing by actively engaging with powerful corporations in order to ensure that they, alongside public agencies, provide essential public goods to all its citizens by 'reversing the policies of privatization and outsourcing that has transferred so many of the functions of the state to the market (Garrard 2022: 184), and rebalancing of public and private power in favour of the former constitutes the priorities for a revived liberal/social democratic state. In all of this, experts will provide the specialist knowledges and skills required to make the 'public interest state' a political reality and will seek to re-establish their legitimate authority based on how they will be judged by states and publics alike in helping to realize this transformation in our collective and individual lives.

Expert authority has always been made and remade through struggles over its legitimacy (Kennedy 2016) and will continue to be so. However, it relies on sufficiently robust sources and mechanisms of 'countervailing power' (Galbraith 1967; Reich 2016) which have been severely weakened during the socio-historical period covered in this book. Along with the return of the liberal/social democratic state, experts will remain a vital source of power and authority interacting with other sources of countervailing power within a pluralistic socio-political order in which private interests are counterbalanced by public agencies. However, they will only be able to do so if they are prepared to respond to the challenges which much more reflexive modes of expert authority and governance demand. Insofar as this book can make a contribution to social democratic revival and the renewal of the countervailing power mechanisms and relations on which it depends through an analysis of ongoing debates about 'expert authority' helping us to interpret it in a more socially and politically realistic light, then it will have done its job.

References

Abbasi, K. (2020). When good science is suppressed by the medical-political complex, people die. *BMJ*, 317. doi: https://doi.org/10.1136/bmj.m4425

Abbott, A. (1988). *The System of Professions: An Essay on the Division of Expert Labour.* Chicago, IL: Chicago University Press.

Abbott, A. (2005). Linked ecologies: states and universities as environments for professions, *Sociological Theory*, 23(3).

Adams, T. L. (2017). Self-regulating professions: past, present, future. *Journal of Professions and Organization*, 4(1): 70 – 87.

Adams, T. L, Clegg, S., Eyal, G., Reed, M. and Saks, M. (2020). Connective professionalism: towards (yet another) ideal type., *Journal of Professions and Organization*, 7(2): 224 – 233.

Adler, P. (2019). *The 99 Per Cent Economy: How Democratic Socialism Can Overcome the Crises of Capitalism.* Oxford: Oxford University Press.

Albrow, M. (1970). *Bureaucracy.* London: Pall Mall Press.

Alwakeel, R. and Demianyk, G. (2021). Has Boris Johnson Really Done 'Everything' To Tackle Coronavirus? Retrieved from https://m.huffingtonpost.co.uk/amp/entry/guided-by-the-science-co ronavirus_uk_5fe46a92c5b6e1ce8338aa72

Amoore, L. (2020). *Cloud Ethics: Algorithms and the Attributes of Ourselves and Others.* London: Duke University Press.

Anderson, E. (2017). *Private Government.* Princeton: Princeton University Press.

Anter. A. (2014). *Max Weber's Theory of the Modern State.* Basingstoke, UK: Palgrave Macmillan.

Anthony, P. (1977). *The Ideology of Work.* London: Tavistock.

Anthony, P. (1986). *Foundations of Management.* London: Tavistock.

Applebaum, A. (2020). *Twilight of Democracy: The Seductive Lure of Authoritarianism.* New Work: Doubleday.

Babones, S. (2018). *The New Authoritarianism: Trump, Populism and the Tyranny of Experts.* Cambridge, UK: Polity Press.

Ball, P. (2022). Muted and deferential, the UK's scientists have failed the pandemic test. Retrieved from https://www.newstatesman.com/politics/2022/01/quiet-uncritical-obedient-how-the-uks-sci entists-failed-the-pandemic-test

Balloux, F. (2022). The best of times, the worst of times...That's science in the age of Covid. Retrieved from https://www.theguardian.com/commentisfree/2022/jul/17/best-of-times-worst-of-times-science-in-age-of-covid

Ban, C. (2016). *Ruling Ideas: How Global Neoliberalism Goes Local.* Oxford, UK: Oxford University Press.

BBC. (2022). Experts had too much power over Covid lockdowns, says Rishi Sunak. Retrieved from https://www.bbc.com/news/uk-politics-62664537.amp

Beck, U. (1992). *Risk Society: Towards a New Modernity.* London; Sage.

Beck, U. (1997). *The Reinvention of Politics.* Cambridge, UK: Polity Press.

Beck, U. (1999). *World Risk Society.* Cambridge, UK: Polity Press.

Beck, U., Giddens, A., and Lash, S. (1994). *Reflexive Modernization: Politics, Tradition and Aesthetics in the Modern Social Order.* Cambridge, UK: Polity Press.

Bell, D. (1960). *The End of Ideology: On the Exhaustion of Political Ideas in the Fifties.* New York: Free Press.

Bell, D. (1973). *The Coming of Post-Industrial Society.* New York: Basic Books.

Bell. D. (1976). *The Cultural Contradictions of Capitalism.* New York: Free Press.

https://doi.org/10.1515/9783110734911-010

Bell. D. (1999). *The Coming of Post-Industrial Society.* Special Anniversary Edition. New York: Basic Books, Pegasus Press.

Bell, E. (2015). *Soft Power and Freedom under the Coalition: State-Corporate Power and the Threat to Democracy.* Kindle Edition, Palgrave Macmillan.

Belton, C. (2020). *Putin's People: How the KGB Took Back Russia and then Took the West.* London: William Collins Harper Collins Publishers.

Benanav, A. (2020). *Automation and the Future of Work.* London: Verso.

Bernstein, B. (2000). *Pedagogy, Symbolic Control, and Identity.* Second Edition. New York: Rowan and Littlefield.

Bevir, M. (Ed.). (2016). *Governmentality after Neoliberalism.* London: Routledge.

Bickerton, C. J., and Accetti, C. I. (2021). *Technopopulism: The New Logic of Democratic Politics.* Oxford, UK: Oxford University Press.

Bingham, K. (2021). Romanes Lecture – Kate Bingham, 'Lessons from the Vaccine Taskforce.' Retrieved from https://www.youtube.com/watch?v=tG_a0P2qybE

Billig, M. (2021). Rhetorical uses of precise numbers and semi-magical round numbers in political discourse about COVID-19: Examples from the government of the United Kingdom. *Discourse & Society,* 32(5): 542–558.

Bishop, B. (2009). *The Big Sort: Why the Clustering of Like-Minded America is Tearing us Apart.* Boston, US: Mariner Books.

Blau, P. (1955). *The Dynamics of Bureaucracy.* Chicago: University of Chicago Press.

Blowers, A., Boersema, J., and Martin, A. (2005). Experts, decision-making and deliberative democracy. *Environmental Sciences,* 2(1): 1–3.

Blyth, M. (2013). *Austerity: The History of a Dangerous Idea.* Oxford: Oxford University Press.

Booth, R. (2020). UK health screening advisers not involved in 'moonshot' Covid plan. Retrieved from https://www.theguardian.com/world/2020/sep/11/uk-health-screening-advisers-not-involved-in-moonshot-covid-plan-mass-testing-coronavirus

Bourgeron, T. (2021). 'Let the virus spread'. A doctrine of pandemic management for the libertarian-authoritarian capital accumulation regime. *Organization,* 29(3): 401–413.

Boussard, V. (2018). Professional closure regimes in the global age: the boundary work of professional services specialized in mergers and acquisitions. *Journal of Professions and Organization,* 5(3): 167–183.

Boussebaa, M., and Morgan, G. (2015). Internationalization of professional service firms. In: L. Empson, D. Muzio, J. P. Broschak, and B. Hinings (Eds.), *The Oxford Handbook of Professional Service Firms* (pp. 71–91). Oxford: Oxford University Press.

Bowman, A., Froud, J., Law, J., Leaver, A, Moran, M and William K. (2014). *The End of the Experiment? From Competition to the Foundational Economy.* Manchester, UK: Manchester University Press.

Bowman, A., Froud, J., Sukhdev, J., Moran, M. and Williams, K. (2015). Business Elites and Undemocracy in Britain: A Work in Progress. In G. Morgan, P. Hirsch and S. Quack (Eds.), *Elites on Trial* (Research in the Sociology of Organizations, Vol. 43), (pp. 305–336). Bingley US: Emerald Group Publishing.

Broad, W. J., and Levin, D. (2020). Trump Muses About Light as Remedy, but Also Disinfectant, Which Is Dangerous. Retrieved from https://www.nytimes.com/2020/04/24/health/sunlight-coronavirus-trump.html

Brooks, R. (2018). *Bean Counters: The Triumph of the Accountants and How They Broke Capitalism.* London, UK: Atlantic Books.

Brown, M. B. (2014). Expertise and deliberative democracy. In S. Elstub and P. McLaverty (Eds.), *Deliberative Democracy: Issues and Cases* (pp. 50–68). Edinburgh: Edinburgh University Press.

Brown, W. (2015). *Undoing the Demos: Neoliberalism's Stealth Revolution.* Cambridge, MA: The MIT Press.

Brown, W. (2019). *In the Ruins of Neoliberalism.* New York City, NY: Columbia University Press.

Buchanan, D., Addicott, R., Fitzgerald, L., Ferlie, E., and Baeza, J. (2007). Nobody in charge: distributed agency in health care'. *Human Relations*, 60(7): 1065–1090.

Bullough, O. (2022). *Butler to the World: How Britain became the Servant of Tycoons, Tax Dodgers, Kleptocrats and Criminals.* London: Profile Books.

Buranyi, S. (2020). How coronavirus has brought together conspiracy theorists and the far right. Retrieved from https://www.theguardian.com/commentisfree/2020/sep/04/coronavirus-con spiracy-theorists-far-right-protests

Burchell, G., Gordon, C., and Miller, P. (Eds). (1991). *The Foucault Effect: Studies in Governmentality.* London: Prentice-Hall.

Burns, E. (2019). *Theorizing Professions: A Sociological Introduction.* London, UK: Palgrave Macmillan.

Burrell, G. (2006). Foucauldian and postmodern thought and the analysis of work. In M. Korcynski, R. Hodson and P. Edwards (Eds.), *Social Theory at Work* (pp. 155–181). Oxford, UK: Oxford University Press.

Burrell, G. (2022). *Organization Theory: A Research Overview.* London: Routledge.

Busch, L. (2017). *Knowledge for Sale: The Neoliberal Takeover of Higher Education.* Cambridge, Mass: The MIT Press.

Cahill, D. (2014). *The End of Laissez-Faire?: On the Durability of Embedded Neoliberalism.* Cheltenham: Edward Elgar.

Cahill, D., and Konings, M. (2017). *Neoliberalism.* Cambridge, UK: Polity.

Callison, W., and Manfredi, Z. (Eds.). (2020). *Mutant Neoliberalism: Market Rule and Political Rupture.* New York City, NY: Fordham University Press.

Calvert, J., and Arbuthnott, G. (2021). *Failures of State: The Inside Story of Britain's Battle with Coronavirus.* London, UK: Harper Collins.

Campbell, J. L and Pedersen, Ove K. (Eds.). (2001). *The Rise of Neoliberalism and Institutional Analysis.* Princeton: Princeton University Press.

Campbell, D., and Walker, P. (2020). Ministers shifting blame to Public Health England for Covid-19 errors, say experts. Retrieved from https://www.theguardian.com/world/2020/jul/01/experts-say-ministers-are-blaming-public-health-england-over-covid-19-errors

Chafetz, M. E. (1995). *The Tyranny of Experts: Blowing the Whistle on the Cult of Expertise.* Maryland, US: Maddison Books.

Chandler, D., and Reid, J. (2016). *The Neoliberal Subject: Resilience, Adaptation and Vulnerability.* Lanham, MD: Rowman & Littlefield.

Channel 4 News. (2021). Instead of... being clapped we are now being told that we are killers, liars, frauds. Retrieved from https://twitter.com/Channel4News/status/1357028256311083008?s=20

Child, J. (1973). Organization: a choice for man. In: J. Child (Ed.), *Man, and Organization* (pp. 234–257). London: Allen and Unwin.

Child, J. (2019). *Hierarchy: A Key Idea for Business and Society.* London: Routledge.

Christensen, J. (2017). *The Power of Economists within the State.* Stanford, US: Stanford University Press.

Christophers, B. (2020). *Rentier Capitalism: Who Owns the Economy and Who Pays for it?* London: Verso.

Clarke, J. (2005). Performing for the public: doubt, desire, and the evaluation of public services. In P. Du Gay (Ed.), *The Values of Bureaucracy*, (pp. 211–232). Oxford: Oxford University Press.

Clarke, J., and Newman, J. (1997). *The Managerial State: Power, Politics and Ideology in the Remaking of Social Welfare.* London: Sage.

Clarke, J., Newman, J., Smith, N., Vidler, E., and Westmarland, L. (2007). *Creating Citizen Consumers: Changing Publics and Changing Public Services.* London: Sage.

Clegg, S. (1998). Foucault, Power and Organization In: A. McKinlay and K. Starkey (Eds.), *Foucault, Management and Organization Theory* (pp. 29–48). London: Sage.

Clegg, S., Harris, M., and Höpfl, H. (2011). *Managing Modernity: Beyond Bureaucracy?* Oxford: Oxford University Press.

Coats, D. (2018). *Fragments in the Ruins: The Renewal of Social Democracy.* London: Rowan and Littlefield.

Cohen, N. (2020). The meritocracy has had its day. How else to explain the rise of Dido Harding? Retrieved from https://www.theguardian.com/commentisfree/2020/sep/19/meritocracy-dido-harding-rise

Cohen, J., and Arato, A. (1992). *Civil Society and Political Theory.* Cambridge, Mass: MIT Press.

Collier, P. (2018). *The Future of Capitalism: Facing the New Anxieties.* New York: Harper Collins Publishers.

Collins, H. (2013). *Tacit and Explicit Knowledge.* Chicago: The University of Chicago Press.

Collins, H. (2019). *Forms of Life: The Method and Meaning of Sociology.* Cambridge, MA: MIT Press.

Collins, H., and Evans, R. (2009). *Rethinking Expertise.* Chicago: The University of Chicago Press.

Collins, H., Evans, R., Durant, D., and Weinel, M. (2020). *Experts and the Will of the People.* London: Palgrave Macmillan.

Collins, R. (2019). *The Credential Society: An Historical Sociology of Education and Stratification.* New York: Columbia University Press.

Collins, R. (1990). Changing conceptions in the sociology of the profession. In M. Burrage, and Torstendahl, R. (Eds.), *Knowledge, State and Strategy: The Formation of Professions in Europe and North America* (pp. 11–23). London: Sage.

Connolly, W. E. (1983). *The Terms of Political Discourse.* Second Edition. Oxford: Martin Robertson and Company.

Cooper, H., and Szreter, S. (2021). *After the Virus: Lessons from the Past for a Better Future.* Cambridge: Cambridge University Press.

Costello, A. (2021). Retrieved from https://twitter.com/globalhlthtwit/status/1447802358424084484?t=LVxd5os62utPi82xnOJPDQ&s=03

Courpasson, D. (2000). Managerial strategies of domination: power in soft bureaucracies. *Organization Studies*, 21, (1): 141–161.

Courpasson, D. (2006). *Soft Constraint: Liberal Organizations and Domination.* Liber: Copenhagen Business School Press.

Courpasson, D., Golsorkhi, D., and Sallaz, J. (Eds.). (2012). *Rethinking Power in Organizations: Institutions and Markets* (Research in the Sociology of Organizations, Vol. 34). Bingley: Emerald Group Publishing.

Courpasson, D., Younes, D., and Reed, M. (2021). Durkheim and the neoliberal organization: taking resistance and solidarity seriously. *Organization Theory*, 2: 1–24.

Cousins, M., and Hussain, K. (1984). *Michel Foucault.* London: Macmillan.

Crawford, K. (2021). *Atlas of AI.* New Haven: Yale University Press.

Crozier, M. (1964). *The Bureaucratic Phenomenon.* Chicago: University of Chicago Press.

Crouch, C. (2016). *The Knowledge Corruptors: Hidden Consequences of the Financial Takeover of Public Life.* Cambridge, UK: Polity Press.

Crouch, C. (2017). *Can Neoliberalism be Saved from Itself?* London: Social Europe Edition.

Cruddas, J. (2021). *The Dignity of Labour.* Cambridge: Polity Press.

Currie, G., and White, L. (2012). Inter-professional barriers and knowledge brokering in an organizational context'. *Organization Studies,* 33(10): 1333–1361.

Currie, G., Lockett, A., Finn, R., Martin, G., and Waring, J. (2012). Institutional work to maintain professional power: recreating the model of medical professionalism. *Organization Studies,* 33(10): 937–962.

Dahl, R. (1971). *Polyarchy, Participation and Opposition.* New Haven, US: Yale University Press.

Daniels, R. J. (2021). *What Universities Owe Democracy.* Baltimore, US: John Hopkins University Press.

Dardot, P., and Laval, C. (2013). *The New Way of the World: On Neoliberal Society.* London: Verso.

Daub, A. (2020). *What Tech Calls Thinking.* New York: FSG Originals x Logic.

Davies, J. (2011). *Challenging governance theory: from networks to hegemony.* Bristol, UK: The Policy Press.

Davies, R. (2020b). A £56 m bill and rising: the cost of Covid consultancy contracts. Retrieved from https://www.theguardian.com/business/2020/sep/29/a-56m-bill-and-rising-the-cost-of-covid-con sultancy-contracts

Davies, W. (2014). *The Limits of Neoliberalism: Authority, Sovereignty and the Logic of Competition.* London: Sage.

Davies, W. (2017). Elite Power under Advanced Neoliberalism. *Theory, Culture & Society,* 34(5–6): 227–250.

Davies, W. (2018). *Nervous States: How Feeling Took Over the World.* New York City, NY: Vintage.

Davies, W. (2020a). *This is Not Normal: The Collapse of Liberal Britain.* London: Verso.

Davies, W., Dutta, S. J., Taylor, N., and Tazzioli, M. (2022). *Unprecedented? How Covid-19 Revealed the Politics of our Economy.* London: Goldsmiths Press.

Davis, A. (2018). *Reckless Opportunists: Elites at the End of the Establishment.* Manchester: Manchester University Press.

Davis, A., and Williams, K. (2017). Introduction: elites and power after financialization. *Theory, Culture and Society,* Special Issue on Elites and Power after Financialization.

Davis, G. (2009). The rise and fall of finance and the end of the society of organizations. *Academy of Management Perspectives,* 23(3): 27–44.

Davis, G. (2009). *Managed by the Markets: How Finance Reshaped America.* Oxford: Oxford University Press.

Dean, M. (1999). *Governmentality: Power and Rule in Modern Society.* London, UK: Sage.

Deetz, S.A. (1992). *Democracy in an Age of Corporate Colonization: Developments in Communication and the Politics of Everyday Life.* New York: SUNY Press.

Dencik, L. (2020). Mobilizing Media Studies in an Age of Datafication. *Television & New Media,* 21(6): 568–573.

Derber, C., Schwartz, W. A., and Magrass, Y. (1990). *Power in the Highest Degree: Professionals and the Rise of a New Mandaring Order.* Oxford: Oxford University Press.

Diamond, J., and LeBlanc, P. (2020). Ex-pandemic preparedness chief resigns from federal government. Retrieved from https://edition.cnn.com/2020/10/06/politics/rick-bright-resigns-nih-whistleblower/index.html?utm_medium=social&utm_source=twCNN&utm_content=2020-10-07T00%3A07%3A04&utm_term=link

Du Gay, P. (2005). *The Values of Bureaucracy.* Oxford: Oxford University Press.

Elster, J. (Ed.). (1998). *Deliberative Democracy.* Cambridge: Cambridge University Press.

Elstub, S., and McLaverty, P. (2014). *Deliberative Democracy: Issues and Cases.* Edinburgh: Edinburgh University Press.

Empson, L., Muzio, D., Broschak, J. P., and Hinings, B. (Eds.). (2015). *The Oxford Handbook of Professional Service Firms.* Oxford: Oxford University Press.

Etzioni, A. (1988). *The Moral Dimension: Towards a New Economics.* New York: Free Press.

Etzioni, A. (1993). *The Spirit of Community: Rights, Responsibilities and the Communitarian Agenda.* London: Fontana.

European Medicines Agency. (2021). AstraZeneca's COVID-19 vaccine: EMA finds possible link to very rare cases of unusual blood clots with low blood platelets. Retrieved from https://www.ema.eu ropa.eu/en/news/astrazenecas-covid-19-vaccine-ema-finds-possible-link-very-rare-cases-unusual-blood-clots-low-blood

Eyal, G. (2019). *The Crisis of Expertise.* Cambridge: Polity.

Ezzamel, M., and Reed, M. (2008). Governance: a code of multiple colours, *Human Relations*, 61(5), Special Issue on Governance in Transition: 597 – 616

Fairclough, N. (2010). *Critical Discourse Analysis: The Critical Study of Language.* Second Edition. London: Longman Pearson.

Farchi, T., Dopson, S., and Ferlie, E. (2022). Do we still need professional boundaries? The multiple influences of boundaries on inter-professional collaboration. Retrieved from doi: 10.1177/01708406221074146

Farnsworth, K. (2014). Public Politics for Private Companies: The British Corporate Welfare State. *Renewal*, 21(4): 51 – 65.

Farr, C. (2020). Why scientists are changing their minds and disagreeing during the coronavirus pandemic. Retrieved from https://www.cnbc.com/2020/05/23/why-scientists-change-their-mind-and-disagree.html

Farrar, J. (2021). *Spike: The Virus vs The People The Inside Story.* London: Profile Books.

Ferlie, E., McGivern, G., Dopson, S., and Fitzgerald, L. (2013). *Making Wicked Problems Governable: The Case of Managed Networks in Health Care.* Oxford: Oxford University Press.

Fieschi, C. (2019). *Populocracy.* Newcastle upon Tyne, UK: Agenda Publishing.

Fischer, F. (2003). *Reframing Public Policy: Discursive Politics and Deliberative Practices.* Oxford: Oxford University Press.

Fleming, P. (2014a). When 'life itself' goes to work: Reviewing shifts in organizational life through the lens of biopower. *Human Relations*, 67(7): 875 – 901.

Fleming, P. (2014b). *Resisting Work: The Corporatization of Life and its Discontents.* Philadelphia: Temple University Press.

Fleming, P. (2022). How biopower puts freedom to work: Conceptualizing 'pivoting mechanisms' in the neoliberal university. *Human Relations*, 75(10): 1986 – 2007.

Fleming, P., and Spicer, A. (2007). *Contesting the Corporation: Struggle, Power and Resistance in Organizations.* Cambridge: Cambridge University Press.

Fletcher, C. (1973). The end of management. In: J. Child, J. (Ed.), *Man, and Organization* (pp. 135 – 157). London: Allen and Unwin.

Fligstein, N., and McAdam, D. (2012). *A Theory of Fields.* Oxford: Oxford University Press.

Florida, R. (2002). *The Rise of the Creative Class.* New York: Basic Books.

Ford, M. (2021). *Rule of Robots: How Artificial Intelligence Will Transform Everything.* London: Basic Books.

Forrester, K. (2019). *In the Shadow of Justice: Post-war Liberalism and the Remaking of Political Philosophy.* Princeton: Princeton University Press.

Foucault, M. (1980). *The History of Sexuality: Volume 1.* London: Vintage Books.

Foucault, M. (1991). Right of Death and Power over Life. In P. Rabinow (Ed.), *The Foucault Reader* (pp. 258–272). London: Penguin.

Foucault, M. (2003). *Society Must Be Defended: Lectures at the Collège De France 1975–1976.* London: Picador.

Foucault, M. (2007). *Security, Territory, Population: Lectures at the Collège De France 1977–1978.* London: Penguin.

Foucault, M. (2008). *The Birth of Bio-politics: Lectures at the Collège de France, 1978–1979.* London: Picador.

Fox, A. (1971). *A Sociology of Work in Industry.* London: Collier Macmillan.

Fox, A. (1974). *Man Mismanagement.* London: Hutchinson and Co.

Fox, A. (1985). *History and Heritage: The Social Origins of the British Industrial Relations System.* London: Allen and Unwin.

Frank, T. (2001). *One Market Under God: Extreme Capitalism, Market Populism and the End of Economic Democracy.* London: Secker and Warburg.

Frank, T. (2020). *People Without Power: The war on Populism and the Fight for Democracy.* London: Scribe.

Freedland, J. (2022). We don't need Sue Gray's report to tell us that Britain is run by a liar. Retrieved from https://www.theguardian.com/commentisfree/2022/jan/28/sue-gray-report-britain-liar-met-police-partygate-report

Freeman, J. B. (2018). *Behemoth: A History of the Factory and the Making of the Modern World.* New York: W.W. Norton and Company.

Freidson, E. (1986). *Professional Powers: A Study of the Institutionalization of Formal Knowledge.* Chicago IL: University of Chicago Press.

Freidson, E. (1994). *Professionalism Reborn: Theory, Prophecy and Policy.* Chicago IL: University of Chicago Press.

Freidson, E. (2001). *Professionalism: The Third Logic.* Cambridge, UK: Polity Press.

Galbraith, J. K. (1952). *American Capitalism: The Concept of Countervailing Power.* Boston, MA: Houghton Mifflin.

Galbraith, J. K. (1967). *The New Industrial State.* Harmondsworth, UK: Penguin Books.

Galbraith, J. K. (1973). *Economics and the Public Purpose.* London: Pelican Books.

Gallagher, S. (2020) Coronavirus: How Effective Are Face Masks At Stopping Spread? Retrieved from https://www.independent.co.uk/life-style/health-and-families/face-masks-coverings-coronavirus-do-they-work-shops-transport-a9617666.html

Gallagher, K. P., and Kozul-Wright, R. (2021). *The Case for a New Bretton Woods.* Cambridge: Polity Press.

Gamble, A. (2009). *The Spectre at the Feast: Capitalist Crisis and the Politics of Recession.* Basingstoke: Palgrave Macmillan.

Gamble, A. (2014). *Crisis without End? The Unravelling of Western Prosperity.* Basingstoke. Palgrave Macmillan.

Garland, D. (1990). *Punishment and Society: A Study in Social Theory.* Oxford: Clarendon Press.

Garrard, G. (2022). *The Return of the State: And why it is Essential for our Health, Wealth and Happiness.* Yale: Yale University Press.

Gendrot, V. (2021). *Cop: A Journalist Infiltrates the Police.* London: Scribe Publications.

Geoghegan, P. (2020). *Democracy for Sale: Dark Money and Dirty Politics.* London: Head of Zeus Limited.

Geoghegan, P., and Fitzgerald, M. (2020). The 'lockdown sceptics' want a culture war, with experts as the enemy. Retrieved from https://www.theguardian.com/commentisfree/2020/may/18/lock down-sceptics-coronavirus-brexit

Gerbaudo, P. (2021). *The Great Recoil: Politics after Populism and Pandemic.* London: Verso.

Giddens, A. (1984). *The Constitution of Society.* Cambridge: Cambridge University Press.

Giddens, A. (1987). *Social Theory and Modern Sociology.* Cambridge: Polity Press.

Giddens, A. (1994). Living in a Post-Traditional Society. In: U. Beck, A. Giddens and S. Lash (Eds.), *Reflexive Modernization: Politics, Tradition and Aesthetics in the Modern Social Order* (pp. 56 – 109). Cambridge, UK: Polity Press.

Giddens, A. (2000). *The Third Way and its Critics.* Cambridge: Polity Press.

Giridharadas, A. (2018). *Winners Take All: The Elite Charade of Changing the World.* New York: Alfred A. Knopf.

Glaser, E. (2018). *Anti-Politics: On the Demonization of Ideology, Authority and the State.* London: Repeater Books.

Goffman, E. (1961). *Asylums.* New York: Doubleday.

Goodhart, D. (2020). *Head, Hand and Heart: The Struggle for Dignity and Status in the 21st Century.* London: Allen Lane Random House.

Goodley, S., and Halliday, J. (2020). Troubled test-and-trace system drafts in management consultants. Retrieved from https://www.theguardian.com/world/2020/sep/18/troubled-covid-test-and-trace-programme-drafts-in-management-consultants

Goodman, J., and Carmichael, F. (2020). Coronavirus: 5G and microchip conspiracies around the world. Retrieved from https://www.bbc.co.uk/news/53191523

Gorman, E. H., and Vallas, S. P. (Eds.). (2020). *Professional Work: Knowledge, Power, and Social Inequalities* (Research in the Sociology of Work, Vol. 34). Bingley: Emerald Publishing Company.

Gouldner, A. (1971). *The Coming Crisis of Western Sociology.* London: Heinemann.

Grace, G. (2014). Professions, sacred and profane: Reflections on the changing nature of professionalism. In: M. Young and J. Muller (Eds.), *Knowledge, Expertise and the Professions* (pp. 18 – 30). London: Routledge.

Gray, J. (2007). *Al Qaeda and What it Means to be Modern.* New Edition with New Introduction. London: Faber and Faber.

Greenhalgh, T., Ozbilgin, M., and Contandriopoulos, D. (2021). Orthodoxy, *illusio,* and playing the scientific game: a Bourdieusian analysis of infection control science in the COVID-19 pandemic [version 3; peer review: 2 approved]. *Wellcome Open Res* 6:126. Retrieved from https://doi.org/10.12688/wellcomeopenres.16855.3

Grove, J. (2021). Public trust in science soared in pandemic, says global survey. Retrieved from https://www.timeshighereducation.com/news/public-trust-science-soared-pandemic-says-global-survey?utm_source=newsletter&utm_medium=email&utm_campaign=editorial-daily&mc_cid=c0035555a5&mc_eid=893017dcad

Grundmann, R. (2021). Covid, Expertise, and Society: Stepping out of the Shadow of Epidemiology? *Discover Society: New Series,* 1(3). Retrieved from https://doi.org/10.51428/dsoc.2021.03.0003

Gruzd, A., De Domenico, M., Sacco, P. L., and Briand, S. (2021). Studying the COVID-19 infodemic at scale. *Big Data & Society,* 8(1). https://doi.org/10.1177/20539517211021115

Guillén, M. F. (2015). *The Architecture of Collapse.* Oxford: Oxford University Press.

Guilluy, C. (2019). *Twilight of the Elites: Prosperity, the Periphery, and the Future of France*. New Haven: Yale University Press.

Gurri, M. (2018). *The Revolt of the Public and the Crisis of Authority in the New Millennium*. California: Stripe Press.

Habermas, J. (1976). *Legitimation Crisis*. London: Heinemann Educational Books.

Habermas, J. (1985). *The Philosophical Discourse of Modernity*. Mass, US: MIT Press.

Hamilton, C., and Ohlberg, M. (2020). *Hidden Hand: Exposing How the Chinese Communist Party is Reshaping the World*. London: Oneworld Publications.

Hanlon, G. (2016). *The Dark Side of Management: A Secret History of Management Theory*. London: Routledge.

Hardt, M., and Negri, A. (2019). *Assembly*. Oxford: Oxford University Press.

Harris, B. (2020). Spread of fake news adds to Brazil's pandemic crisis. Retrieved from https://www.ft.com/content/ea62950e-89c0-4b8b-b458-05c90a55b81f

Harvey, D. (2005). *A Brief History of Neoliberalism*. Oxford: Oxford University Press.

Harvey, D. (2011). *The Enigma of Capital and the Crises of Capitalism*. London: Profile Books.

Harvey, D. (2015). *Sixteen Contradictions and the End of Capitalism*. London: Profile Books.

Hay, C. (2001). The 'crisis' of Keynesianism and the rise of neoliberalism in Britain: an ideational institutionalist approach. In J. L. Campbell and Ove K. Pedersen (Eds.), *The Rise of Neoliberalism and Institutional Analysis* (pp. 193–218), Princeton: Princeton University Press.

Heazle, M., and Kane, J. (Eds.). (2016). *Policy Legitimacy, Science and Political Authority: Knowledge and action in Liberal Democracies*. London: Routledge.

Hennessey, P. (2022). *A Duty of Care: Britain Before and after Covid*. London: Allen Lane, Penguin Random House.

Heusinkveld, S., Gabbioneta, C., Werr, A., and Sturdy, A. (2018). Professions and (new) management occupations as a contested terrain: Redefining jurisdictional claims. *Journal of Professions and Organization*, 5(3): 248–261.

Hibou, B. (2016). Neoliberal bureaucracy as an expression of hybrid rule. In S. Hurt and B. Lipschutz (Eds.), *Hybrid Rule and State Formation: Public-Private Power in the 21st Century* (pp. 59–78). London: Routledge.

Hirst, P. (1994). *Associative Democracy: New Forms of Economic and Social Governance*. Cambridge: Polity Press.

Ho, K. (2009). *Liquidated: An Ethnography of Wall Street*. London: Duke University Press.

Hochschild, A. R. (2016). *Strangers in their Own Land: Anger and Mourning on the American Right*. New York: The New Press.

Holst, C., and Molander, A. (2020). Public deliberation and the fact of expertise: making experts accountable. *Social Epistemology*, 31(3): 235–250.

Hoogenboom, M., and Ossewarde, R. (2005). From iron cage to pigeon house: the birth of reflexive authority. *Organization Studies*, 26(4): 601–619.

Hook, D. (2007). *Foucault, Psychology and the Analytics of Power*. Hampshire: Palgrave Macmillan.

Hopkin, J. (2020). *Anti-System Politics: The Crisis of Market Liberalism in Rich Democracies*. Oxford: oxford University Press.

Horton, R. (2020). *The COVID-19 Catastrophe: What's Gone Wrong and How to Stop it Happening Again?* Cambridge, UK: Polity Press.

Horton, J., and Mendus, S. (Eds.). (1994). *After MacIntyre: Critical Perspectives on the Work of Alasdair MacIntyre*. Cambridge: Polity Press.

House of Commons. (2021). *Coronavirus: lessons learned to date*. London: House of Commons.

Hurt, S., and Lipschutz, R. (Eds.). (2016). *Hybrid Rule and State Formation: Public-Private Power in the 21st Century.* London: Routledge.

Hutton, W. (2015). *How Good We Can Be: Ending the Mercenary Society and Building a Great Country.* London: Abacus.

Independent SAGE (2021). The 'Following the Science' Timeline: What SAGE and Independent SAGE advised as key behavioural mitigations versus what the Westminster Government did January 2020 – July 2021. Retrieved from https://www.independentsage.org/wp-content/uploads/2021/08/IS-Timeline-Complete-1.pdf

Jackall, R. (1998/2010). *Moral Mazes: The World of Corporate Managers.* First Edition and Twentieth Anniversary Edition. Oxford: Oxford University Press.

Jessop, B. (1994). The Schumpeterian Workfare State. In R. Burrows and B. Loader (Eds.), *Towards a Post-Fordist Welfare State?* (pp. 13 – 37). London: Routledge.

Jessop, B. (2008). *State Power.* Cambridge, UK: Polity.

Jessop, B. (2010). Constituting another Foucault Effect: Foucault on States and State Craft. In U. Brockling, S. Krasmann and T. Lemke (Eds.), *Governmentality: Current Issues and Future Challenges* (pp. 56 – 73). New York: Routledge.

Jessop, B. (2016). *The State: Past, Present and Future.* Cambridge, UK: Polity.

Johannessen, J. A. (2019). *The Workplace of the Future: The Fourth Industrial Revolution, the Precariat and the Death of Hierarchies.* London: Routledge.

Johnson, T. (1994). Expertise and the state. In M. Gane and T. Johnson (Eds.), *Foucault's New Domains* (pp. 139 – 152). London, UK: Routledge.

Johnson, T. (2016). *Professions and Power.* Abingdon: Routledge Revivals.

Jones, L. (2021). From Rolls Royce to Skoda: How the pandemic has exposed Britain's failed 'regulatory state'. Retrieved from https://www.telegraph.co.uk/global-health/science-and-disease/rolls-royce-skoda-pandemic-has-exposed-britains-failed-regulatory

Judis, J. B. (2016). *The Populist Explosion: How the Great Recession Transformed American and European Politics.* New York: Columbia Global Reports.

Kahl, C., and Wright, T. (2021). *Aftershocks: Pandemic Politics and the End of the Old International Order.* New York: Saint Martin's Press.

Karkowsky, C. (2021). Vaccine Refusers Risk Compassion Fatigue. Retrieved from https://www.theatlantic.com/ideas/archive/2021/08/health-care-workers-compassion-fatigue-vaccine-refusers/619716/?s=03

Kellogg, K. C., Valentine, M. A., and Christin, A. (2020). Algorithms At Work: The New Contested Terrain of Control. *Academy of Management Annals,* 14(1): 366 – 410.

Kennedy, D. (2016). *A World of Struggle: How Power, Law, and Expertise Shape Global Political Economy.* Princeton: Princeton University Press.

Kinder, T., and Plimmer, G. (2020). UK government paid £1.7bn to private groups for coronavirus contracts. Retrieved from https://www.ft.com/content/7fe7c2d5-24df-431b-9149-50417fa0236a

Kirkpatrick, I., Ackroyd, S., and Walker, R. (2005). *The New Managerialism and Public Sector Professionals.* London: Palgrave.

Kirkpatrick, I., and Noordegraaf, M. (2015). Organizations and Occupations: Towards Hybrid Professionalism in Professional Service Firms, In L. Empson, J. Broschak and B. Hinings (Eds.), *The Oxford Handbook of Professional Service Firms* (pp. 92 – 112). Oxford: Oxford University Press.

Kirkpatrick, I., Aulakh, S., and Muzio, D. (2021). The evolution of professionalism as a mode of regulation: evidence for the United States. *Work, Employment and Society,* September: 1 – 18.

Koppl, R. (2018). *Expert Failure.* Cambridge, UK: Cambridge University Press.

Kotkin, J. (2020). *The Coming of Neo-Feudalism: A Warning to the Global Middle Class.* New York: Encounter Books.

Krastev (2020). Tyrants Hate a Plague. But Covid cripples democracies too. Which system works best against a pandemic? Retrieved from https://www.persuasion.community/p/ivan-krastev-tyrants-hate-a-plague

Krause, E. (1996). *Death of the Guilds: Professions, States and the Advance of Capitalism, 1930 to the present.* New Haven, US: Yale University Press.

Krzyżanowski, M., and Krzyżanowska, N. (2022). Narrating the 'new normal' or pre-legitimising media control? COVID-19 and the discursive shifts in the far-right imaginary of 'crisis' as a normalisation strategy. *Discourse & Society,* 33(6): 805–818.

Kupferschmidt, K. (2021). The pandemic turned them into celebrities. Now, scientists are grappling with new power – and internet hate. Retrieved from https://www.science.org/content/article/pandemic-turned-them-celebrities-now-scientists-are-grappling-new-power-and-internet-hate

Kyriakidou, M., Morani, M., Cushion, S., and Hughes, C. (2022). Audience understandings of disinformation: navigating news media through a prism of pragmatic scepticism. *Journalism.* Retrieved from https://doi.org/10.1177/14648849221114244

Lapavitsas, C. (2013). *Profiting without Producing: How Finance Exploits Us All.* London: Verso.

Larson, M. (1977). *The Rise of Professionalism: Monopolies of Competence and Sheltered Markets.* Berkley, CA: University of California Press.

Larson, M. (1990). On the matter of experts and professionals: or how its is impossible to leave nothing unsaid. In Torstendahl, R., and Burrage, M. (Eds.), *The Formation of Professions: Knowledge, State and Strategy* (pp. 11–23). London: Sage.

Larson, M. S. (2013). *The Rise of Professionalism: Monopolies of Competence and Sheltered Markets.* New Introduction. New Brunswick New Jersey: Transaction Publishers.

Lawrence, P., and Lorsch, J. (1967). *Organization and Environment.* Cambridge Mass: Harvard University Press.

LeBlanc, P. (2020). Trump rebukes Fauci's coronavirus assessment: 'I think we are in a good place.' Retrieved from https://edition.cnn.com/2020/07/06/politics/fauci-coronavirus-us-response/index.html

Leicht, K. (2016). Market fundamentalism, cultural fragmentation, post-modernism, scepticism, and the future of professional work. *Journal of Professions and Organization,* 3(1): 103–117.

Lemke, T. (2011). *Bio-politics: An advanced introduction* (translated by E. F.Trump). New York and London: New York University Press.

Levitsky, S., and Ziblatt, D. (2018). *How Democracies Die: What History Reveals About Our Future.* London: Viking, Penguin Random House.

Liu, S. (2020). Professional impurities. In E. H. Gorman and S. P. Valls (Eds.), *Professional Work: Knowledge, Power, and Social Inequalities* (Research in the Sociology of Work,Vol. 34), (pp. 147–168). Bingley: Emerald Publishing Company.

Liu, J., Shahab, Y., and Hoque, H. (2022). Government Response Measures and Public Trust during the COVID-19 Pandemic: Evidence from Around the World. *British Journal of Management,* 33(2): 571–602.

Loveridge, R. (2013). Designing Legitimacy: The Rise of the Global Advocacy Coalitions and the Emergence of the Proselytizing Think Tank. Unpublished MS. Cardiff. Business School, Cardiff, UK.

Lukes, S. (1975). *Emile Durkheim: His Life and Work, A Historical and Critical Study.* Harmondsworth: Penguin Books Limited, Peregrine Books.

Macdonald, K. (1995). *The Sociology of the Professions.* London: Sage.

MacIntyre, A. (1981). *After Virtue: A Study in Moral Theory.* London: Duckworth.

MacIntyre, A. (1988). *Whose Justice? Which Rationality?* London: Duckworth.

Mair, P. (2013). *Ruling the Void: The Hollowing of Western Democracy.* London: Verso.

Malin, N. (2020). *De-professionalism and Austerity: Challenges for the Public Sector.* Bristol, UK: Policy Press.

Martí, I., Mumby, D., Seidl, D., and Thomas, R. (2017). Introduction to Special Issue Resistance, Resisting and Resisters in and around Organizations. *Organization Studies,* 38(9): 1157 – 1183.

Marquand, D. (2004). *Decline of the Public.* Cambridge, UK: Polity.

Mathers, M. (2020). Ministers using 'following the science' defence to justify decision-making during pandemic, says Prof Brian Cox. Retrieved from https://www.independent.co.uk/news/uk/politics/coronavirus-brian-cox-minister-follow-science-comments-a9520041.html

Matthews, D. (2020a). Science 'risks coronavirus backlash' as it is drawn into politics. Retrieved from https://www.timeshighereducation.com/news/science-risks-coronavirus-backlash-it-drawn-politics

Matthews, D. (2020b). French trust in science drops as coronavirus backlash begins. Retrieved from https://www.timeshighereducation.com/news/french-trust-science-drops-coronavirus-backlash-begins

Mau, S. (2019). *The Metric Society: On the Quantification of the Social.* Cambridge, UK: Polity Press.

Maxmen, A., and Subbaraman, N. (2021). Biden's ambitious COVID plan: what scientists think. Retrieved from https://www.nature.com/articles/d41586-021-00220-x

McKelvey, T. (2020). Coronavirus: Why are Americans so angry about masks? Retrieved from https://www.bbc.co.uk/news/world-us-canada-53477121

Merquior, J.G. (1991). *Foucault.* Second Edition. London: Fontana.

Miller, D. (2005). What is best value? Bureaucracy, virtualism and local governance. In P. Du Gay (Ed.), *The Values of Bureaucracy* (pp. 233 – 254). Oxford: Oxford University Press.

Miller, P., and Rose, N. (2008). *Governing the Present: Administering Economic, Social and Personal Life.* Cambridge, UK: Polity Press.

Milstein, B. (2021). What does a legitimation crisis mean today? Financialized capitalism and the crisis of consciousness. In B. Vormann and M. D. Weinman (Eds.), *The Emergence of Illiberalism: Understanding a Global Phenomenon* (pp. 27 – 42). London: Routledge.

Mirowski, P. (2013). *Never Let a Serious Crisis Go to Waste: How Neoliberalism Survived the Financial Meltdown.* London, UK: Verso Books.

Mizruchi, M. S. (2013). *The Fracturing of the American Corporate Elite.* Cambridge Mass: Harvard University Press.

Moffitt, B. (2020). *Populism.* Cambridge. Polity.

Moore, A. (2017). *Critical Elitism: Deliberation, Democracy, and the Problem of Expertise.* Cambridge: Cambridge University Press.

Moore, G., and Beadle, R. (2006). In search of organizational virtue in business: agents, goods, practices, institutions and environments. *Organization Studies,* 27(3): 369 – 389.

Moran, M. (2007). *The British Regulatory State: High Modernism and Hyper-Innovation.* Oxford: Oxford University Press.

Morani, M., Cushion, S., Kyriakidou, M., and Soo, N. (2022). Expert voices in the news reporting of the coronavirus pandemic: A study of UK television news bulletins and their audiences. *Journalism.* Retrieved from https://doi.org/10.1177/14648849221127629

Morgan, G., Hirsh, P., and Quack, S. (Eds.). (2015). *Elites on Trial* (Research in the Sociology of Organizations, Vol. 43). Bingley, US: Emerald Group Publishing.

Mouffe, C. (2018). *For a Left Populism*. London: Verso.

Mudde, C., and Kaltwasser, C. R. (2017). *Populism: A Very Short Introduction*. Oxford: Oxford University Press.

Müller, J.-W. (2016). *What is Populism?* Philadelphia: University of Philadelphia Press.

Müller, J.-W. (2021). *Democracy Rules*. London: Allen Lane, Penguin Random House.

Munck, R. (2005). Neoliberalism and politics, and the politics of neo-liberalization. In A. Saad-Filho and D. Johnston (Eds.), *Neoliberalism: A Critical Reader* (pp. 60–69). London: Pluto Press.

Muzio, D., Aulakh, S., and Kirkpatrick, I. (2019). *Professional Occupations and Organizations*. Cambridge: Cambridge University Press.

Navidi, S. (2017). *Superhubs: how the Financial Elite and their Networks Rule our World*. Boston, US: Nicholas Brealey Publishing.

Newman, J. (2013). Professionals, power and the reform of public services. In M. Noordegraaf and B. Steijn (Eds.), *Professionals Under Pressure: The Reconfiguration of Professional Work in Changing Public Services* (pp. 41–53). Amsterdam: Amsterdam University Press.

Newman, J., and Clarke, J. (2009). *Publics, Politics and Power: Remaking the Public in Public Services*. London. Sage.

Nichols, T. (2017). *The Death of Expertise: The Campaign against Established Knowledge and Why it Matters*. Oxford: Oxford University Press.

Nielsen, R. P. (2006). Introduction to the special issue: In Search of Organizational Virtue. *Organization Studies*, 27(3): 317–321.

Nisbet, R. A. (1969). *The Quest for Community*. Oxford: Oxford University Press.

Nisbet, R. A. (1970). *The Sociological Tradition*. London: Heinemann.

Nogrady, B. (2021). 'I hope you die': how the COVID pandemic unleashed attacks on scientists. Retrieve from https://www.nature.com/articles/d41586-021-02741-x?s=03

Noordegraaf, M. (2007). From pure to hybrid professionalism: present-day professionalism in ambiguous public domains. *Administration and Society*, 39(6): 761–785.

Noordegraaf, M. (2011a). Remaking professionals? How associations and professional education connect professionalism and organizations. *Current Sociology*, 59(4): 465–488.

Noordegraaf, M. (2011b). Risky business: how professionals and professional fields (must) deal with organizational issues. *Organization Studies*, 32(10): 1349–1371.

Noordegraaf, M. (2015). Hybrid professionalism and beyond: (new) forms of public professionalism in changing organizational and societal contexts'. *Journal of Professions and Organization*, 2(2): 187–206.

Noordegraaf, M. (2020). Protective or connective professionalism? How connected professionals can (still) act as autonomous and authoritative experts. *Journal of Professions and Organization*, 7(2): 205–223.

Noordegraaf, M., and Steijn, B. (Eds.). (2013). *Professionals under Pressure: The Reconfiguration of Professional Work: Changing Public Services*. Amsterdam: Amsterdam University Press.

Norris, P., and Inglehart, R. (2019). *Cultural Backlash: Trump, Brexit, and Authoritarian Populism*. Cambridge: Cambridge University Press.

O'Dwyer, M. (2021). Deloitte UK profits boosted by public sector pandemic work. Retrieved from https://www.ft.com/content/d00f5495-c664-41fc-ab50-ab40a1c74b89

O'Flynn, I. (2022). *Deliberative Democracy*. Cambridge: Polity.

O'Neil, J. (1986). The disciplinary society. *British Journal of Sociology*, 3: 42–60.

O'Reilly, D., and Reed, M. (2011). The grit in the oyster: professionalism, managerialism and discourses of public service modernization. *Organization Studies*, 32(8): 1079–1101.

Oreskes, N. (2019). *Why Trust Science?* Princeton: Princeton University Press.

Oreskes, N., and Conway, E. M. (2010). *Merchants of Doubt: How a Handful of Scientists Obscured the Truth on Issues from Tobacco Smoke to Global Warming.* New York: Bloomsbury.

Owen, D., and Strong, T. B. (Eds.). (2004). *Max Weber: The Vocation Lectures.* Indianapolis, US: Hackett Publishing Company.

Padgett, J. F., and Powell, W. P. (2012). *The Emergence of Organizations and Markets.* Princeton: Princeton University Press.

Paiva, E. L., and Miguel, P. L. S. (2022). Overcoming enduring inequalities in Global Value Chains? Interpreting the case of Brazil's Covid-19 vaccine supply through a chess metaphor. *Organization*, 29(3): 414 – 425.

Parkin, F. (1979). *Marxism and Class Theory: A Bourgeois Critique.* London: Tavistock.

Parkin, F. (1982). *Max Weber.* London; Routledge.

Pasquale, F. (2015). *The Black Box Society: The Secret Algorithms that Control Money and Information.* Cambridge, Mass: Harvard University Press.

Payne, S. (2020). Jeremy Hunt says Sage gave 'wrong' advice at start of pandemic. Retrieved from https://www.ft.com/content/fe2442ce-ffc5-478b-b7b5-9240ccf2ffcf

Peck, J. (1996). *Workplace: The Social Regulation of Labour Markets.* New York: Guilford Publications.

Peck, J. (2010). *Constructions of Neoliberal Reason.* Oxford, UK: Oxford University Press.

Peck, J., and Theodore, N. (2015). *Fast Policy: Experimental Statecraft at the Thresholds of Neoliberalism.* Minneapolis: University of Minnesota Press.

Perrow, C. (1984). *Normal Accidents: Living with High-Risk Technologies.* New York: Basic Books.

Perrow, C. (1986). *Complex Organizations: A Critical Essay.* Third Edition. New York: McGraw-Hill.

Perrow, C. (2008). Conservative radicalism. *Organization*, 16(6): 915 – 21.

Phillips, T. (2021). Brazil set to lose its third health minister amid pandemic as Covid death toll rises. Retrieved from https://amp.theguardian.com/world/2021/mar/16/brazil-loses-third-health-minister-pandemic

Phillips, T., Sadiq, M., and Chulani, N. (2020). Why has Brazil been so badly hit by coronavirus? – video explainer. Retrieved from https://www.theguardian.com/world/video/2020/may/22/why-has-brazil-been-so-badly-hit-by-coronavirus-video-explainer

Picard, C.-F., Durocher, S., and Gendron, Y. (2021). Office design: neoliberal governmentality and professional service firms. *Organization Studies*, 42(5): 739 – 760.

Pick, D. (2022). *Brainwashed: A New History of Thought Control.* London: Profile Books Limited.

Pollitt, C., and Bouckaert, G. (2011). *Public Management Reform: A Comparative Analysis.* Oxford: Oxford University Press.

Pollock, A. (2004). *NHS Plc: The Privatisation of our Health Care.* London: Verso.

Plehwe, D., Slobodan, Q., and Mirowski, P. (Eds.). (2020). *Nine Lives of Neoliberalism.* London: Verso.

Quack, S., and Schüßler, E. (2015). Dynamics of regulation of professional service firms: national and transnational developments. In P. Empson, D. Muzio, J. P. Broschak and B. Hnings (Eds.), *The Oxford Handbook of Professional Service Firms* (pp. 48 – 70). Oxford: Oxford University Press.

Raco, M. (2013). *State-Led Privatization and the Demise of the Democratic State: Welfare Reform and Localism in an Era of Regulatory Capitalism.* London, UK: Routledge.

Ransom, J. S. (1997). *Foucault's Discipline: The Politics of Subjectivity.* London: Duke University Press.

Rawls, J. (1971). *A Theory of Justice.* Harvard: Harvard University Press.

Ray, L., and Reed, M. (Eds.). (1994). *Organizing Modernity: New Weberian Perspectives on Work, Organization and Society.* London: Routledge.

Reed, C., and Reed, M. (2022). Expert authority in crisis: making authority real through struggle, *Organization Theory*.

Reed, M. (1985). *New Directions in Organizational Analysis.* London: Tavistock Publications.

Reed, M. (1996). Expert power and control in late modernity: an empirical review and theoretical synthesis. *Organization Studies*, 17(4): 573 – 597.

Reed, M. (1999). From the Cage to the Gaze? The Dynamics of Organizational Control in Late Modernity. In G. Morgan and L. Engwall (Eds.), *Regulation and Organizations* (pp. 17 – 49). London: Routledge.

Reed, M. (2001). Organization, trust and control: a realist analysis. *Organization Studies*, 22(2): 201 – 213.

Reed, M. (2005). Beyond the Iron Cage? Bureaucracy and Democracy in the Knowledge Economy and Society. In P. Du Gay (Ed.), *The Values of Bureaucracy* (pp. 115 – 140). Oxford: Oxford University Press.

Reed, M. (2011). The post-bureaucratic organization and the control revolution. In S. Clegg, M. Harris and H. Höpfl (Eds.), *Managing Modernity: Beyond Bureaucracy?* (pp. 230 – 256). Oxford: Oxford University Press.

Reed, M. (2012). Masters of the universe: power and elites in organization studies. *Organization Studies*, 33(2): 203 – 222.

Reed, M. (2018). Elites, professions, and the neoliberal state: critical points of intersection and contention. *Journal of Professions and Organization*, 5(3): 297 – 312.

Reed, M. (2019). Managing Public Service Professionals Under New Public Management. In A. Sturdy, S. Heusinkveld, T. Reay and D. Strang (Eds.), *The Oxford Handbook of Management Ideas* (pp. 443 – 457). Oxford, UK: Oxford University Press.

Reed, M. (2020). Connective professionalism: towards (yet another) ideal type' with T. Adams, S. Clegg, G. Eyal and M. Saks. *Journal of Professions and Organization*, 7(2): 214 – 233.

Reed, M. (2022). Metaphors and organization studies: a critical realist view'. In A. Ortenblad (Ed.), *The Oxford Handbook of Metaphor in Organization Studies.* Oxford: Oxford University Press.

Reed, M., and Burrell, G. (2018). Theory and organization studies; the need for contestation. *Organization Studies*, 40(1): 39 – 54.

Reed, M., and Wallace, M. (2015). Elite discourses and institutional innovation: making the hybrid happen in English public services. In G. Morgan, P. Hirsch and S. Quack (Eds.), *Elites on Trial* (Research in the Sociology of Organizations, Vol. 43), (pp. 269 – 301).

Reich, R. (2016). *Saving Capitalism: For the Many, Not the Few.* London: Icon Books Limited.

Reicher, S. (2021). Retrieved from https://twitter.com/ReicherStephen/status/1447989081430953991?t= ue14u7N_Wkb12ZWIIhOb3g&s=03

Roberts, A. (2021). Retrieved from https://twitter.com/theAliceRoberts/status/1441290512023973895?s= 03

Roberts, J., Lightbody, R., Ragne, L., and Elstub, R. (2020). Experts and evidence in deliberation: scrutinizing the role of witnesses and evidence in mini publics, a case study. *Policy Sciences* 53: 3 – 32.

Rosenfeld, S. (2019). *Democracy and Truth: A Short History.* Philadelphia: University of Pennsylvania Press.

Runciman, D. (2013). *The Confidence Trap: A History of Democracy in Crisis from World War 1 to the Present.* Princeton: Princeton University Press.

Runciman, D. (2019). *How Democracy Ends.* London: Profile Books.

Runciman, G. (2002). *A Critique of Max Weber's Philosophy of Social Science*. Cambridge, UK: Cambridge University Press.

Saks, M. (2021). *Professions: A Key Idea in Business and Society*. London, UK: Routledge.

Saks, M., and Brock, D. (2018). Professions and organizations: a European perspective. In S. Siebert (Ed.), *Management Research: European Perspectives*. Abingdon: Routledge.

Sample, I. (2021). UK government's Covid advisers enduring 'tidal waves of abuse'. Retrieved from https://www.theguardian.com/world/2021/dec/31/uk-governments-covid-advisers-enduring-tidal-waves-of-abuse

Sample, I., and Walker, P. (2021). Covid response 'one of UK's worst ever public health failures'. Retrieved from https://www.theguardian.com/politics/2021/oct/12/covid-response-one-of-uks-worst-ever-public-health-failures

Sandel, M. J. (2020). *The Tyranny of Merit: What's Become of the Common Good?* London: Allen Lane.

Savage, M., and Williams, K. (Eds.). (2008). *Remembering Elites*. Oxford: Blackwell Publishing.

Schneider, S., Schmidtke, H., Haunss, S., and Gronau, J. (Eds.). (2017). *Capitalism and its Legitimacy in Times of Crisis*. Switzerland: Palgrave Macmillan Imprint published by Springer Nature.

Schön, D. (1990). *Educating the Reflective Practitioner: Towards a New Design for Teaching and Learning in the Professions*. San Francisco: Jossey Bass.

Scott, J. S. (2020). *Seeing Like a State: How Certain Schemes to Improve the Human Condition Have Failed*. New Haven: Yale University Press.

Selznick, R. (1949/1966). *TVA and the Grass Roots*. Second Edition. New York: Harper.

Seymour, R. (2014). *Against Austerity*. London: Pluto Press.

Shafik, M. (2021). *What We Owe Each Other: A New Social Contract*. London: The Bodley Head, Penguin Random House.

Silverman, D. (1970). *The Theory of Organizations*. London: Heinemann.

Simons, J. (2020). Why the UK government's approach to coronavirus modelling is dangerous. Retrieved from https://www.newstatesman.com/politics/health/2020/03/uk-government-approach-coronavirus-modelling-dangerous

Singh, N., and Banga, G. (2022) Media and information literacy for developing resistance to 'infodemic': lessons to be learnt from the binge of misinformation during COVID-19 pandemic. *Media, Culture & Society*, 44(1): 161 – 171.

Smets, M., Morris, T., and von Nordenflych, A. (2017). 25 years since P2; Taking Stock and Charting the Future of Professional Firms. *Journal of Professions and Organization*, 4(3): 261 – 281.

Smith, G. D., Blastland, M., and Munafò, M. (2020). Covid-19's known unknowns. *BMJ*, 371. Retrieved from doi: doi.org/10.1136/bmj.m3979

Snyder, B. H. (2016). *The Disrupted Workplace: Time and the Moral Order of Flexible Capitalism*. Oxford: Oxford University Press.

Sodha, S. (2020). Bias in 'the science' on coronavirus? Britain has been here before. Retrieved from https://www.theguardian.com/commentisfree/2020/jul/23/bias-science-bse-coronavirus-crisis

Sokhi-Bulley, B. (2011). Government(ality) by Experts: Human Rights as Governance. *Law and Critique*, 22(3): 251 – 271.

Sozudogru, E. (2020). Coronavirus: government advisory groups should include a wider range of experts. Retrieved from https://theconversation.com/coronavirus-government-advisory-groups-should-include-a-wider-range-of-experts-137734

Spence, C., Voulgaris, G., and Maclean, M. (2017). Politics and the professions in a time of crisis. *Journal of Professions and Organization*, 4(3): 261 – 281.

Springer, S. (2016). *The Discourse of Neoliberalism: An Anatomy of a Powerful Idea.* Lanham, MD: Rowman & Littlefield.

Sridhar, D. (2022). *Preventable: How a Pandemic Changed the World and How to Stop the Next One.* London: Penguin.

Srnicek, N., and Williams, A. (2015). *Inventing the Future: Postcapitalism and a World Without Work.* London: Verso.

Stehr, N., and Grundmann, R. (2011). *Experts: The Knowledge and Power of Expertise.* London: Routledge.

Stiglitz, J. E. (2013). *The Price of Inequality: How Today's Divided Society Endangers our Future.* New York: Norton Paperback.

Streeck, W. (2014). *Buying Time: A Delayed Crisis of Democratic Capitalism.* London; Verso.

Streeck, W. (2016). *How Will Capitalism End?* London: Verso.

Sturdy, A., and Mahoney, J. (2018). Explaining national variation in the use of management consulting knowledge: a framework. *Management Learning*, 49(5): 521–558.

Sturdy, A., Wright, C., and Wylie, N. (2016). *Management as Consultancy: Neo-Bureaucracy and the Consultant Manager.* Cambridge: Cambridge University Press.

Strittmatter, K. (2019). *We Have Been Harmonized: Life in China's Surveillance State.* Exeter, UK: Old Street Publishing.

Styhre, A. (2014). *Management and Neoliberalism: Connecting Policies and Practices.* London: Routledge.

Suddaby, R., and Muzio, D. (2015). Theoretical perspectives on the professions. In Empson, L., Muzio, D., Broschack, J., and Hinings, B. (Eds.), *The Oxford Handbook of Professional Service Firms* (pp. 25–47). Oxford: Oxford University Press.

Susskind, J. (2020). *Future Politics: Living Together in a World Transformed by Tech.* Oxford: Oxford University Press.

Susskind, J. (2022). *The Digital Republic: On Freedom and Democracy in the 21ˢᵗ Century.* London: Bloomsbury Publishing.

Susskind, R., and Susskind, D. (2015). *The Future of the Professions: How Technology Will Transform the Work of Human Experts.* Oxford: Oxford University Press.

Swarts, J. (2013). *Constructing Neoliberalism: Economic Transformation in Anglo-American Democracies.* Toronto, Canada: University of Toronto Press.

Sylvia, J. J., and Andrejevic, M. (2016). The Future of Critique: Mark Andrejevic on Power/Knowledge and the Big Data-Driven Decline of Symbolic Efficiency. *International Journal of Communication*, 10: 3230–3240.

Taylor, A. (2019). *Democracy May Not Exist but We'll Miss it When it's Gone.* London: Verso.

Thompson, G. (2003). *Between Hierarchies and Markets: The Logic and Limits of Network Forms.* Oxford: Oxford University Press.

Thornton, P. H., Ocasio, W., and Lounsbury, M. (2012). *The Institutional Logics Perspective: A New Approach in Culture, Structure and Process.* Oxford: Oxford University Press.

Tooze, A. (2021). *Shutdown: How Covid Shook the World's Economy.* London: Allen and Lane: Penguin Random House.

Tourish, D. (2019). *Management Studies in Crisis: Fraud, Deception and Meaningless Research.* Cambridge: Cambridge University Press.

Turner, B. (1976). The organizational and interorganizational development of disasters. *Administrative Science Quarterly*, 21: 378–97.

Turner, B. (1978). *Man Made Disasters.* London: Wykeham.

Turner, B. S. (1993). *Max Weber: From History to Modernity.* London: Routledge.

Turner, S. P. (2014). *The Politics of Expertise.* London: Routledge.

VanHeuvelen, J. S. (2020). Professional engagement in articulation work: implications for experiences of clinical and workplace autonomy. In E. H. Gorman and S. P. Vallas (Eds.), *Professional Work: Knowledge, Power, and Social Inequalities* (Research in the Sociology of Work, Vol. 34), , (pp. 11 – 32). Bingley: Emerald Publishing Limited.

Vaughan, D. (1996). *The Challenger Launch Decision: Risky Technology, Culture, and Deviance at NASA.* Chicago: University of Chicago Press.

Visser, L. M., Bleijenbergh, I. L., Benschop, Y. W. M., and Van Riel, A. C. R. (2018). Prying Eyes: A Dramaturgical Approach to Professional Surveillance. *Journal of Management Studies*, 55(4): 703 – 727.

Vogl, J. (2017). *The Ascendancy of Finance.* Cambridge: Polity.

Vormann, B., and Weinman, M. (Eds.). (2021). *The Emergence of Illiberalism: Understanding a Global Phenomenon.* London, UK: Routledge.

Walker, P. (2021). Cummings right about 'false groupthink', says Covid inquiry chair. Retrieved from https://www.theguardian.com/world/2021/oct/12/cummings-right-about-false-groupthink-says-covid-inquiry-chair

Wallace, M., Reed, M., O'Reilly, D., Tomlinson, M., Morris, J., and Deem, R. (2023). *Developing Public Service Leaders: Elite Orchestration, Change Agency, Leadership and Neoliberalism.* Oxford: Oxford University Press.

Waugh, P. (2021a). Johnson And Gove 'Ripped Up The Rules' On Covid PPE Contracts For Private Firms. Retrieved from https://m.huffingtonpost.co.uk/amp/entry/johnson-gove-ppe-procurement-private-firms-high-priority-nao_uk_5fb41773c5b6f79d601b99ee/

Waugh, P. (2021b). 'No Clear Evidence' Test And Trace Has Cut Covid Rates Despite £22bn Cost, Spending Watchdog Says. Retrieved from https://m.huffingtonpost.co.uk/amp/entry/test-and-trace-treats-taxpayers-like-cash-machine dido harding_uk_6047b1eec5b6cf72d09264ad/

Wedel, J. (2011). *Shadow Elite.* New York, NY: Basic Books.

Wedel, J. (2014). *Unaccountable: How Elite Power Brokers Corrupt our Finances, Freedom and Security.* New York: Pegasus Books.

West, D. (2020). REVEALED: NHS Test and Trace top team includes just one public health expert. Retrieved from https://www.lgcplus.com/services/health-and-care/revealed-top-leadership-team-at-nhs-test-and-trace-includes-just-one-public-health-expert-15-09-2020/

White, A. (2016). *Shadow State: Inside the Secret Companies that Run Britain.* London: Oneworld Publications.

Whitley, R. (2000). *Divergent Capitalisms: The Social Structuring and Change of Business Systems.* Oxford: Oxford University Press.

WHO. (2020). Coronavirus disease (COVID-19): Herd immunity, lockdowns and COVID-19. Retrieved from https://www.who.int/emergencies/diseases/novel-coronavirus-2019/question-and-answers-hub/q-a-detail/herd-immunity-lockdowns-and-covid-19?gclid=CjwKCAjw0dKXBhBPEiwA2bmObY-WPA82Ti6_Wb1uLiW0xU7EEOYJTG-oZ22VK6YW37WIaFIWm1XdKBoCtaIQAvD_BwE

Wickham, A., and Baker, K. J. M. (2020). Scientists Advising The UK Government On The Coronavirus Fear Boris Johnson's Team Is Using Them As "Human Shields". Retrieved from https://www.buzzfeed.com/alexwickham/coronavirus-uk-scientists-human-shields

Wilks, S. (2013). *The Political Power of the Business Corporation.* Cheltenham, UK: Edward Elgar.

Willmott, H. (2011). Making sense of the financial meltdown. *Organization*, 18(2): 239 – 260.

Winston, B., and Law, G. R. (2021). Great on scandals, useless on science. *British Journalism Review*, 32(3): 14–20.

Wiseman, E. (2022). The dark side of wellness: the overlap between spiritual thinking and far-right conspiracies. Retrieved from https://www.theguardian.com/lifeandstyle/2021/oct/17/eva-wiseman-conspirituality-the-dark-side-of-wellness-how-it-all-got-so-toxic?

Witztum, A. (2019). *The Betrayal of Liberal Economics*, Volumes 1&11. London: Palgrave Macmillan.

Wolin, S. (2004). *Politics and Vision.* Expanded Edition. Princeton: Princeton University Press.

Wooldridge, A. (2021). *The Aristocracy of Talent: How Meritocracy Made the Modern World.* London: Allen Lane Random House.

Young, M. (1958). *The Rise of the Meritocracy.* Harmondsworth: Penguin Books.

Young, M., and Muller, J. (2014). From the sociology of professions to the sociology of professional knowledge. In Young, M., and Muller, J. (Eds.), *Knowledge, Expertise and the Professions* (pp. 3–17). London: Routledge.

Zuboff, S. (2019). *The Age of Surveillance Capitalism.* London, UK: Profile Books.

Index

Abbasi, Kamran   113
Abbott, Andrew   5, 7, 80, 95 – 96, 100 – 102, 104, 138
Accetti, Carlo   36, 38, 48 – 49, 68, 91, 125, 128, 153, 159, 166 – 169
Adams, Tracey   82, 177
Adler, Paul   148
Albrow, Martin   6
Alwakeel, Ramzy   113
Amoore, Louise   28
Anderson, Elizabeth   25, 41, 62
Andrejevic, Mark   73
Anter, Andreas   6, 61, 104
Anthony, Peter   93, 190
Applebaum, Anne   22, 37, 153
Arato, Andrew   131
Arbuthnott, George   111, 116, 122 – 123, 125 – 126
Aulakh, Sundeep   77 – 78, 199

Babones, Salvatore   23, 48, 153
Baker, Katie   113
Ball, Philip   124
Balloux, Francois   116, 118
Ban, Cornel   24, 34 – 35, 66 – 67, 82
Banga, Gagndeep   110
BBC   108, 113, 124
Beadle, Ron   191
Beck, Ulrich   3, 12, 14, 22, 39 – 40, 93, 139 – 142, 144, 157, 186 – 187, 195, 197
Bell, Daniel   30
Bell, Emma   60
Belton, Catherine   30
Benanav, Aaron   26
Bernstein, Basil   137
Bevir, Mark   48
Bickerton, Christopher   36, 38, 48 – 49, 68, 91, 125, 128, 153, 159, 166 – 169
Billig, Michael   112
Bingham, Kate   118
Bishop, Bill   20, 22, 45
Blastland, Michael   116
Blau, Peter   101

Blowers, Andrew   150
Blyth, Mark   14, 24 – 25, 83
Boersema, Jan   150
Booth, Robert   115
Bouckaert, Geert   15
Bourgeron, Théo   115
Boussard, Valérie   82
Boussebaa, Mehdi   81
Bowman, Andrew   41, 66 – 67, 83
Broad, William   108
Brock, David   82
Brooks, Richard   67
Brown, Mark   154, 159
Brown, Wendy   9, 15, 25, 41, 48, 55 – 58, 62, 73, 83, 154
Buchanan, David   43
Bullough, Oliver   198
Buranyi, Stephen   110
Burchell, Graham   55
Burns, Edgar   5, 7, 66, 80, 104, 137 – 139, 143, 200
Burrell, Gibson   54, 57, 63, 74, 179
Busch, Lawrence   33

Cahill, Damien   25 – 26, 33 – 34, 82
Callison, William   14, 36 – 37, 48 – 49, 61, 166
Calvert, Jonathan   111, 116, 122 – 123, 125 – 126, 199
Campbell, Denis   113
Campbell, John   178
Carmichael, Flora   110
Chafetz, Morris   1
Chandler, David   57 – 58, 62
Channel 4 News   110
Child, John   86, 101, 122, 128
Christensen, Johan   41, 66
Christophers, Brett   42, 57, 66, 198
Clarke, John   15, 25, 131, 149, 160, 171 – 174
Clegg, Stewart   61, 143, 177
Coats, David   193
Cohen, Jean   131
Cohen, Nick   114
Collier, Paul   131, 188, 190, 193

https://doi.org/10.1515/9783110734911-011

Collins, Harry   5, 11, 50, 94, 120, 134, 136 – 138, 145, 154, 180, 182, 201 – 203
Collins, Randall   161 – 162, 177,
Connolly, William   201
Conway, Erik   135
Cooper, Hilary   48, 114, 188, 197 – 199, 206 – 207.
Costello, Anthony   118
Courpasson, David   32, 87 – 88, 143, 188, 190
Cousins, Mark   59
Crawford, Kate   26 – 27
Crouch, Colin   14, 24, 43, 67, 84 – 85, 149
Crozier, Michel   101
Cruddas, Jon   193
Currie, Graeme   32, 43, 85, 174

Dahl, Robert   65
Daniels, Ronald   1
Dardot, Pierre   33, 48, 58, 83
Daub, Adrian   28, 146 – 148
Davies, Jonathan   54, 57, 60 – 62, 65
Davies, Rob   115
Davies, William   5, 10 – 11, 14, 22 – 23, 26, 33 – 34, 48, 55, 57, 62, 66 – 68, 70, 83, 106, 114, 126, 153, 166, 189
Davis, Aeron   14, 22, 30, 33, 82
Davis, Gerald   66
Dean, Mitchell   54, 57, 73
Deetz, Stanley   124
Demianyk, Graeme   113
Dencik, Lina   73
Derber, Charles   104
Diamond, Jeremy   108
Dopson, Sue   174
Du Gay, Paul   35
Durant, Darrin   120
Durocher, Sylvain   161

Elster, Jon   131 – 132
Elstub, Stephen   150
Empson, Laura   87, 89
Etzioni, Amitai   131, 191, 193
European Medicines Agency   117
Evans, Robert   120, 136 – 138, 180
Eyal, Gil   5, 12, 15, 26, 35, 41, 83, 149 – 150, 157 – 158, 177, 179, 182 – 183, 188, 204, 206
Ezzamel, Mahmoud   151 – 152

Fairclough, Norman   65, 73
Farchi, Tomas   174
Farnsworth, Kevin   67
Farr, Christina   116
Farrar, Jeremy   107, 110, 112 – 113, 118, 120 – 122, 124, 127
Ferlie, Ewan   93, 149, 174
Fieschi, Catherine   36 – 37
Fischer, Frank   150
Fitzgerald, Mary   110
Fleming, Peter   32, 59 – 60
Fletcher, Colin   92 – 93
Fligstein, Neil   16, 61, 95 – 96
Florida, Richard   45
Ford, Martin   26 – 27
Forrester, Katrina   188, 190 – 191
Foucault, Michel   55 – 56, 58 – 61, 200, 204
Fox, Alan   188, 190
Frank, Thomas   20, 34, 36 – 38, 45, 153, 160, 193
Freedland, Jonathan   131
Freeman, Joshua   146
Freidson, Eliot   7 – 8, 80, 100, 138

Galbraith, John Kenneth   20, 25, 31, 147 – 148, 207
Gallagher, Kevin   81
Gallagher, Sophie   116
Gamble, Andrew   33, 65, 67, 84
Garland, David   57
Garrard, Graeme   194, 206 – 207
Gendron, Yves   161
Gendrot, Valentin   87
Geoghegan, Peter   14, 22, 110
Gerbaudo, Paolo   188, 191, 194 – 196, 206
Giddens, Anthony   3, 8, 11 – 12, 14, 39, 91, 129, 139 – 140, 144, 157, 186 – 187, 195, 197
Giridharadas, Anand   29
Glaser, Eliane   153
Goffman, Erving   92
Golsorkhi, Damon   143
Goodhart, David   162 – 163
Goodley, Simon   115
Goodman, Jack   110
Gordon, Colin   55
Gorman, Elizabeth   7, 85, 87, 137
Gouldner, Alvin   103

Grace, Gerald   19, 93, 138
Gray, John   22
Greenhalgh, Trisha   116
Gronau, Jennifer   52
Grove, Jack   121
Grundmann, Reiner   118, 155–156, 188, 202
Gruzd, Anatoliy   110
Guillén, Mauro   23
Guilluy, Christophe   30
Gurri, Martin   28

Habermas, Jürgen   21, 51–, 154
Halliday, Josh   115
Hamilton, Clive   30
Hanlon, Gerard   39
Hardt, Michael   27, 76
Harris, Brian   109
Harris, Martin   143
Harvey, David   24, 33
Haunss, Sebastian   52
Hay, Colin   178
Heazle, Michael   202–203
Hennessy, Peter   191, 193, 206
Heusinkveld, Stefan   26, 66, 90, 99
Hibou, Béatrice   32, 83
Hirst, Paul   131
Ho, Karen   66, 87–88
Hochschild. Arlie   23
Holst, Cathrine   133
Hoogenboom, Marcel   139–140
Hook, Derek   60
Höpfl, Harro   143
Hopkin, Jonathan   39–40
Horton, John   131, 190
Horton, Richard   108–109, 112–113, 118
House of Commons   114
Hurt, Shelley   14, 25, 27, 36–37, 61, 166
Hussain, Athar   59
Hutton, Will   193

Independent SAGE   113, 125
Inglehart, Ronald   196

Jackall, Robert   92
Jessop, Bob   21, 23–24, 47, 49, 55, 61, 65, 70, 73–74
Johannessen, Job-Arild   26, 67

Johnson, Terry   7, 10, 35, 54, 57, 123, 125–126
Jones, Lee   115
Judis, John   36

Kahl, Colin   188
Kaltwasser, Cristóbal   36
Kane, John   202–203
Karkowsky, Chavi   111
Kellogg, Katherine   73
Kennedy, David   23, 170, 207
Kinder, Tabby   115
Kirkpatrick, Ian   43, 67, 77–78, 86, 95, 103, 138–139, 165, 175, 177, 188, 199–200
Konings, Martijn   25–26, 33, 82
Koppl, Roger   15, 39–40, 153
Kotkin, Joel   30
Kozul-Wright, Richard   81
Krastev, Ivan   126
Krause, Elliott   7, 10
Krzyżanowska, Natalia   110
Krzyżanowski, Michal   110
Kupferschmidt, Kai   111
Kyriakidou, Maria   111

Lapavitsas, Costas   25, 66–67, 146
Larson, Magall   5, 7 8, 10–11, 35, 80, 101
Lash, Scott   14, 39, 139–140, 144, 157, 186–187, 197
Laval, Christian   33, 48, 58, 83
Law, Graham   112
Lawrence, Paul   86
LeBlanc, Paul   108
Leicht, Kevin   7, 31, 33, 138–140
Lemke, Thomas   59–60
Levin, Dan   108
Levitsky, Steven   21, 29
Li, Jiawei   107
Lipschutz, Ronnie   14, 25, 27, 36–37, 61, 166
Liu, Jia   111
Liu, Sida   96, 98, 101–102
Lorsch, Jay   86
Lounsbury, Michael   16, 178, 200
Loveridge, Ray   65
Lukes, Steven   188–189

Macdonald, Keith   5, 7
MacIntyre, Alasdair   131, 190–191

Maclean, Mairi   66, 82
Mair, Peter   22, 163
Malin, Nigel   25 – 26, 35, 41, 83
Manfredi, Zachary   14, 36 – 37, 48 – 49, 61, 166
Marquand, David   5, 11
Martí, Ignasi   63
Martin, Adrian   150
Mathers, Matt   111
Matthews, David   113, 118
Mau, Steffen   73, 83 – 84
Maxmen, Amy   109
McAdam, Doug   16, 61, 95 – 96
McKelvey, Tara   110
McLaverty, Peter   150
Mendus, Susan   131, 190
Merquior, Jose   59
Miguel, Priscila   121
Miller, Daniel   172
Miller, Peter   54 – 58, 60, 69 – 70
Milstein, Brian   51 – 52
Mirowski, Philip   23, 26, 34, 37, 47, 64, 82
Mizruchi, Mark   15, 29, 93
Moffitt, Benjamin   36 – 37
Molander, Anders   133
Moore, Alfred   160, 178 – 183, 186, 188, 202
Moore, Geoff   191
Moran, Michael   5, 11, 35
Morani, Marina   121, 124
Morgan, Glenn   65 – 66, 81, 84
Mouffe, Chantal   36, 193
Mudde, Cas   36
Müller, Jan-Werner   21 – 22, 36 – 37, 44 – 45
Muller, Johan   94, 136 – 137
Munafò, Marcus   116
Munck, Ronaldo   82
Muzio, Daniel   77 – 78, 82, 199 – 200

Navidi, Sandra   14
Negri, Antonio   27, 76 – 77
Newman, Janet   15, 25, 32, 41, 43, 85, 96 – 97,
    149, 171, 174
Nichols, Tom   33
Nielsen, Richard   190
Nisbet, Robert   131, 184, 191
Nogrady, Bianca   127

Noordegraaf, Mirko   15, 18, 67, 96 – 97, 105,
    132, 160, 174 – 179
Norris, Pippa   196

Ocasio, William   16, 178, 200
O'Dwyer, Michael   114
O'Flynn, Ian   131, 133
Ohlberg, Mareike   30
O'Mahoney, Joe   26, 87 – 89
O'Neil, John   204
O'Reilly, Dermot   32
Oreskes, Naomi   135, 151 – 152
Ossewaard, Ringo   139
Owen, David   206

Padgett, John   86, 103
Paiva, Ely   121
Parkin, Frank   6 – 7
Pasquale, Frank   27, 146 – 147
Payne, Sebastian   113
Peck, Jamie   24, 33 – 35, 43, 47, 64, 67 – 68, 72,
    83, 101, 169 – 170
Pedersen, Ove   178
Perrow, Charles   86, 104, 141
Phillips, Tom   109
Picard, Claire-France   161
Pick, Daniel   92
Plehwe, Dieter   35
Plimmer, Gill   115
Pollitt, Christopher   15
Pollock, Allyson   84
Powell, Walter   86, 103

Quack, Sigrid   89

Raco, Mike   14, 26, 31, 35, 41, 57, 83
Ransom, John   64
Rawls, John   191
Ray, Larry   6
Reed, Cara   188
Reed, Michael   6, 8, 18, 26, 31 – 32, 34 – 37, 41,
    43, 48, 63 – 65, 74, 83, 85 – 88, 101, 103,
    109, 138, 143, 151 – 152, 170, 172, 174, 177 –
    179, 188, 190, 204
Reich, Robert   193, 207
Reicher, Stephen   124
Reid, Julian   57 – 58, 62

Roberts, Alice   111
Roberts, Jennifer   133
Rose, Nik   54 – 58, 60, 69 – 70
Rosenfeld, Sophia   180
Runciman, David   21, 30, 91, 153
Runciman, Garry   6

Saks, Mike   5, 7, 66, 82, 101, 104, 137 – 139, 143, 177, 200
Sallaz, Jeffrey   143
Sample, Ian   114, 127
Sandel, Michael   20, 38, 45 – 46, 149, 160, 193
Savage, Mike   30, 65
Schmidtke, Henning   52
Schneider, Steffen   21, 24, 52
Schön, Donald   137
Schüßler, Elke   89
Scott, James   21
Selznick, Philip   101, 122
Seymour, Richard   153, 193
Shafik, Minouche   188, 191 – 193, 206
Silverman, David   86
Simons, Joshua   112
Singh, Nirmal   110
Slobodian, Quinn   35
Smets, Michael   33
Smith, George   116
Snyder, Benjamin   93
Sodha, Sonia   112 – 113
Sokhi-Bulley, Bal   63
Sozudogru, Erman   118
Spence, Crawford   31, 66, 82
Spicer, André   32
Springer, Simon   26, 33, 47, 56, 58, 61 – 62, 64
Sridhar, Devi   106 – 112, 114, 116 – 118, 120 – 121, 123, 127
Srnicek, Nick   36, 193
Stehr, Nico   155, 188, 202
Stiglitz, Joseph   153
Streeck, Wolfgang   15, 21, 24, 26, 31, 33, 48
Strittmatter, Kai   23, 30
Strong, Tracy   206
Sturdy, Andrew   26, 31, 41, 66 – 67, 87 – 89, 96 – 98
Styhre, Alexander   83, 92
Subbaraman, Nidhi   109
Suddaby, Roy   82

Susskind, Daniel   26
Susskind, Jamie   23, 26 – 27
Susskind, Richard   26
Swarts, Jonathan   14, 24, 34 – 35, 66, 82
Sylvia, J.J   73
Szreter, Simon   48, 114, 188, 197 – 199, 206 – 207

Taylor, Astra   145 – 146, 149, 153, 160 – 161
Theodore, Nik   33 – 35, 47, 64, 67 – 68, 83, 169 – 170
Thompson, Grahame   30
Thornton, Patricia   16, 178, 200
Tooze, Adam   22, 106, 120, 188, 191, 194 – 195, 206
Tourish, Dennis   161
Turner, Barry   141
Turner, Bryan   6
Turner, Stephen   165 – 166, 188, 202, 204

Vallas, Steven   7, 85, 87, 137
VanHeuvelen, Jane   98
Vaughan, Diane   92, 141
Visser, Laura   73
Vogl, Joseph   25, 33, 84, 146
Vormann, Boris   21, 36 – 37, 48, 61, 68, 166
Voulgaris, Georgios   31, 66, 82

Walker, Peter   113 – 114, 124
Wallace, Mike   32, 41, 43, 65, 85, 174, 178
Waugh, Paul   115
Wedel, Janine   14, 26, 65 – 67
Weinel, Martin   120
Weinman, Michael   21, 36 – 37, 48, 61, 68, 166
Werr, Andreas   66
West, Dave   114
White, Alan   42, 84,
White, Leroy   43, 85, 174,
Whitley, Richard   15
WHO   106, 113, 116 – 117, 121, 123
Wickham, Alex   113
Wilks, Stephen   14, 35, 41, 67, 84, 146
Williams, Alex   36, 193
Williams, Karel   30, 33, 65, 82
Willmott, Hugh   67
Winston, Brian   112
Wiseman, Eva   110

Witztum, Amos   189
Wolin, Sheldon   29, 131, 146, 188 – 189
Wooldridge, Adrian   159, 164 – 165
Wright, Christopher   26, 31, 41, 67, 83, 87 – 88,
    96 – 98
Wright, Thomas   188
Wylie, Nick   26, 31, 41, 67, 83, 87 – 88, 96 – 98

Younes, Dima   32, 87 – 88, 188, 190
Young, Michael   94, 136 – 137, 160

Ziblatt, Daniel   21, 29
Zuboff, Shoshana   23, 26, 28 – 29, 73, 146 – 147